Nzoputa Uwa

The Holy Ankhuwa Abstracts Vol. 2

By
Chukwudi Okeke Maduno

Ekumeku Communication Systems
A Subsidiary of
EKUMEKU Universal Foundation

NZOPUTA UWA

EKUMEKU UNIVERSAL FOUNDATION NUMBER 006
FIRST EDITION * FIRST PRINTING

Copyright ©18 N.U. (2011) by Chukwudi Okeke Maduno

All rights reserved. No section of this book may be reproduced or utilized in any form of by any means, electronic or mechanical, including photocopying, recording or by an information storage and retrieval system, without the written permission of the Publisher.

ISBN: 0-9644596-5-5

Printed in the United States of America

Published by Ekumeku Communication Systems,
P.O. BOX 11311
Port Harcourt
Rivers State, Nigeria.

NZOPUTA UWA

TABLE OF CONTENT

Foreword- - - - - - 5

Preface - - - - - 6

Introduction- - - - - 16

Chapter One - - - - - 23
The Origins of the Ekwueme Calendar

Chapter Two - - - - - 64
Come Out of the Historical Process of Oge Nzuzu

Chapter Three - - - - 77
The Doctrines of Ignorance and Falsehood

Chapter Four - - - - 93
The Doctrine of ISFET

Chapter Five - - - - 113
The New Human Paradigm

Chapter Six - - -- - 133
We Are The Ekwueme People of Kemet

Chapter Seven - - -- - 149
The Chronology of the Life of Chukwudi

Chapter Eight - - - - 158
The Chosen One Has Come For Human Freedom

Chapter Nine - - - - 178
The Humble Beginnings of the Ekwueme World Historical Era

Chapter Ten - - - - 185
The Origins of the Kemetic World Identity

Chapter Eleven - - - - 201
The Revolution of the Ekwueme Civilization of Kemet

Chapter Twelve - - - - 222
The Movement of Nzoputa Uwa is Universal

FOREWORD

For over 20 years, I have been exposed to the teachings of the Chosen One for the mission of **Nzoputa Uwa** in Atlanta GA. Since this time, the truthfulness of the mission has been revealed over a long period to me. Furthermore, over my lifetime, I have been able to bear witness to the falsehoods, deception and disinformation driven by the promulgation of that contraption of skin color espoused by the followers of the religions of ISFET.

Those who preach what they have never practiced and practiced what they never preach will lead the human spirit to destruction of the Planet. They do not have the answers, and as such shall remain the Ekwensu people until they repent from Nsi. Amongst other reasons, I have become a devoted follower of the Divine Plan of AMUN in whom we must trust.

In other words, let this stand as my living testimony against the skin color contraption of the religions of ISFET.

Today, being the 31st of the month of Hatshepsut 18 **Nzoputa Uwa,** I bear witness to the Truth of the divine birth of EKUMEKU on the Second year of **Nzoputa Uwa** as follows:

I, Abiodun Aladiokuma Adekunle, believe without any shadow of doubt that the Creator of the universe of life is One. I believe that the One Creator of the universe is AMUN in whom I must trust. And, I believe that EKUMEKU is the Divine Plan of AMUN in whom I trust.

Hotepu!

PREFACE

Nzoputa Uwa: The Holy Ankhuwa Abstracts Vol. 2 is a fundamental text of the Ekwueme People of Truth. The Chosen One of **Nzoputa Uwa** is a daily worker of **Nzoputa Uwa**, teaching and spreading the Almighty Spirit of EKUMEKU. Whosoever that follows in the footsteps of the Chosen One shall not perish, but rather shall realize life everlasting.

The whole world of Ekwensu is ignorant of EKUMEKU. This ignorance has created anxieties which are the result of the lack of moral certainty. Without the **Vision of Nzoputa Uwa**, the Way would be uncertain since the goal cannot be certain. It is through the **Movement of Nzoputa Uwa** can the Way become a certainty because it has defined the Universal Aim of the human life. It is in relation of the Aim of the **Movement of Nzoputa Uwa** that the moral certainty of the Ekwueme is realized by the individual.

The Chosen One of **Nzoputa Uwa** is the Servant of Humanity in humility and truth, who does not fear evil of any kind. Why? This is because the eternal Truth of the divine birth of EKUMEKU is the greatest, greater than error, in opposition to ignorance, falsehood and deception. The Ekwueme is the Universal Being who exists in the wholeness of eternity in disagreement with Nsi. No doubt, the historical life of the **Chosen One of Nzoputa Uwa** gave voice and form to the longing and need of humanity, in the moral necessity of displacing ISFET and restoring MAAT as the dominant consciousness of life in the universe.

Without any doubt, **Nzoputa Uwa** is a fundamental text that must be applied to get rid of the obstacles which have shackled the life of humanity in aimlessness. With the supreme vision of **Nzoputa Uwa**, the universal aim of the human life is now realizable through the devotion of purpose in EKUMEKU.

Let it then be known that from the beginning of creation, the Divine Plan of the One Creator of the universe has always been and would always be the Truth of creation. But the religions of ISFET, in their dogmas of creation, distorted the Truth of creation with their false concepts of one God. They failed to realize that there is only One Creator of the universe; and as a result, the religions of ISFET misinterpreted the Divine Plan of creation because of their ignorance of EKUMEKU. They then falsely identified these created images as if to say that they were one and the same reality with the Truth of the One Creator of the universe. But the dogma of a created image of the human mind can never be synonymous with the Truth of the One Creator of the universe. A created image cannot speak and cannot create anything not to talk of creating life in the universe. Yet, the Ekwensu people in their ignorance of EKUMEKU were deceived into believing that a created image of the human mind can save them from the vicious circle of eternal death. The divine birth of EKUMEKU on the Second year of **Nzoputa Uwa** has vouschafed the everlasting Truth of the One Creator of the universe.

It is only with the Living Truth can the human spirit worship the One Creator of the universe; whereas, it is only with the poisonous lies of a dogma can those who are ignorant of EKUMEKU worship a created image of the human mind. Therefore, the followers of the religions of ISFET are the Ekwensu people who worship the created images of the human mind instead of the One Creator of the universe. That is why, every religion of ISFET can only exist in agreement with Nsi. But whatever that is in agreement with Nsi, is mortal and perishable. Thus, the religions of ISFET with their created images of the human mind are perishable.

Wherefore, the worship of any created image of the human mind has never and would never serve any real purpose of salvation whatsoever. The created images of the human mind could not speak and can never speak for they are dead in Nsi. As a result, they cannot hear; neither can they grant petitions of worship, prayer or meditation. This is the reason why it is foolishness to worship any God or to believe in any God whatever. Indeed, the followers of the religions of ISFET are abusing human morality with their skin color contraption.

If the human spirit cannot agree with the Living Truth that there is only One Creator of the universe, it means that the human spirit lives in opposition to the Divine Plan of the One Creator of the universe as an Unbeliever. Whatever that can exist in thought, word or deed against the Divine Plan of the One Creator of the universe is Nsi or is agreeable to Nsi. Whatever that exists in agreement with Nsi is perishable and is bound to be destroyed by the Almighty Spirit of EKUMEKU. Because the religions of ISFET exist to create forms of separation from the Divine Plan of the One Creator of the universe, they are bound to be destroyed by the Almighty Spirit of EKUMEKU.

Behold, the Almighty Spirit of EKUMEKU is the Destroyer of what is evil and the Restorer of what is good. We were thirsty and EKUMEKU Has given us water to drink. We were naked and EKUMEKU Has clothed our nakedness. We were hungry and EKUMEKU Has fed us. We were weak and EKUMEKU Has made us strong. We were hopeless and EKUMEKU Has given us the eternal message of salvation. We were worshipers of a created image of the human mind and it is through the devotion of purpose that we have renounced ISFET by living MAAT in our worship of the One Creator of the universe. We were blind and EKUMEKU Has given us sight. We were deaf and EKUMEKU Has made us to hear. We were dumb and EKUMEKU Has given us the Word of Truth for our good speech.

Thus, in the creation of the universe, the Divine Plan of AMUN in whom we trust is the Truth of all creation. In other words, the Truth of life and death is EKUMEKU. The Truth of good and evil is EKUMEKU. The Truth of day and night is EKUMEKU. The Truth of male and female is EKUMEKU. The Truth of MAAT and ISFET is EKUMEKU. The Truth of darkness and lightness is EKUMEKU. Whoever desires to suppress the Truth by spreading all sorts of malicious and false dogmas against the eternal Truth of the divine birth of EKUMEKU would be unto himself or herself like a thief who ignorantly believes that everybody else is a thief like himself or herself.

Because the Almighty Spirit of EKUMEKU is the Truth of every aspect of creation, it is EKUMEKU that can destroy what is evil and it is the Living Truth that can restore what is good. Between the living and the dead, it is the Almighty Spirit of EKUMEKU that is the Living Truth that can bring the living out of the dead and the dead out of the living.

In a word, EKUMEKU means Devotion. It is the devotion of purpose to the Divine Plan of the One Creator of the universe. Our Redeemer manifests the devotion of purpose to live MAAT by renouncing ISFET through the Ekwueme. Devotion of purpose is not the mere lip-worship or verbalized ritual of the religions of ISFET; instead, it is the wrestling of life against death. A single-minded devotion of purpose is undivided in consciousness; and it is the process of realizing the oneness of being. The attainment of the devotion of purpose to the supreme principle of EKUMEKU is the true victory of the faculty of MAAT against the faculty of ISFET.

No doubt, the Almighty Spirit of EKUMEKU is the Truth of the devotion of purpose to destroy evil in order to restore good. For, it is only the truthfulness of EKUMEKU that can destroy evil and restore good in the universe of life through the worship of the One Creator of the universe. Thus, it is only through the Divine Plan of the One Creator of the universe can the true knowledge of good and evil be mastered by the human spirit. And, it is only by following the Divine Plan of AMUN in whom we trust can evil be destroyed and good restored in human life.

No doubt, it is only by following the Divine Plan of the One Creator of the universe can the human spirit be saved from Nsi. Although every human spirit is born in agreement with Nsi in the world of Ekwensu, the human spirit can never become conscious of Nsi without being born again. The human spirit who is not born again cannot overcome evil by doing good. The human spirit who lives in agreement with Nsi can never realize the Truth of human freedom without the repentance from Nsi. Anybody who lives in opposition to the Divine Plan of the One Creator of the universe is a slave in bondage whose life has neither meaning nor purpose. Without the repentance from Nsi, such a life is worthless and the Biafra Ocha can be waged against it.

O Ekwueme, beware of any life that is actively lived in opposition to the Divine Plan of the One Creator of the universe for it may be destroyed by the Almighty Spirit of EKUMEKU. Whatever you do, never you accept any life that lives actively in opposition to the Divine Plan of the One Creator of the universe because such a life is bound to be destroyed by the Almighty Spirit of EKUMEKU.

But if there is the repentance from Nsi by such a life and the human spirit has publicly declared the **Nkwekolita** of the Ekwueme Universal Life and the repentance from Nsi is without any doubt genuine, the human spirit should be redeemed from the life of living in agreement with Nsi that it may become liberated from the dead end nature of the world of Ekwensu. If the human spirit cannot agree with the eternal Truth of the divine birth of EKUMEKU that there is only One Creator of the universe, it means that the human spirit lives in opposition to the Divine Plan of the One Creator of the universe as an Unbeliever, that is to say an Ekwensi. Because the religions of ISFET exist to create forms of separation from the Divine Plan of the One Creator of the universe, they are bound to be destroyed by the Almighty Spirit of EKUMEKU.

To the extent that even evil also exists to advance the Divine Plan of the One Creator of the universe, it is to that extent that any human spirit who repents from Nsi can be redeemed from the vicious circle of eternal death. Say: Whoever rejects ISFET by living MAAT is capable of realizing the Truth of the One Creator of the universe. But whomever that follows any religion of ISFET is beyond redemption for the Truth is the diametrical opposite of error. The Almighty Spirit of EKUMEKU is the Restorer of what is good and the Destroyer of what is evil. It is the Dispensational Judgment of the time of **Oge Nzuzu** that would destroy what is evil and restore what is good in the Holy Name of AMUN in whom all Truth resides.

It has been revealed and it is written in ***THE HOLY ANKHUWA*** that it is only the One Creator of the universe that is worthy of worship. There is nothing hidden under the sun. Whatever that is under the sun must exist according to the Divine Plan of the One Creator of the universe. There is nothing under the sun that is not under the dominion of the Almighty Spirit of EKUMEKU. What then is the true worship according to the Divine Plan of the One Creator of the universe?

Let it be known that true worship is the self-realization of life everlasting in the Living Truth. It is to be born again in the image of EKUMEKU. True worship is the unconditional surrender of the human spirit to the Divine Will of the One Creator of the universe. However, true worship is unrealizable without the liberation of the human spirit from the dead end nature of the world of Ekwensu.

In other words, true worship is the attainment of the devotion of purpose to the supreme principle of EKUMEKU. It is the liberation of the individual Chi from the vicious circle of eternal death. True worship is the struggle of the human spirit to displace ISFET and restore MAAT as the dominant consciousness in the universe of life. It is the fellowship of every Ekwueme in an established Haremakhet for the realization of the Living Truth.

True worship is to have constant intercourse or intimacy in consciousness with the One Creator of the universe through the devotion of purpose to the supreme principle of EKUMEKU. It is to become the devoted follower of the Divine Plan of AMUN in whom we trust. And, it is following in the footsteps of the Chosen One who was chosen by the One Creator of the universe for the mission of **Nzoputa Uwa**. Therefore, true worship leads to the Salvation of the individual Chi from the dead end nature of the world of Ekwensu.

Without any doubt whatsoever, the worship of only the One

Creator of the universe essentially means the devotion of purpose to the supreme principle of EKUMEKU. There is nothing else worthy of worship except the One Creator of the universe. Thus, it is the worship of the One Creator of the universe that separates the Ekwueme who is the manifest expression of EKUMEKU in the flesh from the Ekwensi who lives in agreement with Nsi, being ignorant of EKUMEKU.

According to the Divine Plan of the One Creator of the universe, the voluntary worship of the One Creator of the universe is the true meaning and purpose of human life. True worship is good for the human spirit because it gives meaning and purpose to the human being. True worship involves a complete identification with the Almighty Spirit of EKUMEKU in the Spirit of MAAT. True worship can only be the voluntary and single-minded worship of the One Creator of the universe which would give the human spirit the knowledge of self. Thus, it is the true worship of the One Creator of the universe that gives the human being the strength of conviction to overcome evil by doing good and to live in disagreement with Nsi.

In order to worship only the One Creator of the universe, the human spirit must never submit to the worship of any created image of the human mind. What is a created image of the human mind? It is any created thing or image that is the creation of the human mind which exists in opposition to the Divine Plan of the One Creator of the universe. Evidently, every created image of the human mind is agreeable to Nsi and whatever that is in agreement with Nsi can never liberate the human spirit from the dead end nature of the world of Ekwensu. Whatever that is a product of the human mind is a created image that must never be worshiped. Every God is a created image of the human mind. There is no God that can create anything. It is the human mind that creates every God in whatever form or shape.

There is no God that is worthy of worship. Those who worship any God are very ignorant of EKUMEKU. Every human spirit who is not a devoted follower of the Divine Plan of the One Creator of the universe is a worshiper of a created image of the human mind. The human spirit who worships a created image of the human mind is not fundamentally different from the human spirit who worships many created images of the human mind. That is to say, that the Ekwensi who worships one God is not fundamentally different from the Ekwensi who worships many Gods. Do not be fooled by the semantic gimmick of the capital "G" as in God and that of a small letter "g" as in god. Fundamentally, a God and a god have the same value since they are both the created images of the human mind. The differences between the God and the gods are only in the view of history and in the struggle for power between one or the other.

The whole world of Ekwensu worships the created images of the human mind instead of the One Creator of the universe. There is no doubt about it. According to the Divine Plan of the One Creator of the universe, anybody who is not a devoted follower of the Divine Plan of the One Creator of the universe can only live in opposition to the Divine Will of AMUN in whom we trust.

It is only those who have gained the mastery of **THE HOLY ANKHUWA** through the worship of AMUN in whom we trust in their devotion of purpose to the supreme principle of EKUMEKU that can realize the supreme consciousness of Chineke. Attaining harmony and balance between the state of being and the state of becoming, the Ekwueme becomes one with the universe of life. This oneness of being an Ekwueme, which is realizable through the devotion of purpose to the supreme principle of EKUMEKU, is the true meaning and purpose of human life. It is in Chineke Consciousness that the One Creator of the universe and human freedom are united in the state of EKUMEKU as the Living Truth of life.

Therefore, the fundamental principle of Chineke is the Truth realized, completed and perfected for everlasting life. Chineke Consciousness is the Truth of the divine birth of EKUMEKU realized in its highest potentiality and possibility and yet it is nothing when compared to AMUN in whom we trust.

The One Creator of the universe is AMUN in whom we trust. The One Creator of the universe is the Truth of Absolute Existence, transcending all the limitations of time and space, noumenal and phenomenal, name and identity, language and sound, form and shape, spirit and matter or gender and mind. The Greatest AMUN in whom we trust is no doubt manifest and unmanifest, transcendent and immanent, visible and invisible; because the One Creator of the universe can only be worshiped through the devotion of purpose to the supreme principle of EKUMEKU.

The Greatest AMUN in whom we trust is very far from those who are separated from the supreme principle of EKUMEKU; and yet Our Creator is very near to those who are the devoted followers of the Divine Plan of the One Creator of the universe. The One Creator of the universe is nearest to those who are pious and devoted to the Holy Cause of **Nzoputa Uwa**. Through the Chosen One, the One Creator of the universe is merciful and reachable since we have been called upon to follow in the footsteps of Chukwudi, *Onye-Nzoputa-Uwa*. The One Creator of the universe is the only One worthy of worship because the Greatest AMUN in whom we trust is the One Creator of all creation.

The Holy Name AMUN is neither wholly a realized experience of the ultimate reality nor wholly an historical Idea because it transcends everything as it expresses the Absolute Existence of the One Creator of the universe. The Holy Name AMUN is the everlasting name that expresses the hidden nature of the One Creator in the universe of life. The Holy Name AMUN is therefore a descriptive reference to the location of the One Creator in the universe of life. The Holy Name AMUN means **THE HIDDEN ONE CREATOR** of the universe in whom all Truth resides.

The One Creator of the universe is hidden in time and space because the Greatest AMUN transcends the limitations of time and space. The One Creator of the universe has neither equal nor partner because the Greatest AMUN in whom we trust has neither equal nor an equivalent. Homage to thee O Greatest AMUN in whom all Truth resides. Homage toThee the One and only Creator of the universe to whom all Truth resides. Homage to Thee my trustworthy and the only One Creator of the universe, that is worthy of worship, in the Spirit of MAAT.

Let us bear witness to the eternal Truth of the divine birth of EKUMEKU, proclaiming that the time of **Nzoputa Uwa** has come. Indeed, *Nkuzimatism* is the teaching, instruction, guidance, doctrine, theory, system, definition, technique, method, deliberation, fellowship, etc., as can be applied on the ultimate reality of **Nzoputa Uwa**. Therefore, this volume embodies the divine inspiration and mental architecture upon which *Nkuzimatism* is made applicable to the supreme **Vision of Nzoputa Uwa**. OTUA-KA-ODI!

In the Spirit of MAAT, I am

YOUR HUMBLE SERVANT.

Chukwudi, Onye-Nzoputa-Uwa.

18th Year of Nzoputa Uwa.

INTRODUCTION

All that is agreeable to Nsi is subject to death, for whatever that is in agreement with Nsi lives in the dead end nature of the world of Ekwensu. But whomever that exists in disagreement with Nsi through the devotion of purpose in EKUMEKU shall never die and will exist forever in the wholeness of eternity in the world of EKUMEKU. ----The Chosen One

When you see a naked man clothe him. When you see a naked woman clothe her. But if she or he refuses to be clothed, let him or her be naked until he or she becomes aware of his or her nakedness. ---- THE HOLY ANKHUWA.

Who is this Man of EKUMEKU? Who is this Humble Servant of EKUMEKU? Who is Chukwudi, *Onye-Nzoputa-Uwa*? Is he a man just like any other man? Or, is he a servant just like every other servant? If he is, what makes him completely devoted to the Divine Plan of the One Creator of the universe? How did he become the manifest expression of the Divine Will of the One Creator of the universe in the flesh? Why are the people who follow in his footsteps being blessed unto themselves? Have you heard about the Chosen One of **Nzoputa Uwa**? If you have, what can you say about the Chosen One from what you have heard about the Humble Servant of EKUMEKU? Is it not amazing that we are fortunate to be alive at this historical time of Nzoputa Uwa when the Chosen One is still physically in our midst?

If you have not yet heard about the Master Teacher, *Mazi* Chukwudi Okeke Maduno, then you are many years behind time. The Chosen One is everywhere, in thought, in word and in deed. Some Ekwensu people said that they have heard about him in Lagos. Some said that they have heard about him in New York. Many said that the Chosen One is even the topic of many discussions in the Vatican. Some said that in Makka the people are discussing about the Chosen One. So many people said that in Jerusalem the Hebrews are asking themselves who is the Chosen One? Is he the *Onye Nzoputa Uwa* (so-called Messiah) that would come at the end of the time of **Oge Nzuzu** to judge everybody?

There are those who believe that the Chosen One lives either in Oba, Onitsha, Awka, Aba, Enugu, Owerri or Kaduna. There are those who said that they have met him in Atlanta. Many Unbelievers would tell you that they know his house in Pitakwa (Port Harcourt). Regardless, those who know *Amadi-Oha* Chukwudi Okeke Maduno very well would always say that he is the Master Teacher and the Servant of Humanity. That is why, he is everywhere.

If you ask the Unbelievers about the Chosen One, they would murmur to themselves from their evil of unbelief. The Unbelievers are afraid of change because they want to continue their life of wickedness in *Ekwensism*, living in agreement with Nsi. But if you ask a devoted follower of the Divine Plan of the One Creator of the universe who has become an Ekwueme about the Chosen One, the human spirit would start with "*OTUA-KA-ODI*". The Ekwueme would not hesitate to tell the questioner that the Master Teacher is the real *Amadi-Oha* whose words and actions are like the thunder in the sky that would always manifest the Truth of human freedom.

Who is this Man of EKUMEKU that is loved and hated by so many people? If you go to Atlanta or Pitakwa, you will find people who love him and people who hate him. Wherever you go the Master Teacher would be there in one form or the other form, spreading the Almighty Spirit of EKUMEKU, being hated by many Unbelievers and being loved by many Believers.

Let it be known that the Master Teacher lives in the world of Ekwensu but exists in the world of EKUMEKU. His life is quite different from the Ekwensi condition of living a life. In other words, the Master Teacher is a man who is on the divine mission of **Nzoputa Uwa**. Today, he is here. Tomorrow, he may be somewhere else planting the seed of **Nzoputa Uwa**.

The Master Teacher is a daily worker of **Nzoputa Uwa**, liberating the individual Chi of the Ekwensu people for EKUMEKU. Few years ago, when the Master was in New York teaching and a celebrated worshiper of a God was with him. The Master was asked: "Why is the Teacher associating with somebody who is known to be a celebrated worshiper of a created image?" The Master Teacher then asked: Have you ever seen a market where there is no trader on the market day? They said no. Then the Master Teacher stated that the world of Ekwensu is like a marketplace and in that marketplace people come to buy different things because people sell many things. He continued, if you go to the marketplace to sell your goods many people may come to buy from you. And then he asked: "Will you reject a buyer because of his nakedness?" It is written in *THE HOLY ANKHUWA*, that "when you see a naked man clothe him" that he may become aware of his nakedness.

Many Ekwensu people talk about the Master Teacher without knowing who they are talking about. Most of those who talk about him in Europe have never met him. But when they talk about him, what they talk about can only be their own Ekwensi imagination of the Master Teacher. There are those in the *Mbadiegwu* (U. S.A.) who talk about him as if to say that they have met him before. Those who have met the Chosen One are many but they do not talk about him carelessly. For they know the worth of the Master Teacher to humanity. But those who have never met *Mazi* Chukwudi Okeke Maduno are making mockery of themselves believing that the *Ochiagha* of the Faithfuls is like them. How can the Master Teacher be like the Unbelievers who are ignorant of EKUMEKU?

The supreme principle of EKUMEKU is greater than any religion that has existed or will ever exist. No doubt, the Divine Plan of the One Creator of the universe has never been realized before in the entire history of human life until the time of **Nzoputa Uwa.** Therefore, it is by following in the footsteps of the Chosen One can the human spirit realize the Divine Plan of the One Creator of the universe in one's life.

The Master Teacher acts in devotional discipline and speaks according to the Divine Plan of the One Creator of the universe. What the Ekwueme seeks out of life is in the true Self; whereas what the Ekwensi seeks out of life is what is outside of the true Self, what has been conditioned by the passions and desires of the Lower Self. In everything, the Ekwueme strives to live according to the Divine Plan of the One Creator of the universe.

In order to overcome evil by doing good, the movement of the Ekwueme must be universal, the Truth of the Ekwueme must be divinely ordained, the conduct of the Ekwueme must follow the universal Law of MAAT and the speech of the Ekwueme must be based on the universal norm of renouncing ISFET by living MAAT. Thus, the basic nature of the Ekwueme's character is the devotion of purpose to the supreme principle of EKUMEKU.

Wherefore, this First Portrait of the Master Teacher has shown that Chukwudi was born during the time of **Oge Nzuzu**. It was at the time when the religions of ISFET had made human morality redundant. The weakening of the moral values of good and evil had created the tendency where it seemingly appeared that there was no room for Truth, Justice or Reciprocity. As a result, before the coming of the Master Teacher, humanity had no conception of the One Creator of the universe; nor did anybody know that it is by following the Divine Plan of the One Creator of the universe can the human spirit be liberated from the dead end nature of the world of Ekwensu.

The masterful teaching of the Chosen One started as an attack against the ignorance, falsehood and deception that the religions of ISFET depended upon to keep the people in slavery and bondage. The Master Teacher while exposing the root of all evil to be the condition of living in agreement with Nsi, was able to offer the entire humanity the spiritual ladder that is needed to climb out of the dead end nature of the world of Ekwensu. Without the devotion of purpose to the supreme principle of EKUMEKU, the human spirit can never be liberated from the vicious circle of eternal death.

II. BEHOLD, THE CHOSEN ONE OF NZOPUTA UWA

On the 29th year of **Oge Nzuzu**, a male child was born in an hospital in Kakuri, one of the suburbs of Kaduna City. The male child was given the name, Chukwudi. His parents were Igbo settlers in Kaduna, having come from the Eastern part of the country.

Few years after he was born, there was a bloody riot in Kaduna, and other major cities and towns in Northern Nigeria, in which Ndi Igbo were targeted and killed by the Muslim followers of a religion of ISFET. Chukwudi's family escaped from their family house in N.E. 10 Forcadoes Road, Kaduna City, and managed to return to their Oba ancestral hometown, soon enough before the Biafran war broke out. The Biafran war was and still is the struggle of life against death.

That was how the youth that was born in Kaduna, having escaped death in Kaduna came to understand the Biafran war that had begun few months after Chukwudi's family had resettled in Oba. The then youthful Chukwudi was being *Nkuzimatized* to the reality of the struggle of life against death. Living in the underground Bunker that was built by the Biafran soldiers who camped in his father's compound at Oba, the youthful Chukwudi was never impressed with the conventional justifications of the War.

But Chukwudi had to wait until he was old enough to search for the answers that would satisfy his yearning for the Truth. After being *Nkuzimatized* on the vices and virtues that exist in the struggle of life against death, Chukwudi embarked on the journey to the hometown of a man he had come across from books in his quest to understand the struggle of life against death. Chukwudi had read that this historical man had preached non-violence as opposed to the violence that he had experienced for more than three years as a youngster, from Kaduna to Oba. Chukwudi had been interested to know more about the Revered Martin Luther King, Jr., who had preached non-violence, but was brutally killed with violence.

Then, Chukwudi settled down in Atlanta and for more than Fifteen years identified with the best of what Atlanta should be known for. Atlanta was his home away from home and now would always be his home. May the One Creator of the universe bless Atlanta with the Almighty Spirit of EKUMEKU. AMEN!

It was in Atlanta that the Living Truth was first realized as the Ultimate Reality. It was in Atlanta that the supreme vision of **Nzoputa Uwa** was first revealed to the Chosen One for the mission of **Nzoputa Uwa** by AMUN in whom we must trust. Also, it was in Atlanta that the Chosen One realized wholly the universal Truth that it is the agreement with Nsi that is the origin of all evil. And yet every human spirit is born in the world of Ekwensu in agreement with Nsi.

If the yoke of Nsi must be broken, then the human spirit must be born again in the image of EKUMEKU. The human spirit ought to become the devoted follower of the Divine Plan of the One Creator of the universe in order to be redeemed from the dead end nature of the world of Ekwensu. The liberation of the human spirit from the vicious circle of eternal death, in its agreement with Nsi, is possible for anyone that can follow in the footsteps of the Chosen One.

The Chosen One was chosen by the One Creator of the universe for the mission of **Nzoputa Uwa**. The Chosen One was born in Kaduna, N*kuzimatized* in Oba and divinely chosen in Atlanta by the One Creator of the universe. Those who have met the Chosen One often said that they know from the moment they were in his presence that he could not be an ordinary man because of his forthright Ekwueme character. But the Chosen One is the most ordinary man that anyone can meet. Many of his female helpers would say that he is unique, noble and handsome without any pretensions whatsoever.

But the Chosen One is nothing but the Humble Servant of EKUMEKU and the Humble Servant of EKUMEKU is the

Servant of Humanity. The Chosen One is humbled by the Divine Will of AMUN in whom we trust which has made him the epitome of what it means to be fully human. Wherever you come from, and whatever color of skin that you have, once you are in the presence of the Chosen One you would recognize that the man represents the total nobility of what it means to be the original human being.

The Chosen One is the original human being who has come to restore the dignity of what it means to be fully human. The Ekwueme is the complete human being and the original human being can no longer be subjected to the Ekwensism that has enslaved the human spirit in the dead end nature of the world of Ekwensu.

Hearken to the Living Truth, repent from Nsi and accept EKUMEKU as your eternal Savior and Redeemer from the dead end nature of the world of Ekwensu. OTUA-KA-ODI!

CHAPTER ONE

THE ORIGINS OF THE EKWUEME CALENDAR

In the world of Ekwensu, what has always been a test for a higher life to be realized, what always should be the essential knowledge concerning the origin, purpose and meaning of life, is ignored because of the condition of living in agreement with Nsi.

> ---- THE HOLY ANKHUWA

Let it be known that the world of Ekwensu is the House of ISFET; and it has been revealed and it's written in *THE HOLY ANKHUWA* that the House of MAAT must be built on the top of the House of ISFET.

> -----THE CHOSEN ONE

I. THE WORLD OF EKWENSU

The world of Ekwensu is the counterpart of the world of EKUMEKU. As the world of EKUMEKU is above, so is the world of Ekwensu below. Every human spirit is born in the world of Ekwensu involuntarily in agreement with Nsi; and just like every other life that is born in agreement with Nsi, it would also die. The world of Ekwensu is the realm of mind, time and space, unlike the world of EKUMEKU that is beyond the realm of mind, time and space.

Without the world of EKUMEKU, the world of Ekwensu is a limited horizon with one dimensional view for every human spirit, either from the point of view of the *Akwunakwuna*, the point of view of the *Akwunaset* or the point of view of the *Sethian*, where between birth and death the human spirit lives for sometime. Much of the life that is lived in the world of Ekwensu, although essential to the experience of life, could not answer or explain the meaning and purpose of human life. The experience of life in the world of Ekwensu has the certainty of death. But if death is the ultimate destiny of human life, whatever experience gained in the course of living a life would be useless. At the same time, if the human life is limited only to the world of Ekwensu, it would be very difficult to distinguish human life from animal life.

The world of Ekwensu is made up of the conditions of the *Akwunakwuna*, conditions of the *Akwunaset* and the conditions of the *Sethian* processes which arise from one or the other against one another. But whatever conditional process that it might be, the rise and fall of one leads to the rise and fall of the other. In other words, the human spirit is born to think, speak and act as the product of the physical, biological and social conditions in the world of Ekwensu in which he is born, becoming basically an environmentally conditioned personality.

With little or no self-awareness, everybody in the world of Ekwensu follows a pattern of thought, speech and behavior that dominates either from the *Pathway of Akwunakwuna*, the *Pathway of Akwunaset* or the *Pathway of Seth* in which the human spirit was born. There is no freedom of consciousness because the individual Chi is in slavery and bondage. The individual Chi has not yet awakened from its deep sleep of slumber in the dead end nature of the world of Ekwensu.

Once the conditions of the pathways in the world of Ekwensu arise against the fall of another, the consequences of living a life within any of them become monotonous and easily predictable. Although the conditions in one can give rise to the conditions in another, there is no liberation from the dead end nature of the world of Ekwensu.

Characterized by the ontological nature of the separateness of being, the liberation of the human spirit from this dead end nature of the world of Ekwensu is humanly impossible without following the Divine Plan of the One Creator of the universe. Without becoming a devoted follower of the Divine Plan of

AMUN in whom we trust, the voluntary effort of the individual to overcome evil by doing good is unattainable. But it is only through the voluntary effort of the individual to renounce ISFET by living MAAT, can the devotion of purpose in EKUMEKU be attained. Thus, the liberation of the human spirit from the dead end nature of the world of Ekwensu is only realizable through the devotion of purpose in EKUMEKU.

Since the rise and fall of one conditional process affects the rise and fall of another conditional process, there can never be freedom of consciousness in the world of Ekwensu. If the life of the human spirit can only be based on the rise and fall of one condition against other conditions, it there means that life has neither meaning nor purpose. The life of the human spirit can then only be understood as the conditions that rise and fall according to the dictates of the mind, time and space. But then, if the human spirit is born again in the image of EKUMEKU, the condition in the world of Ekwensu under which he or she was born becomes subordinated and would no longer determine what he or she is or what the human spirit would become.

With the freedom of consciousness, the human spirit becomes an Ekwueme who is a devoted follower of the Divine Plan of the One Creator of the universe. The life of the Ekwueme is no doubt the life that has transcended the conditioning process that embodies the world of Ekwensu. Regardless of what may be the conditions in the world of Ekwensu upon which the human spirit is born, the life of the Ekwensi is in vain without any meaning or purpose. Without being born again in the image of EKUMEKU, the human spirit will only live and die in the world of Ekwensu in ignorance, falsehood and deception.

In the world of Ekwensu, the human spirit is born in agreement with Nsi, to live for sometime and die. Living in agreement with Nsi, the human spirit mistakes the living of life as the life itself. Being ignorant of the Divine Plan of the One Creator of the universe, the life of the Ekwensi is in vain without the devotion of purpose. The Ekwensi being entirely ignorant of EKUMEKU is possessed by the passions and desires of the flesh in the dead end nature of the world of Ekwensu.

Ruled by the passions and desires of the Lower Self, the Ekwensi is ignorant of the Higher Self. Without the knowledge of EKUMEKU, the Ekwensi is incapable of thinking in terms of the Higher Self. As a result, the individual consciousness of the Chi is in slavery and bondage in the dead end nature of the world of Ekwensu.

But when the Ekwensi is no longer satisfied with being agreeable to Nsi, with the worship of the created images of the human mind, with the life of vanity upon vanity, with the life of slavery and bondage, the human spirit would repent from Nsi and become a devoted follower of the Divine Plan of the One Creator of the universe. It is only when the human spirit has become a devoted follower of the Divine Plan of AMUN in whom we trust can the human spirit realize that the life of the Ekwensi has neither meaning nor purpose. For it is only when the human spirit is born again in the image of EKUMEKU can the Ekwueme nature emerge to dominate the Ekwensi conditions of living a life.

The Ekwueme lives in the world of Ekwensu; and yet the Ekwueme exists in the wholeness of eternity in the world of EKUMEKU. The world of Ekwensu is the House of ISFET. It is the House of War because it is built on the agreement with Nsi and based on the separateness of being. In the world of Ekwensu, what has always been a test for a higher life to be realized, what always should be the essential knowledge concerning the origin, purpose and meaning of life, is ignored because of the agreement with Nsi. The whole world of Ekwensu worships the created images of the human mind instead of the One Creator of the universe. OTUA-KA-ODI!

II. THE MOVEMENT OF THE EKWUEME IS NZOPUTA UWA

The Movement of Nzoputa Uwa is the life of eternity in the Time of Ausar and Auset. ----THE HOLY ANKHUWA

Let it be known that the movement of the Ekwueme is **Nzoputa Uwa**. The movement of **Nzoputa Uwa** is the mission of blessing to all humanity in the wholeness of eternity. There has never been and there will never be any movement of the human spirit that can be compared to the **Movement of Nzoputa Uwa**. The *Movement of Nzoputa Uwa* stands on its own Truth, comparable to nothing except its own universal awareness of what it means to be fully human. Wherefore, the Movement of **Nzoputa Uwa** is the voluntary expression of what it truly means to be a human being.

Since the beginning of creation, the **Movement of Nzoputa Uwa** has been divinely ordained by the One Creator of the universe for the liberation of the human spirit from the dead end nature of the world of Ekwensu. Without any doubt whatsoever, the Movement of Nzoputa Uwa is universal and has been ordained by the One Creator of the universe for the deliverance of the human spirit from the yoke of living in agreement with Nsi.

That is why, the **Movement of Nzoputa Uwa** is against the worship of any God for any reason or purpose. The Movement of **Nzoputa Uwa** is no doubt diametrically opposed to the worship of any created image of the human mind. The Movement of Nzoputa Uwa is thus the universal expression of the eternal Truth of the divine birth of EKUMEKU, which has revealed that good can overcome evil when the human spirit is a devoted follower of the Divine Plan of AMUN in whom we trust.

Evidently, the **Movement of Nzoputa Uwa** is the battle against every agreement with Nsi--*Ekwensism*--of the human spirit. The Movement of Nzoputa Uwa embodies the mighty struggle to overcome evil by doing good. Therefore, the Movement of Nzoputa Uwa is the displacement of ISFET and the restoration of MAAT as the dominant consciousness in the universe of life. Thus, the **Movement of Nzoputa Uwa** is the Chineke Consciousness of life that is essential in the building of the House of MAAT on the top of the House of ISFET.

No doubt, the **Movement of Nzoputa Uwa** is the subordination of the world of Ekwensu according to the Divine Plan of the One Creator of the universe to the world of EKUMEKU. Again, the **Movement of Nzoputa Uwa** is the Revelaton of EKUMEKU in the life of Chukwudi, *Onye-Nzoputa-Uwa*. Therefore, let it be known that anybody who is not with the Chosen One is against the mission of **Nzoputa Uwa**; and whomever is against the **Movement of Nzoputa Uwa** can only live in opposition to the Divine Will of the One Creator of the universe. Whoever lives in opposition to the Divine Plan of the One Creator of the universe is the *Ekwensi*, an Unbeliever. Whosoever is an *Ekwensi* can only live in agreement with Nsi, in the dead end nature of the world of Ekwensu. Consequently, the human spirit which is dead in Nsi is an Ekwensi who does not have any moral law or reality that can claim any form of boundary for itself against the **Movement of Nzoputa Uwa.**

In other words, the **Movement of Nzoputa Uwa** is the Ekwueme moral struggle against the *Ekwensism* of the world of Ekwensu; and it is through this eternal struggle against every agreement with Nsi can the human spirit develop the morality of repentance from Nsi.

We know that the whole world of Ekwensu is ignorant of EKUMEKU. We know that the Ekwensu people do not practice what they preach. We know that there is no God in any form or shape that is worthy of worship. We know that every God is a created image of the human mind. We reject the preaching without practice of the Ekwensu people because the Ekwensu people preach law while they practice lawlessness. They preach love while they practice hate. They preach peace while they practice war.

On the contrary, what the Ekwueme preaches is what the Ekwueme practices. But the Ekwensi says one thing and does another thing. The Ekwensu people are devoid of the morality of repentance from Nsi that is essential for the human spirit to practice what is being preached.

How can one preach about law and at the same time be lawless? How can one preach about love and at the same time live in hate? How can one preach about peace and at the same time live a life of a war monger? What the Ekwueme preaches is the Truth and what the Ekwueme practices is the Truth of the divine birth of EKUMEKU.

Wherefore, the Movement of the Ekwueme People of Truth is Nzoputa Uwa. TheMovement of Nzoputa Uwa is what brought the Ekwueme People of Truth into existence. **Nzoputa Uwa** is the Movement of the Ekwueme People of Truth. Therefore, the Movement of the Ekwueme People of Truth would always be **Nzoputa Uwa**.

Without the devotion of purpose to the supreme principle of EKUMEKU, the Movement of Nzoputa Uwa would not have come into existence. Without the devotion of purpose to the supreme principle of EKUMEKU, the vision of **Nzoputa Uwa** would never have been realized. Without the devotion of purpose to the supreme principle of EKUMEKU, the mission of **Nzoputa Uwa** cannot stand on its own Truth comparable to nothing except its Universal Life. Without the devotion of purpose to the supreme principle of EKUMEKU, the Movement of Nzoputa Uwa can never be the universal expression of the truthfulness of life. Therefore, without the absolute trust in AMUN in whom we must always trust, the One & Only Creator of the universe is the only one worthy of worship, the Ekwueme People of Truth would never have been on the mission of **Nzoputa Uwa**.

Let it be known that it is through the movement of the Ekwueme People of Truth can the human spirit realize the supreme vision of **Nzoputa Uwa** in every region of the planet. Without the mission of **Nzoputa Uwa**, the movement of the Ekwueme People of Truth would not have been universal. It is the **Movement of Nzoputa Uwa** that makes the Ekwueme a universal being through the devotion of purpose to the supreme principle of EKUMEKU.

In order for the human spirit to self-realize the *supreme vision of Nzoputa Uwa*, the individual must have attained the devotion of purpose to the supreme principle of EKUMEKU. The attainment of the devotion of purpose to the supreme principle of EKUMEKU is the Master Key to the self-realization of the vision of **Nzoputa Uwa.**

The **Movement of Nzoputa Uwa** is fundamental in the understanding of the differences that would always exist between the time of **Oge Nzuzu** and the time of **Nzoputa Uwa.** The distance that would always exist between the time of **Oge Nzuzu** and the time of **Nzoputa Uwa** can never be recognized without the movement of the Ekwueme People of Truth.

It is the **Movement of Nzoputa Uwa** that is ordained in the reckoning of the Ekwueme Calendar. In other words, the Movement of Nzoputa Uwa determines the distance between the time of **Oge Nzuzu** and the time of **Nzoputa Uwa.** Consequently, it is through the **Movement of Nzoputa Uwa** can human history be properly understood according to the Divine Plan of the One Creator of the universe. Therefore, the movement of the Ekwueme People of Truth is **Nzoputa Uwa**; and it is the movement of life everlasting that would always exist in the wholeness of eternity for the liberation of the human spirit from the dead end nature of the world of Ekwensu. No doubt, the Movement of Nzoputa Uwa would always exist in the wholeness of eternity for the salvation of the individual Chi of the Ekwensu people.

THE CREATOR IS ONE. THE ONE IS AMUN AND THE DIVINE PLAN IS EKUMEKU. OTUA-KA-ODI!

III. **THE SIGNIFICANCE OF ATLANTA**

Let it be known that there is only one single Truth underlying every aspect of creation. This one single Truth that underlies every aspect of life is the Truth of the divine birth of EKUMEKU on the Second year of Nzoputa Uwa.

---THE HOLY ANKHUWA

The historical process of the time of **Nzoputa Uwa** is the chronological order upon which the Truth of the divine birth of EKUMEKU is made manifest and acted upon. The significance of Atlanta in the **Movement of Nzoputa Uwa** is very profound. Atlanta is the city where the Movement of Nzoputa Uwa began in the experience of time. Atlanta is the city where the divine birth of EKUMEKU became the ultimate reality. Atlanta is the city where the One Creator of the universe intervened and the Truth was revealed on the First Year of **Nzoputa Uwa**. Also, it was in Atlanta that the first battle was fought between the followers of the Divine Plan of the One Creator of the universe and the worshipers of the created images of the human mind. The enemies of the Spirit of Truth came with their evil of unbelief to turn back the water when it should flow. But the One Creator of the universe intervened and the inspiration to move to the Holy Land made the effort of the enemies of MAAT futile for they did not know what they were doing.

Living for many years at 657 Lawton Street, Apartment #4, S.W., Atlanta, Georgia, and Chukwudi was not happy about the Ekwensu world condition of his people. There was hopelessness and despair. There were many signs of self-hatred. The feeling of being a victim of history was all pervading. The atmosphere was filled with the fear of the other person who must never be trusted. There was ignorance, falsehood and deception as the dominant consciousness. The agreement with Nsi was the celebrated way of life in death. All around him, in the mist of the facade of trying to catch up, Chukwudi noticed that his people saw life as a tragedy and saw themselves as the victims of life's tragedy. Being that most of them were the followers of the religions of ISFET, there was confusion as to the relationship that ought to exist between fact and truth. Many confused faith with Truth and did not understand that faith is the inward realization of the Truth of the One Creator of the universe. This was during the time of **Oge Nzuzu** when there was no knowledge of EKUMEKU.

But as Chukwudi was meditating about the Ekwensu world

condition in his Apartment, which was later turned into the first Ekwueme Haremakhet in Atlanta, he heard a distinct Voice, *the Voice of Salvation*, in a devotional experience saying: ***"THE CREATOR IS ONE. THE ONE IS AMUN AND THE DIVINE PLAN IS EKUMEKU."*** The Voice continued to speak to his heart and mind saying: ***"THERE IS NO OTHER CREATOR OF THE UNIVERSE BUT AMUN IN WHOM YOU MUST TRUST"***. As can be understood, Chukwudi was very much perplexed until his innermost being heard: ***"THE WHOLE WORLD OF EKWENSU IS IGNORANT OF EKUMEKU"***.

Evidently, the Ekwensu people do not realize that there is a fundamental difference between the One Creator of the universe and the creation of the universe. The Ekwensu people worship the created out of ignorance, falsehood and deception. They confuse the created to be the One Creator of the universe. They lack the knowledge of AMUN in whom all Truth resides because they worship the created instead of the One Creator of the universe. They do not know that the One Creator of the universe transcends every form or shape that the human mind would ever conceive. They do not know that AMUN in whom we trust is both manifest and unmanifest. They worship the created images of the human mind. They are in the need of EKUMEKU because there can never be moral liberation without ethical salvation.

It was in Atlanta on that First Year of **Nzoputa Uwa** that the Truth of the divine birth of EKUMEKU was known through the divine intervention of the One Creator of the universe. On that fateful day, Chukwudi was awakened from his deep sleep of slumber and he did not know where to begin. He did not know what to do about the Truth that has been revealed unto him for many months. It was not until the Second Year of **Nzoputa Uwa**, after the divine birth of EKUMEKU, that Chukwudi became convinced without any doubt that he had been chosen by the One Creator of the universe for the mission of **Nzoputa Uwa** through the Almighty Spirit of EKUMEKU. Although the First Year of **Nzoputa Uwa** was the year of separation from the world of Ekwensu, it was on the Second year of **Nzoputa Uwa** that Chukwudi began to teach with divine authority as the Chosen

One of **Nzoputa Uwa**

The Chosen One for the mission of **Nzoputa Uwa** was chosen by the One Creator of the universe and it must be understood that *Chukwudi Okeke Maduno* did not choose himself for this extraordinary program of human redemption. Instead, the Chosen One was chosen by the One Creator of the universe to serve humanity through the Holy Cause of **Nzoputa Uwa**. Initially, Chukwudi was overwhelmed by the overpowering majesty of the Almighty Spirit of EKUMEKU and was alone in the knowledge of the *Eziokwu* before the Spirit of Truth made it possible for him to completely reconcile himself with the Word of Truth.

It is AMUN in whom we trust that chose Chukwudi for the mission of **Nzoputa Uwa**, in accordance with the Divine Purpose, as it has been ordained in the Divine Plan of creation. *It was there in Atlanta that Chukwudi was chosen by the One Creator of the universe to become the first historical Ekwueme, the living Haremakhet, in the history of human life and the human model of self-transformation for those who would follow in his footsteps.*

This realization that there is only One Creator of the universe removed every doubt in his mind about the substantial nature of the universe. His acceptance of the Call to serve the Divine Will of the One Creator of the universe was made manifest when he began to proclaim the **Ozioma of Truth** publicly. This acceptance to bear witness that there is only One Creator of the universe began with his public declaration that there is no God in any form or shape that is worthy of worship. His testimony to the Truth is the **Ozioma of Truth** and it is from the **Ozioma of Truth** can every human spirit declare publicly the **Nkwekolita** of the Ekwueme Universal Life.

Therefore, the Chosen One was chosen by the One Creator of the universe so that those who believe in his **Ozioma of Truth** shall realize the truthfulness of EKUMEKU. There is no other Creator of the universe but AMUN in whom we must trust. No doubt, the truthfulness of EKUMEKU transcends everything that has been or will ever be in the history of human life. This Advent of EKUMEKU is the new moral and ethical dispensation that can only be understood through the historical process of **Nzoputa Uwa**.

What began in Atlanta on the First Year of **Nzoputa Uwa**, at #657 Lawton Street, was a new beginning for all humanity with a future and implication that may have not been fully recognized by the Ekwensu world multitude. This is because it has only begun and its consequences would be far reaching. What it represents is the New World Order of the Ekwueme People of Truth that is bound to transform human thought and behavior. The end of the time of **Oge Nzuzu** was the beginning of the time of **Nzoputa Uwa**. We are on the threshold of the New Era in human consciousness. The Old shall pass away with time and the New shall emerge to dominate the human consciousness in the universe.

The mission of *Nzoputa Uwa* would affect every aspect of the human condition and everything that applied before would never be the same again. Whoever follows in the footsteps of the Chosen One shall not perish but rather will realize everlasting life. ***WHEREFORE, the significance of Atlanta is that those who cannot come to the Holy Land for pilgrimage but can afford to go to Atlanta should go to Atlanta***. From Ralph Abernathy Blvd, coming from WestEnd mall, on the left of Lawton Street, should be preserved and developed for the Third Most Holy Haremakhet. That was the area where the first battle between the forces of MAAT and the forces of ISFET took place in the early years of the time of **Nzoputa Uwa**. The forces of ISFET were defeated because the Chosen One was chosen by the One Creator of the universe for the mission of **Nzoputa Uwa**.

After their defeat, the forces of ISFET became terrorists. These Ekwensu people who were preaching "love" and yet in actuality were practicing hate and bigotry, when confronted by the Almighty Spirit of EKUMEKU, became terrorists, blocking the road and terrorizing innocent people. But their terror did not affect the devoted followers of the Divine Plan of AMUN in whom we trust. Because everything ought to happen according to the Divine Plan of AMUN in whom all Truth resides, the inspiration came for us to migrate to our present abode. We are now in the Holy Land, but the eternal struggle between the forces of MAAT and the forces of ISFET has only begun. The enemies of MAAT must surrender unconditionally to the Divine Will of the One Creator of the universe. OTUA-KA-ODI!

IV. THE CONSCIOUSNESS OF TIME

Time is the point of measurement of the definite movement of consciousness for the realization of life's destiny, in the knowledge of what has happened in the past, what is happening in the present and what is going to happen in the future. The essence of time is consciousness. This is why, one can never understand time without the consciousness of what has made time realizable. No doubt, it is the consciousness of time that gives value to the Ekwueme mastership of life. Therefore, the measurement of time cannot exist without the consciousness of time.

Every Ekwueme master is a time conscious human being who can never take time for granted. Why? This is because time does not exist in a vacuum. It is the consciousness of what IS and what is NOT that gives value to the reality of time. An Ekwueme master may seem like everybody, but the master is different because through the devotion of purpose to the supreme principle of EKUMEKU his consciousness of time is a reality that radiates like the sun.

The consciousness of time must be realized by the human spirit before the devoted follower of the Divine Plan of AMUN in whom we trust can realize the wholeness of eternity. If one has not realized the consciousness of time, it is humanly impossible to realize the timelessness of eternity. If the human spirit has no life in EKUMEKU, how can such a human spirit realize life everlasting? It is what has been realized here that would lead the human spirit to the realization of the life in the Hereafter. If one has not realized the consciousness of time with the body, the human spirit can never realize the consciousness of timelessness, with or without the body. There is nothing that can be greater than its consciousness.

When you are told that there is the time of **Oge Nzuzu** and the time of **Nzoputa Uwa**, you must ask yourself: Which historical process do I belong to? Do I belong to the time of **Oge Nzuzu** or do I belong to the time of **Nzoputa Uwa** in consciousness? Never deceive yourself with a false answer. If your answer is that you belong to the time of **Oge Nzuzu** in consciousness, you should know that you are living in agreement with Nsi, in ignorance of EKUMEKU. But if you belong to the time of **Nzoputa Uwa** in consciousness, you ought to realize the vision of **Nzoputa Uwa** through the devotion of purpose to the supreme principle of EKUMEKU.

Without the consciousness of time, the human spirit would be wasting time in life instead of using time in life to realize life everlasting. Do not waste your time because your time is limited in life. Those who waste their time, would always say "Had I known" before the end of their life. The life of the Unbelievers would have neither meaning nor purpose. They would live and die for nothing like animals and eternal punishment shall be upon them. If you are not conscious of the time of **Nzoputa Uwa**, it is better that you are yet to be born than to be a living dead in the time of **Nzoputa Uwa**.

In order to become conscious of the time of **Nzoputa Uwa**, we must accept EKUMEKU as our eternal Savior and Redeemer from the dead end nature of the world of Ekwensu. We must renounce ISFET by living MAAT through the devotion of purpose to the supreme principle of EKUMEKU. We must follow in the footsteps of the Chosen One for the mission of Nzoputa Uwa by becoming the devoted followers of the Divine Plan of the One Creator of the universe. We must declare publicly the **Nkwekolita** of the Ekwueme Universal Life. And, we must reject the worship of any created image of the human mind.

Therefore, in order to become conscious of the time of **Nzoputa Uwa**, we must worship only the One Creator of the universe through the devotion of purpose to the supreme principle of EKUMEKU. In other words, we must become an Ekwueme master of life in order to become conscious of the time of **Nzoputa Uwa**. No doubt, the time of **Nzoputa Uwa** is everlasting because it has been ordained from the beginning of creation by the One Creator of the universe.

The consciousness of the time of **Nzoputa Uwa** cannot exist without the Truth of the divine birth of EKUMEKU, which is acted upon by the Ekwueme in order to produce the change in consciousness that would make the time of **Oge Nzuzu** the subordinate opposite of the time of **Nzoputa Uwa.**

Without any doubt, the concept of time is based on the consciousness of what IS against what is NOT. It is the distance that exists between what IS and what is NOT that is the true meaning of time. The separateness of being that is the embodiment of the time of **Oge Nzuzu** can never be truly understood without the recognition of the oneness of being that embodies the time of **Nzoputa Uwa**. Since the end of the time of **Oge Nzuzu** is the beginning of the time of **Nzoputa Uwa**, the Movement of **Nzoputa Uwa** is the fundamental basis of realizing the differences that would always exist between the time of **Oge Nzuzu** and the time of **Nzoputa Uwa**.

My brothers and sisters in EKUMEKU, let it be known that the consciousness of time in the world of Ekwensu is fundamentally different with the consciousness of time in the world of EKUMEKU. During the time of **Oge Nzuzu**, the Spirit of EKUMEKU was hidden in the world of Ekwensu because of Nsi. There was ignorance, falsehood and deception as a result. The time of **Oge Nzuzu** was the historical period when evil dominated good due to the ignorance of EKUMEKU. It was the time when the faculty of ISFET dominated the faculty of MAAT because of the worship of the created images of the human mind. The entire humanity was practicing Ekwensism in one form or the other. The peoples of the planet were not conscious of the time of **Nzoputa Uwa**. There was neither existence nor non-existence due to the fear of Nsi. Because those who fear Nsi cannot overcome evil by doing good, the Ekwensu people of the planet were entangled with evil in the vicious circle of eternal death, living in agreement with Nsi.

There is no true consciousness of time except that which is defined by the Truth of the divine birth of EKUMEKU. It is the measurement of the distance between the time of **Oge Nzuzu** and the time of **Nzoputa Uwa** that is the true consciousness of time. On the contrary, during the time of **Oge Nzuzu**, the religions of ISFET preached many things that were based on ignorance, falsehood and deception. The Ekwensu people were made to believe in Dogmas which were in opposition to the Divine Plan of the One Creator of the universe. The Ekwensu people's reckoning of time had no relationship with the consciousness of what it means to know the Truth. Wherefore, the religions of ISFET do not have the true consciousness of time because of the ignorance of EKUMEKU

Note: For those Unbelievers who are using the Calendar of Julius Caesar that was later amended by Pope Gregory, to measure time, let it be known that it can never be an accurate reckoning of time. Did your Ekwensu Calendar start at the birth of Julius Caesar or at his death? What is the consciousness that underlies such a Calendar? Did Julius Caesar renounce ISFET by living MAAT? Was he an Ekwueme master of life? What is the Julius Caesar Calendar based on? Why do you say that A.D. is After the Death of Caesar and B.C. is Before Caesar? Why do you then turn around to say that your Calendar is a Christian Calendar? Was Julius Caesar a Christian follower of this religion of ISFET? To the Ekwueme, the Calendar of Julius Caesar is based on nothing as far as the consciousness of time is concerned. Thus, the religions of ISFET pretend to themselves with the false belief that their Calendar is genuine.

V. THE END OF THE TIME OF OGE NZUZU

The end of the time of **Oge Nzuzu** was the beginning of the time of **Nzoputa Uwa**. On that original point of beginning, at the

Spring Equinox, the Sun from its path along the ecliptic crossed the celestial equator, making the length of the day and the night to be equal, attaining perfect equilibrium, thus marking the First New Year of the time of **Nzoputa Uwa**. In other words, the beginning of the time of **Nzoputa Uwa** is situated at the time of the Spring Equinox, when what is hidden was revealed to the Chosen One for the mission of **Nzoputa Uwa**, which led to the emergence of this new cycle in time. The precession of the Equinoxes changed the position of the Sun, which began the emergent cycle of MAAT in the universe because the cycle of ISFET has accomplished its time. Because its time has expired, the forces of ISFET would gradually cease to remain as the dominant force and the forces of MAAT would gradually emerge to give meaning and purpose to the Spirit. Therefore, the divine birth of EKUMEKU has inaugurated this struggle in time, between the forces of ISFET and the forces of MAAT, for the power of the Spirit.

No doubt, the end of the time of **Oge Nzuzu** has come from the advent of the time of **Nzoputa Uwa**. This time of **Nzoputa Uwa** is the dispensation of the moral repentance of the human spirit from Nsi. Without any doubt, this is the time for the repentance of the human spirit to reconcile itself with the Truth of the divine birth of EKUMEKU. In this evolution of the time of **Nzoputa Uwa**, the course of the future history of humanity has begun to emerge in this new dimension of the human consciousness. The Divine Plan of Salvation is the revealed Truth which has been divinely inspired, conceived and manifested in order that it would be fulfilled by AMUN in whom we trust through the mission of **Nzoputa Uwa**. So, the Master Key to the future of this universe of life is EKUMEKU and the future itself belongs to those who have this Master Key.

During the time of **Oge Nzuzu**, there was no unity of human existence. The concept of unity was a euphemism used by one group against another group. There was the rampant abuse of human morality and the misapplication of the universal principles of life. Thus, whatever that existed during the time of **Oge Nzuzu** can only be understood in its separateness of being.

Separation, division, strife are the definite nature of the Ekwensi condition. That is why, there was dilemma. There was contradiction in what was preached and what was practiced; and there was strife overwhelmingly during the time **Oge Nzuzu**. The separateness of being was the dominant way of life because the whole world of Ekwensu was ignorant of EKUMEKU. The worship of the created images of the human mind was the celebrated way of life.

But in this time of **Nzoputa Uwa**, the oneness of being an Ekwueme would dominate the separateness of being an Ekwensi. All dilemmas and contradictions of being an Ekwensi would be reconciled and the oneness of being an Ekwueme would become a reality that could never be doubted. The Ekwueme then becomes the human spirit who has experienced the supreme vision of **Nzoputa Uwa** as the ultimate meaning and purpose of human life through the devotion of purpose in EKUMEKU. In other words, the Ekwueme is the devoted follower of the Divine Plan of the One Creator of the universe.

Thus, the end of the time of **Oge Nzuzu** is the end of the time of worshipping the created images of the human mind. The judgment of the time of **Oge Nzuzu** is the beginning of the time of **Nzoputa Uwa**. For, it is the time of Nzoputa Uwa that would judge the time of **Oge Nzuzu**. Also, it is from the judgment of the time of **Oge Nzuzu** that the morality of repentance from Nsi would be made realizable for every human spirit. Let it be known that the time of repentance from Nsi is at hand. Those who have repented from Nsi and are living according to the Divine Plan of the One Creator of the universe would inherit the New World Order of EKUMEKU. They would live in the world of Ekwensu and yet would exist in the wholeness of eternity in the world of EKUMEKU, where there is neither suffering nor death.

To whom that is repentant to Nsi and has become the devoted follower of the Divine Plan of AMUN in whom we trust, shall be rewarded with the Life of Truth in this life and eternal life in the hereafter. But to whom that is unrepentant from Nsi, who lives in the dead end nature of the world of Ekwensu, even the life that is lived in agreement with Nsi shall be taken away and eternal death shall be cast upon it. It is of no benefit to the human spirit to reject the Truth of the divine birth of EKUMEKU on the Second Year of **Nzoputa Uwa** for the Truth is the life itself. Whomever lives in agreement with Nsi cannot know the life in Truth for as the human spirit is living in death there can never be life in Truth without the repentance from Nsi.

The life in Truth is a divine ordinance from the One Creator of the universe that derived its historical impetus from the supreme vision of **Nzoputa Uwa**, with its belief in the resurrection of the human spirit from the dead end nature of the world of Ekwensu and the promise of life everlasting, if one can follow in the footsteps of the Chosen One through the devotion of purpose in EKUMEKU. This life in Truth is the life of repentance from Nsi and Nsi is whatever that can exist in thought, word or deed against the Divine Plan of the One Creator of the universe, or in opposition to the Truth thereof.

The divine birth of EKUMEKU, no doubt, has ended the mindless euphemism of the Ekwensu people with the end to the epoch of the time of **Oge Nzuzu**. Now, in this time of **Nzoputa Uwa**, there would no longer be any separation between Igbo and Hausa, between black and white, between male and female because through the devotion of purpose in EKUMEKU everybody is one. For it is in EKUMEKU that all things were formed and all things come into existence according to the Divine Plan of the One Creator of the universe. Wherefore, the reconciliation or harmony that can exist between the world of Ekwensu and the world of EKUMEKU is the Truth made manifest in human life. The time of **Nzoputa Uwa** is the Movement of the Spirit of Truth against the dead end nature of the world of Ekwensu in its time of **Oge Nzuzu**. But life has gone out of the time of **Oge Nzuzu**. It no longer has any movement and can only be understood in its relationship with the time of **Nzoputa Uwa**.

Consequently, the distance between the time of **Oge Nzuzu** and time of **Nzoputa Uwa** is determined by the Movement of the

Spirit of Truth according to the Ekwueme Calendar. Thus, the Ekwueme starting point in history would be from the beginning of the time of **Nzoputa Uwa**. But since the time of **Nzoputa Uwa** was divinely generated from the time of **Oge Nzuzu**, the measurement or reckoning of time would be based on the distance that would always exist between the time of **Oge Nzuzu** and the time of **Nzoputa Uwa**. It is the Movement of the time of **Nzoputa Uwa** that would act upon the time of Oge Nzuzu. This is because the time of **Oge Nzuzu** can offer no resistance to the Movement of **Nzoputa Uwa** and can only give way continually as its nature demands.

Let it then be known that our starting point in the historical process is the First Year of **Nzoputa Uwa**. Whatever happened before the Ekwueme starting point in time belongs to the time of **Oge Nzuzu** and can only be reconciled according to the Divine Plan of AMUN in whom we trust. Whatever it is that is not based on the devotion of purpose to the supreme principle of EKUMEKU can only be understood from the standpoint of the time of **Oge Nzuzu**. It is the historical process of **Nzoputa Uwa** acting on its accord that would separate itself from the non-existent life of the time of **Oge Nzuzu** in order to fulfill the Divine Plan of AMUN in whom we trust. OTUA-KA-ODI!

VI. THE EKWUEME CALENDAR

The Ekwueme Calendar is the compass that every devoted follower of the Divine Plan of the One Creator of the universe should use to locate himself or herself in the map of universal consciousness of what it means to be human.   ---The Chosen One

O you, the seeker of Truth, live MAAT by renouncing ISFET through the devotion of purpose in EKUMEKU, and thine life shall be a blessing unto thee in this Time of Ausar and Auset. ---THE HOLY ANKHUWA

The reckoning of time cannot exist without the unity of consciousness in time. What makes the unity of consciousness to exist in time is the self-certainty of its origin, of its purpose, of its nature and of its destiny. Because time in itself is neither wholly an object nor is it wholly a subject, it cannot stand on its own without the self-certainty of consciousness of its unity of being, which gives it form in human experience. Therefore, the reckoning of time is an expression of the **Movement of Nzoputa Uwa** in its expansion of experience in time and space.

There can never be an Ekwueme Calendar without the **Eternal Wheel of Nzoputa Uwa** which has separated itself from the experience in time during the time of **Oge Nzuzu**. That is why, the Ekwueme Calendar began its forward reckoning of time at that point in time when the **Eternal Wheel of Nzoputa Uwa** was set in motion by the One Creator of the universe, through the Almighty Spirit of EKUMEKU. Whereas, the backward or descending reckoning of the time of **Oge Nzuzu** is calculated based on the measurement of the distance that will always exist between the point in time when the **Eternal Wheel of Nzoputa Uwa** was set in motion and the experience in time before the time of **Nzoputa Uwa**. Thus, it is the **Eternal Wheel of Nzoputa Uwa** that has broken the vicious cycle of living in a dead time, of living on a borrowed time, in the experience of life and of living on a spooky time.

Before the time of **Nzoputa Uwa**, the reckoning of time in the world of Ekwensu was (and it is still presently) based on ignorance, falsehood and deception. For an example: If you ask the Ekwensu people about the origin or purpose of their reckoning of time, many would tell you that their Calendar was instituted by Julius Caesar. But if you were to ask them to explain the historical event that led to the institution of their Calendar, they would speak from another side of their mouth by saying that their Calendar is based on "Before their God was born" and "After their God was born". And when you ask them a very simple question: **Your God and your Calendar which one came first?** Whatever response that you would get from them would always contradict the existence of such a Calendar.

If the Calendar was instituted by their God, they can claim that their Calendar is an expression of their consciousness of the created image in the experience of time. But if their Calendar was instituted Before their God was born, how can such a Calendar represent the experience of real time in the self-certainty of unified consciousness? What if the man who instituted the Calendar had lived many years before their God was born? What then is the justification for such a Calendar? Their Calendar no doubt was instituted Before their God was born. The origin of the Calendar was not when their God was born because the Calendar was already in use when their God was born.

When the Calendar was instituted, the purpose was not to reckon time in the self-certainty of unified consciousness of worshiping only the One Creator of the universe through the devotion of purpose in EKUMEKU. If they claim that their reckoning of time had been divided between the time "Before their God was born" and the time "After their God was born", there is no truth in such a bogus claim. Even if their God is made to be born on the first year of their Calendar, was their God worshiped from the moment he was born? The self-certainty of unified consciousness that he is their God, was it a consciousness that began in the experience of time from the first year of their Calendar? How can such a Calendar be recognized when there is no self-certainty of its origin or purpose? When a Calendar is not based on the movement of the **Eternal Wheel of Nzoputa Uwa**, it can only be based on ignorance, falsehood and deception.

Wherefore, the Ekwueme Calendar began its forward reckoning of time at that point in time when the self-certainty of unified consciousness was originally realized. In the reckoning of time, the self-certainty of unified consciousness in the experience of time can never be overemphasized. This self-certainty of unified consciousness in the experience of time has its origin at that point in time when the One Creator of the universe intervened, through the Almighty Spirit of EKUMEKU, by setting in motion the **Eternal Wheel of Nzoputa Uwa**. That historical moment in time was the first Ekwueme New Year and had been generically known as the Day of the Spring Equinox.

The Ekwueme yearly Calendar is divided into 12 months. Every year that is divisible by four {4} will have an **Abnormal year** of 366 days, and on that year the month of Shabaka will have 31 days. The Ekwueme Calendar reckoning will be 365 days for **Normal year** and 366 days for the **Abnormal year**.

THE EKWUEME CALENDAR:

FIRST MONTH = THE MONTH OF **AUSAR**/ 31 DAYS

SECOND MONTH = THE MONTH OF **SEKHMET**/ 30 DAYS

THIRD MONTH = THE MONTH OF **SEBEK**/ 30 DAYS

FOURTH MONTH = THE MONTH OF **TEHUTI**/ 30 DAYS

FIFTH MONTH = THE MONTH OF **NEKHEBET**/ 31 DAYS

SIXTH MONTH = THE MONTH OF **HERUKHUTI**/ 30 DAYS

SEVENTH MONTH = THE MONTH OF **MAKHEPERU**/ 31 DAYS

EIGHTH MONTH = THE MONTH OF **MESKHENET**/ 30 DAYS

NINTH MONTH = THE MONTH OF **HATSHEPSUT**/ 31 DAYS

NZOPUTA UWA

TENTH MONTH = THE MONTH OF **SHABAKA**/30(N) 31(A) DAYS

ELEVENTH MONTH= THE MONTH OF **AKHENATEN** /30 DAYS

TWELFTH MONTH = THE MONTH OF **AUSET** /31 DAYS

An other name for the **Ekwueme Calendar** is **The Time of Ausar and Auset**. When an Ekwueme says in the **Time of Ausar and Auset**, he or she means according to the reckoning of the **Ekwueme Calendar**. This is partly because the month of **Ausar** is the first month and the month of **Auset** is the twelfth month. Thus, whenever one hears the **Time of Ausar and Auset**, it means the **Unbroken Cycle of the Eternal Wheel of Nzoputa Uwa**. For the experience in time of every Ekwueme can only be understood from the standpoint of the **Time of Ausar and Auset**, which is the self-certainty of unified consciousness in its ultimate reality.

Also, when an Ekwueme says that something happened in the **Time of Ausar and Auset,** it means that the event took place during the time of **Nzoputa Uwa.** In other words, in the world of EKUMEKU, every bonafide Ekwueme exists in the wholeness of eternity in the **Time of Ausar and Auset.** And, it is only through the devotion of purpose in EKUMEKU can the human spirit live in the wholeness of eternity in the **Time of Ausar and Auset**.

In every generation, the legitimate authority to protect, preserve, regulate and to reckon time according to the Divine Plan of AMUN in whom we trust has been bestowed on The Great Haremakhet in the movement of the **Eternal Wheel of Nzoputa Uwa**. Every Ekwueme community and every established Haremakhet can produce its own Ekwueme Calendar based on the authorized reckoning of **The Great Haremakhet.**

Whenever necessary, **The Great Haremakhet** can institute minor adjustment in the scheme of the number of days in the month of Shabaka based on precise calculation of the movement of the **Eternal Wheel of Nzoputa Uwa**. In the 100th year interval, the month of Shabaka shall be 30 days except on every 4th 100th year interval when it will be 31 days. In every 400 years, the years ending in 00 will have three 31 number of days, while one shall have 30 number of days in the month of Shabaka.

Therefore, the Ekwueme Calendar has 365 days on a Normal year and 366 days on an Abnormal year. Although in general, the Ekwueme Calendar recognizes the cycle of a year and reckons it to be 365 1/4 days. In every 100th year, there is a minor adjustment except on the 4th of every 100th year. That is to say, that the year 100 N.U. instead of being 366 days will be 365 days, the same thing with the year 200 N.U., and 300 N.U.; but the year 400 N.U. will be 366 days.

Again, the reckoning of the time of **Oge Nzuzu** is based on the measurement of the distance of the experience in time before the time of **Nzoputa Uwa**, to the point in time when the **Eternal Wheel of Nzoputa Uwa** was set in motion. **As a result, the Movement of Nzoputa Uwa is the life of eternity in the Time of Ausar and Auset**. OTUA-KA-ODI!

VII. THE PUBLIC DECLARATION OF NKWEKOLITA

Do not wait until it is too late to declare your Nkwekolita with the Truth of the divine birth of EKUMEKU. Declare your Nkwekolita now and shame the Ekwensu people. ---THE CHOSEN ONE.

The public declaration of **Nkwekolita** is the first step in the right direction of becoming a devoted follower of the Divine Plan of AMUN in whom we trust. In order to break the yoke of Nsi in which we are all born in the world of Ekwensu, the human spirit must voluntarily struggle to become disagreeable with Nsi by renouncing ISFET and living MAAT. There is nobody that can be able to break the agreement with Nsi without the public declaration of Nkwekolita through the devotion of purpose in EKUMEKU.

The morality to repent from Nsi is fundamental in the public declaration of Nkwekolita. The public declaration of Nkwekolita ought to be done through the voluntary effort of the individual to renounce ISFET by living MAAT. There ought not to be any compulsion in the voluntary effort of the human spirit to overcome evil by doing good.

However, if a human spirit after the public declaration of Nkwekolita goes back to recant what the individual has freely declared publicly in word, thought and deed, to the best knowledge of the living Haremakhet, the human spirit would become guilty of apostasy. The *Biafra Ocha* can be waged against any apostate according to the Divine Plan of the One Creator of the universe. Every apostate is an enemy of the Living Truth and ought to be treated as an Ekwensi who is actively engaged in opposition to the mission of Nzoputa Uwa. But when the human spirit repents from Nsi in the Spirit of MAAT, the individual should be forgiven after being ritually cleansed because the One Creator of the universe is All-Knowing of the past, present and future of every life in the universe.

The Ekwueme is not born again in the image of EKUMEKU to become entangled with evil, but instead to overcome evil by doing good. Without any doubt, the mission of **Nzoputa Uwa** exists in the wholeness of eternity so that every human spirit, in the Spirit of MAAT, can overcome evil by doing good. Therefore, any human spirit who has publicly declared the *Nkwekolita* of the Ekwueme Universal Life in the Spirit of MAAT ought to be considered as an Ekwueme with all due respect and regard to the human spirit's rights and privileges as a follower of the Divine Plan of AMUN in whom we trust.

Prior to the time of the public declaration of **Nkwekolita** by a New Believer, the human spirit ought to have apprehended the

Spirit of EKUMEKU before making the spiritual commitment to become a follower of the Divine Plan of AMUN in whom we trust. The public declaration of *Nkwekolita* is a voluntary spiritual commitment by a human spirit who has freely decided to become a follower of the Divine Plan of the One Creator of the universe.

Without the public declaration of *Nkwekolita*, the human spirit would not be capable of renouncing ISFET by living MAAT. In order to become aware of the morality of repentance from Nsi, the human spirit ought to detach itself from the worship of any created image of the human mind. The following meditation can be used by the human spirit in solitude and silence to detach the mind, body and spirit from the evil of unbelief:

MEDITATION
Homage to thee my One and only Creator of the universe in whom all Truth resides. I have come to Thee in whom I trust and have devoted my life to Thy worship that I may become a follower of Thy Divine Plan of creation. In humility and Truth, have I come into Thy attunement, in repentance from Nsi, that I may be blessed with thy Almighty Spirit of EKUMEKU, my eternal Savior and Redeemer. Thank You My Creator for Saving Me in the Spirit of MAAT. AMEN!

Evidently, *Nkwekolita* is of the heart and of the tongue. Wherefore, let us have an agreement with you the unbeliever in the Living Truth that there is only One Creator of the universe. Let us have an agreement with you the Ekwensi that the One Creator of the universe is the only One worthy of worship. Let us have an agreement with you who are in slavery and bondage in the dead end nature of the world of Ekwensu that the One Creator of the universe is AMUN in whom we must trust. Let us have an agreement with you who are entangled with evil in the vicious circle of eternal death that the Divine Plan of the One Creator of the universe is EKUMEKU.

Indeed, let us have an agreement with you who are searching for the Truth that when you accept EKUMEKU as your eternal

Savior and Redeemer in the Spirit of MAAT, you would realize the Truth within you and around you. Let us have an agreement with you who are oppressed that when you become a devoted follower of the Divine Plan of AMUN in whom we trust, you would voluntarily become free from oppression. Let us have an agreement with you who are naked in the spirit that when you declare your Nkwekolita publicly you would be clothed in the Spirit of MAAT. Let us have an agreement with you who are hopeless and in despair that when you have attained the devotion of purpose to the supreme principle of EKUMEKU, you would become the master of your life's destiny. Let us have an agreement with you who live in agreement with Nsi that when you renounce ISFET by living MAAT, you would develop the morality of repentance from Nsi.

Certainly, let us have an agreement with you that there is no God in any form or shape that is worthy of worship and you would not fear evil of any kind. Let us have an agreement with you who are in doubt that the Chosen One was chosen by the One Creator of the universe for the mission of Nzoputa Uwa and you would be divinely guided to follow in his footsteps.

Consequently, let us all declare publicly and individually the **Nkwekolita** of the Ekwueme Universal Life, as follows:

"I BELIEVE IN THE TRUTH OF THE ONE CREATOR OF THE UNIVERSE. I BELIEVE THAT THE ONE CREATOR OF THE UNIVERSE IS AMUN IN WHOM I TRUST. I BELIEVE THAT THE DIVINE PLAN OF THE ONE CREATOR OF THE UNIVERSE IS EKUMEKU. OTUA-KA-ODI! "

This public declaration of **Nkwekolita** constitutes the declaration of intention to become an Ekwueme, the statement of conviction of the Truth of what it means to be an Ekwueme and the willingness to attain the devotion of purpose to the supreme principle of EKUMEKU. In the public declaration of Nkwekolita, the need for the fellowship with at least one bonafide Ekwueme who can bear witness to the Truth of the divine birth of EKUMEKU ought not to be ignored.

The children of Ekwueme parents should be exposed from childhood to the basic tenets of the Ekwueme Universal Life; but they should be allowed to reach the age of maturity before they can decide for themselves on the public declaration of **Nkwekolita. Every child ought to be nurtured in the Spirit of MAAT;** but no child should be allowed to declare publicly the Nkwekolita of the Ekwueme Universal Life until maturity. Although the Ekwueme Universal Life expresses fundamental opposition to the Ekwensi condition, everybody should be allowed to decide for itself, under normal circumstances.

Declare your **Nkwekolita** now. Do not wait for your wife, husband, father, mother, brother, sister or friend to do so first before you can muster the courage to make known to the public what is already in your heart. Your ability to realize human freedom depends a lot on how you made the unfettered declaration on your own. Of course, this is a matter of degree. However, it is healthy to ask an Ekwueme any question that you may have before the public declaration of **Nkwekolita**. OTUA-KA-ODI!

VIII. THE BASIC TRUTH OF NZUKO

Let it be known that the purpose of Nzizo is to realize Nzuko: NZIZO + NZUZU = NZUKO. The eternal struggle between MAAT and ISFET is Nzizo. That is to say, that the eternal struggle between good and evil is Nzizo. The state of society where ISFET dominates MAAT is Nzuzu. All differentiation in consciousness is inherently a negation of **Nzuko**. At the very best, this would lead to Nzizo. And at the very worst, this would lead to Nzuzu.

What then is **Nzuko**? The world of EKUMEKU is the realization of the divine order of MAAT which has been ordained by the One Creator of the universe for the complete human being. As long as there is Nzuzu, there would always be Nzizo. It is through Nzizo can the Ekwueme realize Nzuko. There can never be Nzuko without Nzizo and there can never be Nzizo without Nzuzu: NZIZO + NZUZU = NZUKO.

The state of human society where ISFET is displaced and MAAT is restored as the dominant consciousness in the universe of life is Nzuko. The state of human society where the world of Ekwensu is subordinated to the world of EKUMEKU is **Nzuko**. The ideal of Nzuko has no division, no separation from the supreme principle of EKUMEKU and no segmentation or splitting of the community of Believers. The Basic Truth of Nzuko is that state of human society where *Nkewa*, division, separation or segmentation, is perceived as Nsi. Since Nsi is anything that can exist in opposition to the Divine Plan of the One Creator of the universe, *Nkewa* is inherently a negation of Nzuko. No doubt, **Nzuko** comprehends and would always fulfill all the modalities of what it means to be an Ekwueme, who is the devoted follower of the Divine Plan of the One Creator of the universe.

The human quest for the realization of Nzuko necessitates that the following fundamental principles must have been realized: First, the human spirit must have become a follower of the Divine Plan of the One Creator of the universe. Second, the human spirit must have attained the devotion of purpose to the supreme principle of EKUMEKU. Third, the human spirit must have begun to follow in the footsteps of the Chosen One for the mission of Nzoputa Uwa. Fourth, the human spirit must renounce ISFET by living MAAT and as such must never worship any God or any created image of the human mind. Fifth, the human spirit must only worship the One Creator of the universe according to the Divine Plan of AMUN in whom we trust. Sixth, the human spirit must have performed the obligatory rites of the Public Declaration of Nkwekolita.

In other words, the quest for the realization of Nzuko necessitates that the human spirit ought to transcend the social, cultural and religious tendencies of the world of Ekwensu; so that it may be inspired by the Almighty Spirit of EKUMEKU for the fulfillment of the Truth of what it means to be an Ekwueme, and the realization of Nzuko thereof. There ought not to be any differentiation or division in consciousness of what it means to be an Ekwueme because the Chosen One was chosen by the One Creator of the universe for the mission of Nzoputa Uwa. The Nzuko Ekwueme is the complete realization of the universal being and must never find itself divided against itself like the Ekwensu groups of Nzuzu societies or any other social, cultural and religious ensembles.

Let it be known that in the absence of **Nzuko**, it would be a return to Nzuzu, a return to the time of **Oge Nzuzu**, when there was nothing in consciousness of what is EKUMEKU. This is to fall into the state of Ekwensu, the state in which the entire human society had been before the divine birth of EKUMEKU and the advent of the movement of Nzoputa Uwa.

The movement of **Nzoputa Uwa** is the life of eternity, unfolding the universality of the Ekwueme World History. The establishment of MAAT as the dominant consciousness and the subordination of ISFET would transform the Ekwensu societies, would guarantee the reign of justice and the realization of Nzuko, for the self-realization of life everlasting.

WHEREFORE, the Basic Truth of Nzuko is the creation of life in abundance through the expansion of the movement of Nzoputa Uwa with a single-minded devotion of purpose to the supreme principle of EKUMEKU.

Woe unto the human spirit who worships the created instead of the One Creator of the universe. Woe unto the Unbeliever in the Living Truth who forsakes the worship of the One Creator of the universe in order to worship a created image of the human mind. Woe unto every enemy of MAAT who condones unbelief, believing in injustice, preaching falsehood and practicing deception. Woe unto those who are fighting against the Living Truth with ignorance, falsehood and deception.

Peace shall be upon those who worship only the One Creator of the universe according to the Divine Plan of AMUN in whom we trust. Peace would be with those who follow in the footsteps of the Chosen One for the mission of Nzoputa Uwa through the devotion of purpose to the supreme principle of EKUMEKU.

May peace be among you, who have become the devoted followers of the Divine Plan of the One Creator of the universe. May the peace of the knowledge of Truth be with the human spirit who is striving to overcome evil by doing good. Without the Peace of the Almighty Spirit of EKUMEKU, the true meaning and purpose of human life can never be fully realized.

There is no God that is worthy of worship and EKUMEKU is the whole Truth. For there is nothing in the universe of life that can have either meaning or purpose without following the Divine Plan of the One Creator of the universe. Without the attainment of the devotion of purpose to the supreme principle of EKUMEKU, the human spirit would be living a life with neither meaning nor purpose. This is the revealed Truth of Nzuko. OTUA-KA-ODI!

IX. WHATEVER IS IN AGREEMENT WITH NSI IS PERISHABLE

The current Ekwueme Calendar year can easily be figured out by substracting 1993 from the current Ekwensu world common/Christian Calendar year, except for the first two months and 19 days or 20 days, as the case may be, of that Calendar.
   ----THE CHOSEN ONE

The Ekwueme symbol of identification is the Ankh. The Ankh is a cross with a loop at the top. The Ankh is the symbol of life according to the Divine Plan of the One Creator of the universe. Every bonafide Ekwueme should possess and defend the Ankh because it signifies the subordination of the Ekwensi condition of living a life by the Ekwueme nature of universal life.
----THE HOLY ANKHUWA

It has been revealed and it is written in **THE HOLY ANKHUWA** that whatever is in agreement with Nsi is mortal and perishable.

This Truth of everlasting life is the whole Truth of salvation for the individual Chi, the only Truth of eternal life and it is comparable to nothing except its own nature. In other words, the agreement with Nsi is the root cause of why the human spirit is born to die. But to live and die just like every other animal is not and ought not be the meaning and purpose of human life.

When the human spirit becomes disagreeable with Nsi and is a devoted follower of the Divine Plan of AMUN in whom we trust, such a life shall never die because of the salvation of the individual Chi. Without any doubt, the human spirit who is a bonafide Ekwueme shall never die. The bonafide Ekwueme will exist forever in the wholeness of eternity in the world of EKUMEKU.

Let it then be known that the human spirit which is separated from the supreme principle of EKUMEKU is an Ekwensi who is mortal and perishable. The human spirit which is not a devoted follower of the Divine Plan of the One Creator of the universe is an Ekwensi, who is ignorant of EKUMEKU. The human spirit which does not struggle to overcome evil by doing good is an Ekwensi, who is the diametrical opposite of the Ekwueme. The human spirit which does not follow in the footsteps of the Chosen One is an Ekwensi, who is an Unbeliever. In short, the human spirit who worships the created images of the human mind instead of the One Creator of the universe is an Ekwensi.

The essential truth of the Ekwensi condition is the human spirit who is agreeable to Nsi or who is dead in Nsi. It means that every Ekwensi is agreeable to Nsi as a result of being dead in Nsi. The human spirit which is dead in Nsi does not have any law or reality that can claim any form of boundary for itself against the mission of **Nzoputa Uwa**. The world of Ekwensu is the battlefield of life; while the world of EKUMEKU exists in the wholeness of eternity to make Chi-Ukwu manifest. Whoever struggles to overcome evil by doing good through the devotion of purpose in EKUMEKU shall be redeemed from all forms of Ekwensism of any kind.

No doubt, it is the separation of the Ekwensi from the supreme principle of EKUMEKU that makes the Ekwensi to be dead in Nsi. The Ekwensi is dead in Nsi because the human spirit has not attained the devotion of purpose in EKUMEKU. The Ekwensi is dead in Nsi because the elemental being is entangled with evil in the vicious circle of eternal death. The Ekwensi is dead in Nsi because the human spirit lives in the world of Ekwensu without existing in the eternity of the world of EKUMEKU. The Ekwensi is dead in Nsi because the elemental being lives in slavery and bondage in the dead end nature of the world of Ekwensu.

The Ekwensi is dead in Nsi because of the ignorance of EKUMEKU. The Ekwensi is dead in Nsi because the human spirit lacks the knowledge of good and evil. The Ekwensi is dead in Nsi because the Unbeliever is not conscious of Nsi. The Ekwensi is dead in Nsi because the human spirit worships the created images of the human mind instead of the One Creator of the universe. The Ekwensi is dead in Nsi because the ignorant Unbeliever secretly or outwardly is blasphemous against the Truth of the divine birth of EKUMEKU. The Ekwensi is dead in Nsi because the human spirit is not a devoted follower of the Divine Plan of AMUN in whom we trust. The Ekwensi is dead in Nsi because the human spirit does not follow in the footsteps of the Chosen One for the mission of Nzoputa Uwa. Therefore, the Ekwensi is dead in Nsi because the human spirit has not yet attained the devotion of purpose in EKUMEKU.

The salvation of the Ekwensi from the vicious circle of eternal death exists only through the devotion of purpose in EKUMEKU. The Ekwensi can never be redeemed from Nsi without following in the footsteps of the Chosen One. The Ekwensi can never be freed from all forms of agreement with Nsi without an unconditional surrender to the Divine Will of AMUN in whom we trust. The Ekwensi can never voluntarily worship the One Creator of the universe without the liberation of the individual Chi from the dead end nature of the world of Ekwensu. Wherefore, the Ekwensi is mortal and perishable because the human spirit lives in agreement with Nsi. Every Ekwensi is mortal and perishable without the repentance from

Nsi. Let every Ekwensi repent from Nsi and confess EKUMEKU as the only eternal Redeemer and Savior of the human spirit from the dead end nature of the world of Ekwensu. OTUA-KA-ODI!

X. THE REVELATION OF EKUMEKU

There is only One Creator of the universe which has been revealed unto us to be AMUN in whom we must trust. This Revelation of EKUMEKU in the life of Chukwudi would always exist in the wholeness of eternity to displace ISFET and restore MAAT as the dominant consciousness in the universe of life. Therefore, the Revelation of EKUMEKU in the life of Chukwudi is the quality and character of a simple and yet complex interrelationship maintaining a perfect coordination of unity in diversity according to its nature of what IS and what is NOT, through its divine authority and legitimate force, as it manifests the divine mastery of existence.

This truthfulness of EKUMEKU transcends the individual consciousness of the human spirit since it is the universal consciousness of life, which can be apprehended and realized by the individual, but it is not limited to the individual because it is the Ultimate Reality of life in the universe. This Chineke Consciousness which is the complete realization of the Divine Plan of the One Creator of the universe is humanly attainable, even though it is from it that human beings can attain within themselves the gifts of knowledge, truth and immortality.

Let it then be known that the Revelation of EKUMEKU in the life of Chukwudi is the **Okaiwu** made manifest. Let it be known that the Revelation of EKUMEKU in the life of Chukwudi is the **Okaome** made manifest. O you the Believer in the Living Truth, let it be known that the Revelation of EKUMEKU in the life of Chukwudi is the **Okaka** made manifest. As a result, the authoritative Law cannot exist without the **Okaiwu**, which is the basis of Outer Uniformity. The authoritative execution of the Law cannot exist without the **Okaome**, which is the basis of the Inner Unity. Wherefore, the authoritative realization of the Law cannot exist as the Ultimate Reality without the **Okaka**, which is the basis of the state where everything has become one in EKUMEKU.

Thus, the attainment of the Outer and the Inner Law without the realization of the Law cannot lead to the supreme consciousness of Chineke. Consequently, the Revelation of EKUMEKU in the life of Chukwudi expresses itself in the three forms of the Ultimate Reality as the Law, its Application and its Realization. But these qualities of the Revelation of EKUMEKU in the life of Chukwudi Onye-Nzoputa-Uwa do not exist completely in separation from the legitimate force of Biafranism. The execution of the Law of MAAT is the legitimate force of Biafranism, which has been ordained from the beginning of creation according to the Divine Plan of the One Creator of the universe.

Evidently, the Revelation of EKUMEKU in the life of Chukwudi is the Truth of what it means to be an Ekwueme. *The Movement of Nzoputa Uwa is the realization of life in eternity because of the Revelation of EKUMEKU in the life of Chukwudi.* In other words, the Revelation of EKUMEKU in the life of Chukwudi is the devotion of purpose to the Divine Plan of the One Creator of the universe. No doubt, the Revelation of EKUMEKU in the life of Chukwudi is the battle against all forms of Ekwensism of any kind. That is why, the Revelation of EKUMEKU in the life of Chukwudi is the living of MAAT by renouncing ISFET. Therefore, the Revelation of EKUMEKU in the life of Chukwudi is the worship of only the One Creator of the universe. No doubt, the Revelation of EKUMEKU in the life of Chukwudi is the ascent of the Haremakhet according to the Divine Plan of AMUN in whom we trust. So, the Revelation of EKUMEKU in the life of Chukwudi embodies the morality of repentance from Nsi of any kind.

Listen O people of the Planet! The Creator is One. The One is AMUN and the Divine Plan is EKUMEKU. This Revelation of EKUMEKU in the life of *Chukwudi Onye-Nzoputa-Uwa is the fulfillment of the Divine Plan of the One Creator of the universe.* And the fulfillment of the Divine Plan of AMUN in whom we trust is the Revelation of EKUMEKU in the life of the Chosen One for the mission of **Nzoputa Uwa**. It is the divine intervention of the One Creator of the universe on the First Year of **Nzoputa Uwa** that has made the Revelation of EKUMEKU in the life of Chukwudi realizable.

The divine birth of EKUMEKU on the Second Year of Nzoputa Uwa is the Truth of the Revelation of EKUMEKU in the life of Chukwudi. Without the divine birth of EKUMEKU on the Second Year of **Nzoputa Uwa**, the liberation of the human spirit from the dead end nature of the world of Ekwensu would be unattainable. Therefore, the Revelation of EKUMEKU in the life of Chukwudi has existed from the beginning of creation but became manifest on the First Year of **Nzoputa Uwa**. Hence, it is the Revelation of EKUMEKU in the life of Chukwudi that has transformed the consciousness of time in the universe of life.

The time before the Revelation of EKUMEKU in the life of Chukwudi became manifest would always be the time of **Oge Nzuzu**; whereas the time when the Revelation of EKUMEKU became manifest would always be the time of **Nzoputa Uwa**. The measurement of time would always be based on the distance that exists between the time of **Oge Nzuzu** and the time of **Nzoputa Uwa**. Because the time of **Oge Nzuzu** ended at the point where the time of **Nzoputa Uwa** began, the reckoning of the time of **Oge Nzuzu** would be for the time period before the time of **Nzoputa Uwa**. Whatever that happened during the time of **Oge Nzuzu** would be reckoned in time according to its distance from the time of **Nzoputa Uwa**.

Let it be known that the time of **Oge Nzuzu** was the time of foolishness; it was the time of ignorance, when there was no human spirit that had attained the devotion of purpose to the Divine Plan of the One Creator of the universe. Say you the Believer in the Living Truth: The time of **Oge Nzuzu** was the time of ignorance, when there was not even one human spirit that worshiped only the One Creator of the universe. The time of **Oge Nzuzu** was the time of falsehood due to the ignorance of

EKUMEKU, when every human spirit has the false belief that a created image of the human mind can be able to save the individual Chi from the vicious circle of eternal death. Without any doubt, the time of **Oge Nzuzu** was the time of deception when the religions of ISFET were used as a weapon or as an instrument of evil to keep the human spirit in bondage and slavery in the dead end nature of the world of Ekwensu. Wherefore, the Revelation of EKUMEKU in the life of Chukwudi is the Truth of the Movement of **Nzoputa Uwa**. OTUA-KA-ODI!

XI. THE TRUTH OF LIFE EVERLASTING

In the beginning was EKUMEKU, which is the Divine Plan of the One Creator of the universe, and on the last Day of Judgment, it will also be EKUMEKU. The creation of the universe is a mystery to those who are ignorant of EKUMEKU. It is AMUN in whom we trust that is the Hidden One Creator of the universe and not any God of the Ekwensu people.

Thus, the Almighty Spirit of EKUMEKU is the only Truth, the whole Truth and nothing but the whole Truth of life everlasting. There is nothing that can be added to it because the Living Truth is the Ultimate Reality.

There is nothing else that can be compared to the Divine Plan of the One Creator of the universe. From the beginning of creation, it was ordained that every life ought to exist according to the Divine Plan of the One Creator of the universe. And by the Last Day, every life must be judged according to the Divine Plan of AMUN in whom we trust. There is no life that can escape the Final Judgment of the Truth according to the Divine Plan of the One Creator of the universe.

Let it be known that anybody who is not a devoted follower of the Divine Plan of AMUN in whom we trust is an Unbeliever who is very ignorant of the Truth. Every Unbeliever is an Ekwensi who lives in agreement with Nsi. The Ekwensi lives in opposition to the Divine Plan of the One Creator of the universe.

There can never be true repentance from Nsi without the human spirit becoming the devoted follower of the Divine Plan of the One Creator of the universe. There can never be Deliverance from the dead end nature of the world of Ekwensu without the attainment of the devotion of purpose to the supreme principle of EKUMEKU. The morality of repentance from Nsi is realized by the human spirit who has been reborn in the image of EKUMEKU. The judgment of the Truth shall be upon every human spirit who lived in agreement with Nsi. Wherefore, the Divine Plan of the One Creator of the universe is perfect, eternal and undifferentiated in consciousness. It is life in its highest potentiality and possibility. And, it is the only Truth, the whole Truth and nothing but the whole Truth of life everlasting. In other words, all differentiation is inherently a negation of the whole Truth, of what it means to be an Ekwueme.

THE NEW WORLD ORDER OF EKUMEKU

This emergence of the New World Order of EKUMEKU, that is within us and is around us, would transform the human spirit and re-order human society to exist according to the Divine Plan of the One Creator of the universe. Living MAAT by renouncing ISFET, the human spirit would worship nothing else except the One Creator of the universe. With the devotion of purpose to the supreme principle of EKUMEKU, the human spirit (society) becomes capable of grappling with the Ultimate Reality of life.

The world of Ekwensu would be subordinated to the world of EKUMEKU, as the Ekwueme battles all forms of Ekwensism of any kind. The ultimate experience in the battle against all forms of Ekwensism is Biafra, that is the devotional discipline of living MAAT by renouncing ISFET.

Therefore, the New World Order of EKUMEKU is the whole Truth of the New Life: THE CREATOR IS ONE. THE ONE IS AMUN AND THE DIVINE PLAN IS EKUMEKU. There is no other Creator of the universe but AMUN in whom we trust. There is no God that is worthy of worship because every God is the created image of the human mind.

THE NEW WOMANHOOD
The harmony that ought to exist between the Ekwueme womanhood and manhood, between male and female, is the epitomy of the New World Order of EKUMEKU. The role of women in the world of EKUMEKU is essential to the legitimate development of every Haremakhet. The Ekwueme men should see the Ekwueme women as people and they must never be used as mere instruments of pleasure or reproduction.

The Chosen One for the mission of **Nzoputa Uwa** is opposed to excessive dowries and divorces of convenience. Marriages should be registered with an established Haremakhet. It is the bridegroom who should pay dowry or brideprice to the parents or guardians of the bride. There should be only one wedding for every marriage. Every marriage ceremony must be done according to the Divine Plan of AMUN in whom we trust.

NZUKO EKWUEME
There is what is called **Nzuko Ekwueme** or Nzuko Ndi Ekwueme. Before anybody can be invited to become a member of the Holy Body, the human spirit must accept that there is only One Creator of the universe and should reject the worship of any created image of the human mind. The human spirit must renounce the worship of any God in any form or shape. And then the human spirit would declare publicly the **Nkwekolita** of the Ekwueme Universal Life:

"I BELIEVE IN THE TRUTH OF THE ONE CREATOR OF THE UNIVERSE. I BELIEVE THAT THE ONE CREATOR OF THE UNIVERSE IS AMUN IN WHOM I TRUST. I BELIEVE THAT EKUMEKU IS THE DIVINE PLAN OF THE ONE CREATOR OF THE UNIVERSE. OTUA-KA-ODI!

The Almighty Spirit of EKUMEKU is the whole Truth. There is

nothing that can be added to it because it is the Divine Plan of the One Creator of the universe. OTUA-KA-ODI! "

CHAPTER TWO

COME OUT OF THE HISTORICAL PROCESS OF OGE NZUZU

*O You who are a seeker of Truth, come out of the historical process of Oge Nzuzu, that you become not agreeable to Nsi and that you shall receive not the final judgment of its destruction....*The Chosen One

Come out of the bondage of Nsi that you may enter into the freedom of Nzoputa Uwa....THE HOLY ANKHUWA

I have come with the Living Truth to set unu apart from the time of Oge Nzuzu....The Chosen One

INTRODUCTION

During the historical time of **Oge Nzuzu,** the spirit of humanity was violated and the fundamental moral values of good and evil were abused by the inhuman application of the universal principles of life. There is no sacrifice greater than the preservation of human life on this planet. The moral and ecological destruction of life on this planet is bound to happen if we are to ignore the timeless Truth of the divine birth of EKUMEKU.

Hearken to the Truth my brothers and sisters in EKUMEKU, for the Living Truth is the ultimate measurement of all things in the universe of life. *THE CREATOR IS ONE. THE ONE IS AMUN AND THE DIVINE PLAN IS EKUMEKU. OTUA-KA-ODI!*

SPIRITUAL BLESSINGS IN EKUMEKU

Let it be known that the immoral character of the time of **Oge Nzuzu** gave rise to the time of **Nzoputa Uwa**; and yet the time of **Oge Nzuzu** has been over since the First year of **Nzoputa Uwa** for the Ekwueme. Without any doubt, the immoral character of the historical process of **Oge Nzuzu** is in its agreement with Nsi.

It is the human condition of living in agreement with Nsi that has separated the Ekwensi from the supreme principle of EKUMEKU. Wherefore, what is unrepentant from Nsi must be acted upon and whatever that must be acted upon is the condition of living in agreement with Nsi. **Are you an Ekwueme or an Ekwensi?** Ask yourself for the judgment day is at hand. The truthfulness of life is the universal nature of the Ekwueme Way of being and becoming. Accept EKUMEKU as your eternal Savior and Redeemer in the Holy Name of AMUN in whom we trust.

With the end of the time of **Oge Nzuzu,** as the result of the divine intervention of AMUN in whom we trust, the New Dispensation of the Age of **Nzoputa Uwa** came into being and the journey of the People of Truth out of the bondage and slavery of Nsi in the dead end nature of the world of Ekwensu into the world of EKUMEKU began in earnest. Those who have come out or would come out of the bondage and slavery of Nsi are the triumphant People of Truth. They are the Ekwueme People of Truth who have resurrected from the dead and have entered into the World of Life. They are no longer in bondage to Nsi because they have become the devoted followers of the Divine Plan of the One Creator of the universe. Therefore, the transformation of all creations into the Living Truth of **Nzoputa Uwa** for the goodness of the World of Life is the moral certainty underlying the ethical imperative of the Movement of Nzoputa Uwa.

Now, we need to understand the immoral character of the historical process of **Oge Nzuzu** without any doubt. Because the historical process of **Oge Nzuzu** is the negation of the historical process of **Nzoputa Uwa**, it will help us to recognize and appreciate the moral certainty underlying the ethical imperative of coming out of the historical process of **Oge Nzuzu.** To overcome the historical process of **Oge Nzuzu** by transcending it, the human spirit must attain the devotion of purpose in EKUMEKU. The human spirit must become an Ekwueme who is the manifest expression of EKUMEKU in the flesh. The human spirit must follow in the footsteps of the Chosen One for the mission of **Nzoputa Uwa**. The human spirit must renounce

ISFET by living MAAT. The human spirit must become aware of Nsi that it may become disagreeable to Nsi of any kind. The human spirit must become a devoted follower of the Divine Plan of AMUN in whom we trust in order to transcend and overcome the historical process of **Oge Nzuzu.**

Let it be known that the moral crisis that had engulfed the world of Ekwensu is due to the violation of human morality and the consequent misapplication of the universal principles of life. Through the divine intervention of the One Creator of the universe, the divine birth of EKUMEKU became the Ultimate Reality of life, bringing the Ekwueme consciousness into being and becoming. The Ekwueme is the Universal Being who is the devoted follower of the Divine Plan of the One Creator of the universe. The Ekwueme is the manifest expression of EKUMEKU in the flesh who is the living Haremakhet. The Ekwueme is the devoted follower of the Divine Plan of AMUN in whom we trust who follows in the footsteps of the Chosen One for the mission of Nzoputa Uwa. The Ekwueme is the human spirit who struggles everyday to overcome evil by doing good. The Ekwueme is the human spirit who has renounced ISFET by living MAAT. The universal consciousness of the Ekwueme is the awareness of yesterday, today and tomorrow in the eternal struggle between good and evil. The Ekwueme is the universal human spirit who has been reborn in the image of EKUMEKU. The Ekwueme is the universal human being who has realized the ultimate reality of the vision of **Nzoputa Uwa,** having transcended in consciousness the historical process of **Oge Nzuzu.**

Because it is from the bottom pit of the world of Ekwensu, that the Voice of Salvation of the CHI has been heard, it is essential that the **Truth of Nzoputa Uwa, Ozioma of Truth,** be realized by all humanity. For, it is at the death of the Ekwensi condition of living a life that the Ekwueme Universal Life has come into being. No doubt, out of the death of the Ekwensi condition of living a life, comes the World of Life of the Ekwueme Universal Being. Therefore, at the end of the historical process of **Oge Nzuzu,** came the origin and the beginning of the historical process of **Nzoputa Uwa**.

Once, we are able to identify with the Truth of the revelation of EKUMEKU in the life of Chukwudi in us, we have moved beyond the realm of death, beyond the realm of agreement with Nsi, that is the abyss of Ekwensism; beyond the historical process of **Oge Nzuzu** to the historical process of **Nzoputa Uwa**; beyond the bondage and slavery of Nsi to the freedom of the Living Truth; beyond the condition of living in agreement with Nsi to the universalism of being in disagreement with Nsi; beyond the condition of being acted upon to the ultimate experience of being actively engaged in the mighty struggle between the world of EKUMEKU and the world of Ekwensu. **No doubt, the Chi-Ukwu-Di in us does not die and can never die as long as we are the devoted followers of the Divine Plan of the One Creator of the universe.**

During the time of **Oge Nzuzu**, we were very ignorant of the Divine Plan of AMUN in whom we trust. We were very foolish and were not conscious of time. At the same time, we were innocent of opposites because we were corrupted by the fear of Nsi and the passions and desires of the body. Thus, we were the living dead who were in bondage and slavery but did not know it. We were living for nothing in borrowed time and space. Consequently, during the time of **Oge Nzuzu**, we were the living dead being acted upon by the Alusi forces of ISFET due to our separation from the supreme principle of EKUMEKU.

Let it be known that the greatest defining moment in the entire history of human life has been the end of the time of **Oge Nzuzu** and the emergence of the historical time of **Nzoputa Uwa**. Since the creation of life by the One Creator of the universe and the unfolding of the human spirit, the world of Ekwensu has been in existence in agreement with Nsi from the beginning of the time of **Oge Nzuzu**. The world of Ekwensu was dominated and controlled by the Alusi forces of ISFET which kept the human spirit in bondage and slavery with Nsi, depriving the human spirit the Truth of everlasting life and keeping the human spirit in perpetual fear of the other.

No doubt, the time of **Oge Nzuzu** is the diametrical opposite of the time of **Nzoputa Uwa**. During the time of **Oge Nzuzu**, the fear of Nsi, as opposed to the morality to repent from Nsi, was the basis upon which the world of Ekwensu interacted with itself; and yet every human spirit is born in agreement with Nsi. As a result, every Ekwensi Unbeliever would always live in agreement with Nsi, due to the ignorance of EKUMEKU. The collective human spirit was in bondage and slavery to Nsi for there was no liberation from the dead end nature of the world of Ekwensu during the time of **Oge Nzuzu**. It was the time of ignorance, falsehood and deception when most things were judged based on their material value for their instant sense-gratification .

As a result, there was no knowledge of good and evil. The human spirit was enslaved to the passions and desires of the flesh because of the absence of human morality. The Divine Plan of the One Creator of the universe was ignored, falsified and overlooked due to the ignorance of EKUMEKU. The curse of death was superimposed as a plague battling against the truthfulness of life. And the supreme principle of Life was ignored, falsified and overlooked; while the notion of light was polarized to be superior to darkness. While the truthfulness of Life was ignored, falsified and overlooked, lightness was made to be the supreme good and darkness was made to become the supreme evil. Both were made to become irreconcilable opposites of each other without recognizing the inherent relationship that exists between them.

The Ekwensi does not reflect upon things very deeply. The Ekwensi's polarization of opposites through {rhetorical} dichotomization can make darkness seem to be evil and lightness seem to be good for those who are ignorant of EKUMEKU; but it has nothing to do with the Living Truth. The Ekwensi is entangled with evil in the vicious circle of eternal death. That is why, the Ekwensi has the tendency of distorting everything to the limitations of the Lower Self in compartmentalization. No doubt, the Ekwensi condition of life is incapable of expressing thoughts beyond all comparison of dark and light, black and white, etc.

The normative judgment implied in the notion that lightness supersedes darkness or that whiteness supersedes blackness is erroneous and yet the issue of skin pigmentation has been tied to this erroneous Ekwensi view of life. The opposition of colors in metaphors such as darkness versus lightness, blackness versus whiteness, etc., is characteristic of many religions of ISFET during the time of **Oge Nzuzu**. It became to the followers of the religions of ISFET the opposition of evil and good without them knowing that darkness and lightness or blackness and whiteness can never have absolute value of being either good or evil because they are identical in nature for none can exist without the other. Let it be known that it is the rhythm of colors that is the Living Truth as opposed to the erroneous notions that express the ideology of opposition in colors.

My brothers and sisters in EKUMEKU, do not allow yourself to be deceived by the Ekwensism of the world of Ekwensu. Do not despise anybody anywhere because of skin color differences. Fight against the Unbelievers based on the strength of your moral conviction. It is the Unbelievers that are unknowing in their lawlessness. The Believers in their single-minded devotion of purpose are the manifest expressions of the Living Truth. **Hearken to the Truth, do not be against anybody because of his or her skin color; instead, be against the Unbelievers because of the evil that they do. It is the evil that the Unbelievers do that you must fight against and not the color of their skin.** No doubt, it is the agreement with Nsi {Ekwensism} of the Ekwensu people that the Ekwueme must fight against because the Ekwueme is the Universal Being.

Every Ekwensi Unbeliever is a worshipper of the created image of the human mind. Because of the ignorance of EKUMEKU, the entire human life was not following the Divine Plan of the One Creator of the universe during the time of **Oge Nzuzu**. Terrorized by the agreement with Nsi upon which human life was based during the time of **Oge Nzuzu** with the plague of death, the *alusigenization* of the skin color differences became an issue that was championed by the *Sethian* people against the *Akwunakwuna* and to a lesser extent the *Akwunaset* to divide and conquer humanity. The notion that the *Akwunakwuna* was inferior was widely propagated as its inferior conditioning was accepted by most of the Ekwensu people.

In the faculties of MAAT and ISFET, there is no form of separation that is absolutely good or absolutely evil. It is only through the devotion of purpose in EKUMEKU can all forms of separation be harmonized into a complete whole. In other words, the eternal struggle between the forces of MAAT and ISFET is, above all, a struggle to determine the ultimate reality of what it means to be fully human. Although the dominant forces of ISFET have erroneously used the metaphoric notions of lightness versus darkness or blackness versus whiteness to express their battle cry against the forces of MAAT, the Truth of the matter is that the mighty struggle is between the forces of MAAT and the forces of ISFET in the ultimate definition of what it is to be fully human. There is no inherent struggle between darkness and lightness or between blackness and whiteness; but rather, there is a rhythmic movement between them for none can exist without the other.

What supersedes darkness and lightness, blackness and whiteness, is the Divine Plan of the One Creator of the universe. For without the Almighty Spirit of EKUMEKU, nothing else can exist. O yes, without the supreme principle of EKUMEKU, there can never be any life. That is why, the Ekwueme would always say, let there be life as against death. **The whole world of Ekwensu is ignorant of EKUMEKU; and as a result, the Ekwensi is unaware of the Truth that the struggle in life is really against Nsi and every agreement with Nsi. It is not about black or white for the Ekwueme; but instead, the mighty struggle is about the world of EKUMEKU battling against the world of Ekwensu because of its agreement with Nsi.** That is why, in the true sense of the word, the struggle is ultimately between the Lower Self {Alusi} and the Higher Self {Chi-Ukwu}. It is not about color even though the religions of ISFET tend to promote the illusion of color opposition which they had erroneously tied to skin pigmentation, polarizing white against black in ignorance, falsehood and deception.

The illusion of conquest that is often expressed in the metaphors such as lightness being triumphant against darkness or the supremacy of whiteness against blackness has been the immoral character of the time of **Oge Nzuzu**. **In Truth, white supremacy is an illusion, for without the blackness of life the condition of whiteness is nothing but death.** Which is to say, that whiteness is the absence of life when it exists in opposition to blackness. Whiteness is incomplete when it does not exist in complementary relationship with blackness.

Wherefore, the delusion of placing absolute value or worth to skin color is without moral conviction and so must never be acceptable to the Ekwueme People of Truth. There is no inherent opposition between lightness and darkness or between blackness and whiteness. The projected opposition between them is a delusional contraption created by the forces of the Lower Self. No doubt, the color opposition during the time of **Oge Nzuzu** was devised by the Sethian people. But it is a delusional contraption that the Ekwueme has overcome. It is a delusional contraption because its boundaries or lines of demarcation were arbitrary, artificial and involuntary. There is only one true humanity under the Universal Motherhood of MAAT and the Universal Fatherhood of EKUMEKU of which the Ekwueme is the only legitimate Child of the Holy Family. The Ekwueme is the Universal Being that is the embodiment of the one humanity under the One Creator of the universe, AMUN in whom we trust. The All is One and the One is the All. The Creator is One. The One is AMUN and the Divine Plan is EKUMEKU. There is no other Creator of the universe but AMUN in whom we trust.

Let it be known that whosoever is not an Ekwueme is an Ekwensi, that is an Unbeliever. Whoever is not an Ekwueme is yet to become fully aware of the infinite worth of human life. The humanity of the Ekwueme is the normative standard of justice upon which human life ought to be recognized, regulated and celebrated. The Ekwueme has rejected the erroneous notion of using the low level of melanin pigmentation as the standard to the justice of what it means to be human. The future of human life belongs to the Almighty Spirit of EKUMEKU and the Ekwueme is the manifest expression of EKUMEKU in the flesh.

Without any doubt, the time of **Oge Nzuzu** had been the embodiment of evil because it elevated whiteness to be the absolute good and debased blackness to be the absolute evil and yet the association of evil was in league with whiteness. What was good was made to become evil and what was evil was made to become good. Evil was in league with whiteness and yet blackness was debased from its reciprocal balance in order to be associated with evil, a flight from reality. There is honor in blackness and yet the historical process of **Oge Nzuzu** tried very much to destroy it.

It goes without saying that the Truth of the divine birth of EKUMEKU makes us devotedly conscious of our individual Chi which transcends the Ekwensi condition of life and yet contradicts the Ekwensi meaning of the instinct of self-preservation. It is in superseding the historical process of **Oge Nzuzu** can we realize the human freedom against all forms of Ekwensism of any kind. The bondage and slavery of the individual Chi in the dead end nature of the world of Ekwensu has chained the Ekwensi to the Lower Self without human freedom, as a result of being entangled with evil in the vicious circle of eternal death. Human life that is limited to the world of Ekwensu is evil because it claims finality when it is clearly incomplete.

The rise of the Ekwueme Civilization is based on the consciousness of the revelation of EKUMEKU in the life of Chukwudi, which has put to an end the historical process of **Oge Nzuzu** and has brought into being the historical process of Nzoputa Uwa, superseding and encompassing whatever that had been in existence before the divine birth of the eternal Savior of all humanity. The Divine Life is self-realizable through the devotion of purpose in EKUMEKU as it exists in the wholeness of eternity for the expansion of the knowledge of what it means to be fully human.

THE PURPOSE OF COMING OUT IS HUMAN FREEDOM

O You who are a seeker of Truth, come out of the historical process of Oge Nzuzu, that you become not agreeable to Nsi and that you shall receive not the final judgment of its destruction. Do not be deceived by the Ekwensism of the Unbelievers whose words and actions are meant to disarm and fool you into accepting words for deeds.

Before the time of **Nzoputa Uwa**, we were kept in bondage and slavery to Nsi in ignorance, falsehood and deception. The Ekwensu people in their ignorance of EKUMEKU tend to distort or manipulate the moral principle of the values of good and evil by associating lightness with what is good and darkness with what is evil in absolute terms. This conditioning was tied to skin color pigmentation in the immoral project of debasing blackness. As a form of *Ekwensism*, the debasement of blackness helped the Unbelievers to associate what is black with evil and what is white with what is good. **But the Unbelievers do not know that the elevation of whiteness and the debasement of blackness when tied to skin color pigmentation is an abuse of human morality.** It is *White Magic*. This is to say, that white magic has contributed tremendously to the abuse of human morality and the consequent misapplication of the universal principles of life. No doubt, it is *White Magic* that affected human morality and gave rise to the New World Order of EKUMEKU.

Without any shadow of doubt, the purpose of coming out of the historical process of **Oge Nzuzu** is human freedom from all forms of Ekwensism of any kind. It is this human freedom that would lead to the liberation of the human spirit from the dead end nature of the world of Ekwensu and the salvation of the individual Chi from the vicious circle of eternal death.

THE DEHUMANIZATION OF THE HUMAN SPIRIT

The dehumanization of the human spirit is the effect of the immoral character of the time of **Oge Nzuzu.** As a consequence of the abuse of human morality and the misapplication of the universal principles of life, many forms of *Ekwensism* came into existence as the dehumanized condition was imposed on the *Akwunakwuna*. But all the spurious arguments (used to justify it) about low melanin pigmentation allegedly being superior to high melanin pigmentation carried no moral conviction. It was foolishness at best; and at worst, it was a crime against humanity. The *Sethians* made a serious error of moral judgment in their abstractions of making the low level of melanin pigmentation the only relevant standard to the justice of what it means to be human.

Although the *Sethian* people have erroneously tied their negation of darkness to skin color, the restoration of justice for all humanity must be based on the Truth of conviction. Those who have made the blunder of tying a particular skin color to be relevant to the justice of what it means to be human and others who lived in agreement with such *Ekwensism* shall be judged according to the Divine Plan of AMUN in whom we trust. But the *Ekwueme* should temper justice with mercy. The judgment of the Truth is already against the whole world of Ekwensu for its agreement with Nsi and the Ekwueme shall act upon them according to the Divine Plan of AMUN in whom we trust, tempering justice with mercy to those who would convert and become the devoted followers of the Divine Plan of the One Creator of the universe. Those who are unrepentant would end up in the abyss of Ekwensism for their final judgment. It is absurd for the Ekwensu people to reject the Truth because the liberation from the bondage and slavery of Nsi into the freedom of the Ekwueme Universal Life would make them partakers in the Truth of the divine birth of EKUMEKU on the Second year of Nzoputa Uwa.

THE CHOSEN ONE HAS COME FOR DELIVERANCE

Despite the immoral character of the historical process of **Oge Nzuzu** and its abuse of human morality, on the 29th year of **Oge Nzuzu**, Chukwudi Okeke Maduno was born. As he grew up in the world of Ekwensu, Chukwudi became aware of Nsi as the root of all evil. He also became aware that the entire humanity were living in agreement with Nsi. He realized that the agreement with Nsi was depriving humanity the moral justice necessary to realize everlasting life. Then, on the First year of **Nzoputa Uwa**, the One Creator of the universe intervened, which led to the divine birth of EKUMEKU on the Second year of **Nzoputa Uwa**. As a result, the Chosen One was chosen by the One Creator of the universe for the mission of Nzoputa Uwa. Confronting the evil of Ekwensism with the Truth of the divine birth of EKUMEKU, the consciousness of what it means to be an Ekwueme became the ultimate reality. Without any doubt, the historical life of Chukwudi gave voice and form to the striving of the human spirit to displace ISFET and restore MAAT as the dominant consciousness in the universe of life.

The transformation of passions and desires of the Ekwensi condition of living a life into the devotion of purpose to the supreme principle of EKUMEKU would lead to the death of the Ekwensi condition and to the birth of the Ekwueme Way of life. Without the death of the Ekwensi condition of living a life, there can never be the birth of the Ekwueme Way of life. The awakening of consciousness of the individual Chi to the timeless Truth of the divine birth of EKUMEKU shall lead to the resurrection of the human spirit from the vicious circle of eternal death. As the Chosen One had undergone the death of the Ekwensi condition and the resurrection of the individual Chi from the dead end nature of the world of Ekwensu, so shall every human spirit be born again through the devotion of purpose to the supreme principle of EKUMEKU.

CONCLUSION

The Ekwueme People of Truth are the devoted followers of the Divine Plan of AMUN in whom we trust, who have transformed themselves from the independent illusion of the time of **Oge Nzuzu** to the interdependent reality of the time of **Nzoputa Uwa**. The creation of the universe brought into being the two powerful and yet opposing forces of MAAT and ISFET which ought to exist in a unity of interrelationship. Because the cause of our existence in this universe of life is predicated on the existence of the opposing forces of good and evil, the Truth of the divine birth of EKUMEKU exists in the wholeness of eternity to redeem us from the eternal struggle that would always exist between the forces of the Lower Self and the forces of the Higher Self. Our consciousness of the universe is therefore based on the spiritual location of the observer in mind, time and space.

Let it be known that the battle against all forms of *Ekwensism* is the struggle of life against death. The human spirit who is not a devoted follower of the Divine Plan of AMUN in whom we trust is dead in Nsi. And, whosoever is dead in Nsi is without life. The resurrection of the dead can never exist without the human spirit following in the footsteps of the Chosen One for the mission of **Nzoputa Uwa**. Accept EKUMEKU as your eternal Savior and Redeemer in the Holy Name of AMUN in whom we trust. OTUA-KA-ODI!

CHAPTER THREE

THE DOCTRINES OF IGNORANCE AND FALSEHOOD

I. THE DOCTRINE OF AKWUNAKWUNA

Who Invented Civilization? page 35, **WHITE MAGIC**.

The absurd aberration of tying skin color to the universal principles of lightness and darkness or blackness and whiteness is a malevolent threat to human morality and an abuse of the equilibrium on the Truth of what it means to be an Ekwueme....The Chosen One

The historical process of Oge Nzuzu had been a death-trap and whosoever can overcome it would enter into the freedom of the World of Life. **THE HOLY ANKHUWA**

I have come with the Living Truth to deliver unu from the furnace fire of light, from the inferno of death in whiteness, to the World of Life, in the Almighty Spirit of EKUMEKU according to the Divine Plan of AMUN in whom we trust....The Chosen One

Chi-Ukwu-Di bu ike bu Ndu na Eziokwu nke EKUMEKU, madu ji ekwu na eme Eziokwu maka mkpali ndi Ekwensu na efe Alusi kparili Chineke bu Ndu Zuruoke. Ya melu, anyi bu madu ji buluzie ndi Nzoputa Uwa site na Ntukwasi obi anyi nwelu na Ama Ama Amasi Amasi bu AMUN, kelu uwa nile dum dina Amasi, bulukwa Ndu na Ndu Ebighebi. Anyi bu madu bu ndi Ekwueme maka na Madu No.....The Chosen One.

INTRODUCTION

The absurd aberration of tying skin color to the universal principles of lightness and darkness or blackness and whiteness is a malevolent threat to human morality and an abuse of the equilibrium on the Truth of what it means to be an Ekwueme. Wherefore, those who use darkness and blackness as the symbol of evil and use whiteness and lightness as the symbol of good have no human morality that the Ekwueme is bound to recognize. They are the Unbelievers who are in the need of EKUMEKU.

SPIRITUAL BLESSINGS IN EKUMEKU

By the principle essential to the Truth of the divine birth of EKUMEKU, black skin means high melanin pigmentation and white skin means low melanin pigmentation. Whosoever would grasp this truth has come to some understanding of what it means to be an Ekwueme. It will never be and there has never been any greater relation between light to white skin than to black skin. Why? Because high melanin pigmentation is produced by the lightness of the Sun; while low melanin pigmentation is produced by the relative absence of light from the Sun. No doubt, it is a violation of the laws of human morality to degrade blackness or darkness and associate it with evil in absolute terms, while whiteness was elevated and associated with good in absolute terms. Let it be known that whiteness is not morally superior to blackness.

In other words, the whiteness of the skin must never be synonymous with lightness and the blackness of the skin must never be synonymous with darkness. **But the religions of ISFET by making lightness superior to darkness in their make-believe doctrines about life, were in error since they were misusing the principles of lightness and darkness and were abusing human morality by their false notions of good and evil**. By associating whiteness with what is good and blackness with what is evil in absolute terms, as they were split and tied to skin color, the followers of the religions of ISFET are abusing the order of creation. Then by the misapplication of these false notions of good and evil to the disadvantage of the Akwunakwuna, the false claim that the Akwunakwuna is intellectually inferior to the Sethian people became entrenched in the world of Ekwensu.

This apparent dehumanization of the human spirit by the religions of ISFET manifested the illusion of white supremacy against blackness. However, the whiteness of the skin, that is the low melanin pigmentation, can never be superior to the blackness of the skin, that is the high melanin pigmentation. Low melanin pigmentation has no exclusive quality that can make it inherently superior to high melanin pigmentation. But this false notion of the Ekwensi was promoted and widely propagated by the religions of ISFET to the detriment of the Akwunakwuna- --due to the ignorance of EKUMEKU.

The Akwunakwuna who becomes disagreeable to this form of Ekwensism is already moving towards the World of Life, and would be born again through repentance from Nsi to become disagreeable to all forms of Ekwensism of any kind.

Let it be known that the creation of the universe did not begin with the Action of Light, neither did it begin with the Word of Light. The creation of the universe began with the Divine Thought of Life. Therefore, lightness does not supersede darkness for it was darkness that became lightness as lightness has also become darkness for the goodness of the **World of Life**, according to the Divine Plan of AMUN in whom we trust.

Those who claim to be the symbol of whiteness may be dead in the blackness of death and those who claim to be the symbol of blackness may be dead in the whiteness of death. The Ekwueme is the Universal Being. The Ekwueme is the only human being. There is no other human being but the Ekwueme. Whomever you are, if you are not an Ekwueme, you are nothing but an Unbeliever who is dead in Nsi. **REPENT FROM NSI!**

So long as the human spirit has not become a devoted follower of the Divine Plan of the One Creator of the universe, such an Ekwensi is dead in Nsi. Let it be known that blackness and whiteness or lightness and darkness are not inherently opposed to each other for they are the primal rhythms of life. Homage to Thee my Greatest AMUN in whom All Truth Resides! AMEN!!!

THE AKWUNAKWUNA IS AT THE CROSSROADS

In the world of Ekwensu, there are the three paths of Ekwensism of which the human spirit is born into the Ekwensi condition of elemental life. They are fundamentally the Sethian's Ekwensism, the Akwunaset's Ekwensism and the Akwunakwuna's Ekwensism. This is because every human spirit is born in agreement with Nsi either in the Path of ISFET, Path of Akwunaset or the Path of Akwunakwuna. When the Ekwensi condition of human life conforms to the Path of Akwunakwuna, it is to be an Akwunakwuna. When the Ekwensi condition of human life conforms to the Path of Akwunaset, it is to be an Akwunaset. When the Ekwensi condition of human life conforms to the Path of ISFET, it is to be a Sethian.

Every human spirit is born into the world of Ekwensu either through the Path of ISFET, Path of Akwunaset or Path of Akwunakwuna. Every human spirit is born in the world of Ekwensu involuntarily in agreement with Nsi. **Whosoever that lives in agreement with Nsi is opposed to the Truth of the divine birth of EKUMEKU and whatever that is opposed to the Truth is mortal and perishable.**

For the human spirit, the struggle is to overcome evil by doing good. Being born in the world of Ekwensu in agreement with Nsi, the human spirit ought to be born again in order to self-realize the meaning and purpose of human life. The choice is to renounce ISFET and to live MAAT, overcome evil by doing good, in the self-realization of what it means to be fully human. It is to say, that when the human spirit has realized the Truth of the divine birth of EKUMEKU it becomes morally capable of living MAAT by renouncing ISFET.

The Akwunakwuna is trapped in a spiritual wilderness, controlled and dominated by the forces of the Lower Self. During the time of **Oge Nzuzu**, there was never a complete surrender to the **Alusi** forces by some few Akwunakwuna thinkers. To that extent, there was hope for the realization of the Higher Self. Through the divine intervention of the One Creator of the universe, what was hoped for became universally manifest through the divine birth of EKUMEKU on the Second year of Nzoputa Uwa. The spiritual equilibrium that is manifest in the revelation of EKUMEKU in the life of Chukwudi became the ultimate reality as a result.

According to the Divine Plan of AMUN in whom we trust, darkness and lightness, blackness and whiteness are the primal rhythms of life. The rhythmic movement of darkness is transformed into lightness and that of whiteness is transformed into blackness manifesting the truthfulness of life. Without life, what is darkness and what is lightness or what is blackness and what is whiteness cannot exist. It is with life can we know these things. Therefore, life supersedes both blackness and whiteness or darkness and lightness even though that the furnace fire of light, **Okumuo**, which has kept the human spirit entangled with evil in the vicious circle of eternal death is the whiteness of death. Whosoever that ignores, falsifies or denies the supreme principle of EKUMEKU is dominated by the involuntary condition of living a life in the dead end nature of the world of Ekwensu.

THE BARRIER THAT HINDERS THE AKWUNAKWUNA IS NSI

Wandering in the spiritual wilderness of **Oge Nzuzu**, the Akwunakwuna lives in agreement with Nsi because of the ignorance of EKUMEKU. Be it the **Alusism** of living in agreement with Nsi of hypocrisy or backbiting or envy or greed or thoughtless speech or filthy tongue or tribalism or bigotry or idiot laughter or sycophancy or filthy food or homosexuality or lesbianism or fornication or wickedness or murder or stealing or empty pride or boasting or maliciousness or covetousness or avarice or rebellion or gossiping or alcoholism or idleness or prostitution or disobedience or untrustworthiness or worshiping the created images of the human mind or any and all unrighteousness, every agreement with Nsi is without any doubt evil.

That is why, the barrier that hinders the Akwunakwuna from the Almighty Spirit of EKUMEKU is Nsi. Living without any devotion of purpose in EKUMEKU, the Akwunakwuna cannot distinguish what is real from what is unreal. The Akwunakwuna is at the crossroads of life and death, moving either towards the **World of Life** or towards the abyss of Ekwensism. It is the Akwunakwuna that must make the choice. Why? Because divine guidance has come to those who would struggle to overcome evil by doing good. Those who would reject the Truth of the divine birth of EKUMEKU would be entangled with evil in the vicious circle of eternal death.

The agreement with Nsi is the source of all the misery that every Akwunakwuna suffers in life. It is the plague of death and the greatest curse on the life of every Akwunakwuna. The Akwunakwuna must be born again in the image of EKUMEKU in order to experience the inner regeneration, Living Truth, that is necessary for the human spirit to realize its fullest potential as a human being. It is the experience of the Living Truth that would transform the Akwunakwuna to become an Ekwueme. It is the evil of living in agreement with Nsi that has kept the Akwunakwuna in bondage and slavery in the dead end nature of the world of Ekwensu; and yet the Akwunakwuna can never be freed from bondage and slavery until the human spirit is morally capable of renouncing ISFET by living MAAT. The Akwunakwuna must struggle to follow in the footsteps of the Chosen One for the mission of **Nzoputa Uwa**. The Akwunakwuna who does not struggle to follow in the footsteps of the Chosen One is doomed to perish

Trapped in the spiritual wilderness of Ekwensism, wandering hither and thither going nowhere without divine guidance, the Akwunakwuna must reject ISFET and accept MAAT in order to realize the wholesome Truth of the divine birth of EKUMEKU. The time of **Nzoputa Uwa** is what matters now and the Akwunakwuna should reckon with the historical process of **Nzoputa Uwa** by letting go of the historical process of **Oge Nzuzu**.

Without aiming to come out of the historical process of **Oge Nzuzu**, the Akwunakwuna would be driven by the passions and desires of the Lower Self, going nowhere, living in a borrowed time and space. Without the vision of **Nzoputa Uwa,** the Akwunakwuna would be living for nothing entangled with evil in the vicious circle of eternal death. Without the attainment of the devotion of purpose in EKUMEKU, every Akwunakwuna worships the created images of the human mind instead of the One Creator of the universe. Without following in the footsteps of the Chosen One for the mission of **Nzoputa Uwa**, every Akwunakwuna is a cultural prostitute being deceived by the Ekwensism of the world of Ekwensu.

Without the knowledge of EKUMEKU, every Akwunakwuna lives for the moment in ignorance, falsehood and deception. Without the Trust in the Truth of the One Creator of the universe, the Greatest AMUN in whom we trust, **THE HIDDEN ONE**, the Akwunakwuna is like a blinded **Alusi** groping in an explosion of light, blinded by the whiteness of death. The Akwunakwuna does not know that there is no fear in the devotion of purpose to the supreme principle of EKUMEKU. No doubt, a single-minded devotion of purpose in EKUMEKU is beyond the fear of all forms of Ekwensism of any kind. Without any doubt, the Akwunakwuna lives in fear and torment because of the ignorance of EKUMEKU.

The Truth of the divine birth of EKUMEKU is my life and my salvation of who shall I be afraid? But the Akwunakwuna is ignorant of the Truth and does not understand the absolute devotion of purpose to the supreme principle of EKUMEKU that is necessary in what it means to be an Ekwueme.

Let it be known that what defiles a man or woman must never be the involuntary condition upon which she or he was born into the world of Ekwensu. Instead, what defiles a woman or a man is the unrepentant life of living in agreement with Nsi. **Without any**

shadow of doubt, what defiles the human spirit is the unrepentant life of living in opposition to the Divine Plan of the One Creator of the universe. What defiles the human spirit is neither the whiteness of the skin nor the blackness of the skin; rather, it is the unrepentant life of living in agreement with Nsi. O yes! What defiles the human life is neither the lightness of the day nor the darkness of the night; but instead, it is the ignorance, falsehood and deception of believing that the lightness of the day supersedes the darkness of the night. What defiles the human spirit is the Ekwensi belief which promotes the illusion that lightness is absolutely good and darkness is absolutely evil. For, just as darkness can represent the process of transformation and assimilation of energy, so also can lightness represent the condition of separation and death of the processed energy in life. Darkness and lightness are not inherently opposed to each other for they are identical in life with different levels of energy.

Guard your life against every form of agreement with Nsi as you struggle against all forms of Ekwensism of many kinds, and the Almighty Spirit of EKUMEKU would be with you at all times.

THE DOCTRINE OF AKWUNAKWUNA

The primal rhythms of life exist to prepare the Akwunakwuna for the struggle to overcome evil by doing good. **Simultaneously with the eternal struggle between the Lower Self and the Higher Self, The Doctrine of Akwunakwuna reveals how the forces of ISFET were able to gain tremendous ground against the forces of MAAT as the Akwunakwuna became a pawn used and abused by the Alusi forces in the mighty struggle to determine what it means to be fully human.** The Akwunakwuna condition of human life is based on ignorance and delusion. No doubt, ignorance is a disease of not being guided by the Truth of the divine birth of EKUMEKU. Ignorance is an Ekwensi sickness of being limited to the functional and carnal instincts. The ignorance of the meaning and purpose of human life is the basis of all human sufferings. The nature of this ignorance has revealed the basic condition of **The Doctrine of Akwunakwuna.**

The Akwunakwuna is ignorant of EKUMEKU but deludes himself or herself that he or she can identify with the Almighty Spirit of EKUMEKU without being born again. Without the repentance from Nsi, the Akwunakwuna is a cultural prostitute who lacks an understanding of the enemy forces that are against the **World of Life**. The Akwunakwuna has a distorted vision of what it means to be fully human and is easily manipulated by the dominant forces of the Lower Self. The Akwunakwuna cannot distinguish the fundamental differences that would always exist between MAAT and ISFET. As a result, the Akwunakwuna lacks the fundamental moral values of good and evil, order and disorder. No doubt, the life of the Akwunakwuna is the epitome of ignorance and it is characterized by a constant self-destructive tendency of treacherous acts. The Akwunakwuna is very unreliable and lacks the knowledge of the principle or vision of **Nzoputa Uwa**, for the elemental being hates the truthfulness of life.

The Akwunakwuna wavers every time there is pressure from any side because the human spirit is a cultural prostitute who is only interested in servicing to the highest bidder. The Akwunakwuna is morally passive and ethically insecure, always afraid to voice his or her true feelings about life because the Akwunakwuna does not want to offend his or her mistaken benefactors. The Akwunakwuna lives for the present in a borrowed time and space and does not understand why people are concerned for the future. The Akwunakwuna tends to be very greedy in little ways and always concerns herself or himself mostly with the comforts of the physical body.

THE TRUTH ABOUT THE AKWUNAKWUNA

The Akwunakwuna has the potential to identify with the Almighty Spirit of EKUMEKU when the human spirit has realized the moral capacity to become a follower of the Divine Plan of AMUN in whom we trust. It is this potential to repent from Nsi that must be acted upon so that the Akwunakwuna may be redeemed from the dead end nature of the world of Ekwensu.

Wherefore, the Akwunakwuna who does not aspire to attain a devotion of purpose to the supreme principle of EKUMEKU is doomed to perish, entangled with evil in the vicious circle of eternal death. Let it be known that the Akwunakwuna worships the created images of the human mind instead of the One Creator of the universe.

The Akwunakwuna is a lawless being because of the ignorance of EKUMEKU. The Almighty Spirit of EKUMEKU is the Law. The Law is the eternal Truth of the divine birth of EKUMEKU on the Second year of **Nzoputa Uwa**. The Akwunakwuna is ignorant of the Law. Therefore, the Akwunakwuna is ignorant of the Truth. But the Akwunakwuna does not know that there is no other Law which can be legitimate without the recognition and realization of the Truth of the divine birth of our eternal Savior. Why? This is because the Law came into universal expression as the result of the divine intervention of the One Creator of the universe.

The Akwunakwuna does not know that the Law exists in the wholeness of eternity and would continue to exist forevermore in order to express the Divine Will of AMUN in whom we trust. The Akwunakwuna does not know that the Law does not have its origins from the created but instead the Law came into universal expression as the result of the divine intervention of the One Creator of the universe. The Akwunakwuna does not know that there could never be justice without the application of the Law because the application of justice is humanly impossible without the devotion of purpose to the supreme principle of EKUMEKU. The Akwunakwuna does not know that the sanctity and legitimacy of the Law exist as the divine ordinance of AMUN in whom we trust because of the divine birth of EKUMEKU.

With the unspoken power of **Nzuko**, the Ekwueme must *Nkuzimatize* the Akwunakwuna, *Biafranize* the Akwunakwuna and *Harembetize* the Akwunakwuna. The Truth of the divine birth of EKUMEKU has brought into existence the forces of **NZUKO** fighting against the forces of **Nzuzu**. The energy of **Nzuzu** is constantly being converted into **NZUKO** and the energy of **NZUKO** into **Nzizo** against **Nzuzu**.

The Akwunakwuna has been given a choice to accept or reject the Truth of the divine birth of our eternal Savior and Redeemer from the dead end nature of the world of Ekwensu. If the Akwunakwuna rejects the Truth of the divine birth of EKUMEKU on the Second year of **Nzoputa Uwa,** by refusing to conform to the Divine Will of the One Creator of the universe, the Unbeliever would become self-destructive and a source of disorder against the Law. Whomever is an Unbeliever should be judged according to the Divine Plan of AMUN in whom we trust.

Without any doubt, the Akwunakwuna who does not aspire to become a devoted follower of the Divine Plan of the One Creator of the universe has no future in the **World of Life**. **If the mighty power and transforming experience of the Living Truth cannot penetrate and transform the heart of the Akwunakwuna, such a human spirit is doomed to perish.**

The Akwunakwuna is a creature with a present and a past without a future so long as the human spirit is unrepentant to Nsi. In order to have a future, the Akwunakwuna must become a devoted follower of the Divine Plan of the One Creator of the universe. The Akwunakwuna who does not follow in the footsteps of the Chosen One is living in ignorance and delusion. Without the hope of a future, the Akwunakwuna is like the fire in the bush during harmattan, **Uguru,** once lighted, it becomes the whitening light that consumes the dried leaves around its path but dies without any purpose.

Let it be known that the House of ISFET is the house of bondage and slavery for the Akwunakwuna and every Akwunakwuna ought to reject it in order to enter into the house of **Freedom**, that is the House of MAAT. The Akwunakwuna ought to seek the goodness of life by overcoming the whitening light that is the harbinger of death, which has kept the human spirit in bondage and slavery in the vicious circle of eternal death.

CONCLUSION

Accept the Almighty Spirit of EKUMEKU as your eternal Savior and Redeemer from the dead end nature of the world of Ekwensu. Declare your **Nkwekolita** in fellowship with the living Haremakhet. Start an EKUMEKU Study Group in your locality to study the Divine Teachings of **THE HOLY ANKHUWA** in order to master the **Omenani** of the Ekwueme People of Truth. OTUA-KA-ODI!

II. THE DOCTRINES OF THE AKWUNASET

The Doctrines of the Akwunasets are immoral because they neither inspired any serious protest against the abuse of human morality; nor were they used to fight against the extermination of many indigenous peoples in the world of Ekwensu. No doubt, the falsehood of the Akwunasets is evil. .....The Chosen One

The Movement of Nzoputa Uwa is the protesting force against all existing religions and creeds which have continued to exist as a curse to the supreme purpose of life. ....THE HOLY ANKHUWA

It is our divine mission to restore balance on the planetary ecosystem, without which we cannot guarantee the future of human life on this plane of life. We are here to serve the universal interest of all humanity. .....The Chosen One

The Ekwueme is the devoted follower of the Divine Plan of the One Creator of the universe. As the Ekwueme people of Truth, we are the devoted followers of the Divine Plan of AMUN in whom we trust to whom the whole Truth of what it means to be human has been vouchsafed. Consequently, we are morally bound by the Almighty Spirit of EKUMEKU to preserve and advance the Living Truth for the benefit of all humanity. As the devoted followers of the Divine Plan of AMUN in whom we trust, let us seek as a family to master the philosophy of all the

Ekwensu people not just in their words but also in their actions as we live MAAT by renouncing ISFET. No doubt, the mission of **Nzoputa Uwa** is divine.

Therefore, let it be known that the Akwunaset is not in the classical sense an Akwunakwuna and is also not a Sethian in the typical sense. The location of the Akwunaset in preaching is within the ontology of the oneness of being and yet in practice the Akwunaset is located within the ontology of the separateness of being. At the same time, there are many Akwunasets who are located within the ontology of the oneness of being in practice; while in preaching they are located within the ontology of the separateness of being.

The *Akwunaset* represents any human spirit whose image does not fit into neither the *Ekwueme*, *Akwunakwuna* nor the *Sethian*. The *Akwunaset* represents an important group in the world of Ekwensu that must not be overlooked in the mission of **Nzoputa Uwa**. The core people of the *Akwunaset* preach Black Magic but practice White Magic. The *Akwunasets* on the periphery preach White Magic but practice Black Magic. The Akwunasets tend to use one illusion against the opposing illusion.

The Akwunasets are not particularly interested in the establishment or maintenance of the much needed delicate balance in the universe of life. The Akwunasets can be very dangerous because they have the ability to play the illusions of Black Magic against the illusions of White Magic or the illusions of White Magic against the illusions of Black Magic. They often use these illusions to deceive the minds of the Ekwensu people. What they preach depends on who is listening and what they practice depends on who is watching. Whatever they do has something to do with their selfish ambition. Their concept of human morality is self-centered and can never be universal.

The Akwunasets can preach Black Magic and practice White Magic or they can preach White Magic and practice Black Magic. Their location in the marketplace of ideas is on the extreme fringes of both the ontology of the oneness of being and separateness of being because they are extreme spiritualists and extreme materialists at the same time and space. Their image can be confusing to those who are ignorant of EKUMEKU because they are all over the marketplace of ideas except in the center where everyone ought to be, by following the Divine Plan of AMUN in whom we trust. They may preach about balance, harmony, or oneness of being; but they lack the experience of the Truth to know and appreciate the divine necessity for a delicate balance because they are not the Ekwueme people of Truth.

The Akwunasets deceive themselves in their notion of the oneness of being since they have failed to recognize the interdependent order of MAAT. Without the realization of the interdependent order of MAAT, the Akwunasets can only live in the falsehood of Ekwensu.

Who are the Akwunasets? The Akwunasets practice or preach the religions or creeds or doctrines such as Hinduism, Buddhism, Sikhism, Yoga, Confucianism, Taoism, Shintoism, and the different indigenous religions or creeds that are still gaining new followers. Those who preach or practice the organized creeds like Hinduism, Buddhism, Confucianism, Taoism, etc., are a people whose extremism is not apperent to the mind of those who are ignorant of EKUMEKU because they use Black Magic against White Magic or White Magic against Black Magic as it suits their selfish interests.

The Akwunasets are not concerned about the maintenance of the delicate balance. That is why, they are known to accept the false propaganda of black inferiority on the one hand; while they preach about the oneness of being on the other. How can one accept the notion that a certain people of color are inferior to another people of color simply because of the differences in skin color and expect an Ekwueme to disregard such contradiction between theory and practice. Are some of them not the same people who are known to uphold a tradition of caste-system that was originally based on the level of melanin on a person's skin, using the lowest level of melanin pigmentation as the model of excellence? Are many of them not the same people that despise blackness and worship whiteness? They confuse themselves when they ignore that there is only One Creator of the universe. How can they expect anybody to accept what they preach when we know that many of them believe in the inferiority or in the evil nature of blackness?

The Akwunasets must be living in a false paradise of bliss because they have imposed absolute values on opposites that are identical in nature. We know the location of the Akwunasets in the marketplace of ideas. The Akwunasets are only interested in their own survival. They are not concerned about human morality and the ecology of the planet because they live in falsehood. The Akwunasets are morally wrong in their acceptance of the alleged biological inferiority of the African people. They are confusing fact with truth because they themselves live in falsehood. They cannot deny the truth that they accepted the propaganda of black inferiority. If they deny their acceptance of this false notion of black inferiority, why is it that none of these creeds came out strongly to denounce it? They cannot deny it because they themselves were benefiting from it. The Akwunasets cannot eat their cake and still have it. Did any of these creeds, religions or doctrines of the Akwunaset protest against the extermination of the Native Americans and Tasmanians? Did any of these creeds, religions or doctrines of the Akwunaset protest against the enslavement of the African people by the followers of the religions of ISFET? Did any of these creeds, religions or doctrines of the Akwunaset fight for the oppressed peoples in the world of Ekwensu? Did any of these creeds, religions or doctrines of Akwunaset rebuke the Sethians when they went into Africa to vandalize, enslave and colonize its people?

This is why, the Movement of Nzoputa Uwa is a protesting force against all existing religions, creeds and doctrines of the Ekwensu people because they have all either by commission or omission contributed to the destruction of human morality and the ecology of the planet. There is no excuse whatsoever to justify the mindless and heartless atrocities committed upon the human spirit while these religions, creeds and doctrines did not have the moral force to stop this anarchy of the religions of

ISFET. We cannot accept their reasons for existence since they have proven incapable of fulfilling the Divine Plan of AMUN in whom we trust by guiding against the abuse of human morality and the ecology of the planet. This violation of the supreme purpose of life has made every existing religion, creed or doctrine complicit in the universal problem of White Magic. The Akwunasets cannot deny the Living Truth because the Ekwueme has emerged to bear witness to the
truthfulness of EKUMEKU. OTUA-KA-ODI!

CHAPTER FOUR
THE DOCTRINE OF ISFET

<u>Whosoever does not see the rhythmic movement of colors is an Unbeliever who is deceitful and unjust</u>....The Chosen One

The process of knowing what is knowable is the continuous, systematic and thorough application and realization of the Truth of the divine birth of EKUMEKU on the Second year of Nzoputa Uwa.

...THE HOLY ANKHUWA

EKUMEKU bu Ike kachasi Ike nile nke Chineke bu Ndu Eziokwu, ji alu olu n'ime Uwa nile dum dina Amasi, site na Ntukwasi obi madu bu onye Ekwueme nwere na Ama Ama Amasi Amasi bu AMUN, kere Uwa nile dum dina Amasi..... Onye Nzoputa Uwa

*The Ekwueme is the devoted human spirit who is against the lawlessness of the Ekwensi. In the World of Life, the Ekwueme uses the symbol of Life, ANKH, to represent the Truth of what it means to be fully human.....*The Chosen One

When you want to talk or write about the Master Teacher, you ought to respect yourself by referring to him as either Chukwudi, *Onye Nzoputa Uwa* or as The Chosen One or as Chukwudi Maduno. If you do not respect the humanity of the Master Teacher, Chukwudi Okeke Maduno, the Ekwueme People of Truth are not morally bound to respect your own humanity. Whatever happens to you when you disrespect yourself, do not say that you were unaware of the historical reality of the Chosen One for the mission of Nzoputa Uwa....COM

INTRODUCTION

The Doctrine of ISFET serves as an ideological and ethical counterpoint to the ethos of MAAT. It is the complementary opposite of MAAT, meaning that the existence of good is presupposed by the existence of evil. The fundamental principle of MAAT is the embodiment of interdependence and the essential principle of everything that is order in the universe. At the same time and space, the Doctrine of ISFET is the recognition of the existence of disorder in the universe of life and thus the need to balance good with evil. But there is moral and ecological balance only when the forces of MAAT are dominant against the forces of ISFET.

The principle of ISFET when it exists in a state of independence from the supreme principle of EKUMEKU is an immoral principle because it will exist in a disunited opposition with the principle of MAAT. Harmony can only be restored in the universe of life when ISFET is subordinated to the principle of MAAT and as MAAT becomes the dominant consciousness. It is only through the devotion of purpose to the supreme principle of EKUMEKU can ISFET be subordinated and MAAT restored as the dominant consciousness. Whenever ISFET is the dominant consciousness, the human spirit would be entangled with evil in the vicious circle of eternal death.

ELEMENTS OF SETHIANISM

In introducing *Sethianism*, let it be known that the first *Sethian* attack against humanity was elemental in its abstraction; but it was not morally justified because it had been based on the false notion of lightness battling against darkness. Initially, however, the light, **Okumuo**, was unable to burn and consume the Other in order to become a living light. So, something has to be done about it. That was why, the one who masterminded it did not take it to its destination. As darkness was degraded, the

Sethians were unable to distinguish it from the black skin. Thus, the elemental attack was then tied to skin color when the Sethian began to associate everything evil with the black skin. Since the yoke was imposed without moral justification, there was the need to create the fable of a curse which has no validity in human history.

Then, with that false notion in mind, came the dominating interest to make the allegedly cursed human spirit to accept the fable as truth. This led to the many versions of the elemental attack against humanity, fundamentally three versions have been dominant. As they were being energized by the ignorance of the Other, who did not understand what was happening, the need arose to reach a final solution. But then something happened: What they had expected did not happen completely as they already had envisioned. There was a loophole, a dilemma. But the dilemma did not come from the Other initially. It came from within the notion itself, with its many versions. What was missing was the truth of moral liberation and ethical salvation.

In the midst of this, after two millennia of suffering and degradation, something else happened. The divine birth of EKUMEKU became the ultimate reality. It is now over for those who can understand. What is now going to happen is another experience in the time of **Nzoputa Uwa**, an experience that would be diametrically opposed to the injustice that had been the historical process of **Oge Nzuzu**. For, the Truth would endure in the wholeness of eternity.

What then is the Law of ISFET as the experience of the historical process of **Oge Nzuzu** has taught us? **The Law of ISFET reminds us that we can get many things that we do not deserve either by hook or by crook but it will not endure.**

THE HEART OF WHITENESS

The heart of whiteness is *white magic*. Let it be known that *white magic* is the extreme materialistic tendency that encourages the abuse of human morality and the consequent misapplication of the universal principles of life. The obstinate lust for power, the enslavement to sense as conditioned by the sensation or passions and desires of the Lower Self and the unquenchable thirst to accumulate dead things and/or gadgets to satisfy the emptiness of worshiping the created images of the human mind have revealed *the heart of whiteness*. The obsession to have control and power over the Other, the tendency to reduce everything to the realm of the dead and the impulse to deny the humanity of the Other manifest the fantastic devotion to light and its transfiguration. Whether this is due to the lack of spiritual genius or to social conditions is not the issue. Without sinking into the whiteness of deception, what is certain is that in the absence of human morality, there can never be moral certainty and ethical security.

In other words, the heart of whiteness is the resultant effect of the ignorance of EKUMEKU. **The heart of whiteness is the obsession to ignore, falsify and deny the Divine Plan of the One Creator of the universe by creating the illusion of the living light. Since it is dead things that are transfigured into light, the illusion becomes to make everything dead that it may be transfigured into light. For what is this light? It is all that burns and consumes dead things.** The *heart of whiteness* is therefore Sethianism, which is a mode or condition of thinking and knowing that can never apprehend the universe of life without the devotion of purpose in EKUMEKU. But the Sethianists are all dead in Nsi and can never resurrect from the vicious circle of eternal death without the repentance from Nsi

Evidently, the heart of whiteness is not concerned with the quality of the *inner life* upon which the devotion of purpose to the supreme principle of EKUMEKU is attained. **The heart of whiteness is the ignorance, falsehood and deception that conditions the elemental being to live in opposition to the Divine Plan of the One Creator of the universe**. The heart of whiteness is the condition of living a life without any devotion of purpose to the supreme principle of EKUMEKU. Based on the self-interest of the individual, the heart of whiteness is the illusion of white supremacy against blackness.

The illusionary power of the exploded light comes from the dead things that it burns and consumes. **When there are no longer dead things to burn and consume, the living light becomes the living dead.** Since the living light cannot burn and consume the Living Truth, the **World of Life** has indeed eclipsed the world of light. No doubt, the whiteness of the world of light has been the plague of death to the Other during the time of **Oge *Nzuzu*** when error reigned supreme. **The heart of whiteness is the whiteness of death with the whitening light that burns and consumes the Other for its own sustenance.** That is why, the heart of whiteness is the negation of life for the living light cannot sustain itself without the transfiguration of the dead things that it burns and consumes. In other words, what this *Okumuo* burns and consumes is only the Other who is considered evil because of the high melanin pigmentation.

The dead end nature of the world of Ekwensu is the world of light made manifest. It is a world that can never exist without the tendency to make-believe that light is greater than life. Yet nothing in life is greater than life itself. But the heart of whiteness is to create the illusion that would make the Other to believe that this light, **Okumuo**. which burns and consumes the dead things in life is greater than life itself. However, it is only by make-believe can the light that burns and consumes dead things compete against the **World of Life**.

No doubt, the world of light is a world of make-believe and it is at the heart of the strife in the whiteness of death. Consequently, every Sethian is heading towards the abyss of Ekwensism if the human spirit is morally incapable of embracing the **World of Life**.

The Chosen One has come for the mission of Nzoputa Uwa with the Ozioma of Truth and he is the thrice greatest of all human spirits in consciousness. **Chukwudi Onye Nzoputa Uwa is he who exists from the beginning of the time of Nzoputa Uwa and will exist to the end of time in the Spirit of MAAT.**

Hearken to the Living Truth, whosoever does not follow in the footsteps of the Chosen One, without any doubt, is doomed to perish. Everybody ought to follow in the footsteps of the Chosen One in order to self-realize the wholesome Truth of what it means to be fully human. The Sethian must surrender unconditionally to the Divine Will of the One Creator of the universe in order to escape the inevitable doom that awaits the Unbeliever in the abyss of Ekwensism.

Let it be known that the Almighty Spirit of EKUMEKU is the ultimate reality of Life and Truth, the ultimate power and cause of all generation and the substantive reality of every seed of life. Many Ekwueme *Nkuzimatists* would emerge from the Mbadiegwu and the *Sethian* would repent from Nsi and become a devoted follower of the Divine Plan of the One Creator of the universe. The Sethian ought to be *Nkuzimatized, Biafranized* and *Harembetized* in the Almighty Spirit of EKUMEKU through the *Eziokwu* Language of the Ekwueme for without the Good Speech of the Ekwueme the Unbeliever may never realize the eternal message of the **Ozioma of Truth**. We know the Sethian for the greatest ambition of the *Sethianists* is to unjustly perpetuate the dominion of Sethianism against the Akwunakwuna through deception.

SPIRITUAL BLESSINGS IN EKUMEKU

In order to become fully human, the Sethian must renounce ISFET and live MAAT through the devotion of purpose to the supreme principle of EKUMEKU. The time of **Oge Nzuzu** has ended and it was the time of ignorance, falsehood and deception.

Let it be known that the Sethian is a lawless being without the Law. The Sethian is a lawless being because the elemental being falsely believes that there is an eternal struggle between lightness and darkness or between blackness and whiteness. The Sethian erroneously believes that there are the forces of lightness and the forces of darkness battling against each other. Above all, the Sethian has committed a grave Nsi when the Unbeliever began to identify lightness with a particular skin pigmentation and darkness with a particular skin pigmentation. So, now to the

Nzuzu mind of the Sethian, the warfare between the forces of darkness and the forces of lightness must be carried on between the white people and the black people until white people have conquered and destroyed the black people. This is not human morality at all. It is a *Sethian absurdity* without any just cause. This is a delusional contraption used by those who are yet to awaken to the everlasting Truth of the divine birth of EKUMEKU to rationalize the evil that they have done against humanity.

Let it be known that whenever the Sethian talks about lightness and darkness, it is tied to skin color. The Sethian is incapable of thinking beyond the skin color contraption. O Yes! The Sethian may deceive the Akwunakwuna with such false notion of good and evil and yet it is an error. How can we have human brotherhood and sisterhood when you already have eternally condemned the significant Other in your make-believe doctrine about life, just because of skin color differences, to be the embodiment of evil and of which you have made yourself the embodiment of good because of your skin color? This skin color contraption has no human morality and it must be abandoned forthwith. Let it be known that the Sethian fallacy of universalism is the skin color contraption of the religions of ISFET.

Without any doubt, there is an eternal struggle. But this mighty struggle is between the forces of MAAT and the forces of ISFET, between the Higher Self and the Lower Self, between the forces of Chi-Ukwu and the forces of Alusi or between the forces of good and the forces of evil. Let it be known the mighty struggle is between the Ekwueme and the Ekwensi, between the wholesome life of disagreement with Nsi and the living of a life in agreement with Nsi, between the **World of Life** and the world of death, between the world of EKUMEKU and the world of Ekwensu. Clearly, the cause of this moral struggle is the existence of Nsi and it can never be understood from the standpoint of the skin color contraption of the religions of ISFET.

To the extent that blackness is not absolutely good, so also is whiteness not absolutely evil. But there is no struggle between darkness and lightness, blackness and whiteness, for they are the primal rhythms of life. If the Sethian maintains that there is an eternal struggle between darkness and lightness or blackness and whiteness, the Sethian should be able to explain the root cause of the struggle. This is because the Ekwensism of the Sethian can never be used to justify the erroneous notion of a moral struggle between lightness and darkness. What then is the root cause of the Sethian's skin color confrontation? Without any doubt, it is Nsi. The Sethian must repent from Nsi.

Wherefore, the Sethian must renounce ISFET and live MAAT in order to self-realize the wholesome Truth of what it means to be human. The choice has been given to the Sethian. If the Unbeliever does not repent from Nsi and is unwilling to surrender unconditionally to the Divine Will of the One Creator of the universe, the elemental being would be doomed to perish.

THE ABSURDITY OF SETHIANISM

The *Sethians* were misguided because of the ignorance of EKUMEKU to believe that there could be white supremacy against blackness. Let it be known that there is no human morality in the religions of ISFET. What the Sethians have is skin color contraption which is nothing but a delusional contraption. Skin color can never be the basis of human morality.

Skin color opposition is a delusional contraption that is incapable of elevating the human spirit. It is a **Sethian error** in Ekwensism and it is inhuman. It is not human morality because it is amoral, incapable of distinguishing between good and evil.

It is morally wrong to attach the values of good and evil to skin color and then by association apply whatever evil that the human mind could conceptualize to one particular skin color, while associating whatever good the human mind could conceptualize as good to the opposite skin color. **By elevating whiteness to be the embodiment of absolute good and degrading blackness to be the embodiment of absolute evil, the followers of the religions of ISFET are abusing human morality.** Then with impunity, without any regards to human morality, whatever that is done by those who claim to be white is supposed to be good and whatever that is done by those who claim not to be white is supposed to be evil. Also, this whiteness of **Alusism** claiming exclusive relationship with light unto itself and imposing exclusive relationship between blackness and darkness, and it came to pass due to the ignorance of EKUMEKU, that this contrived split between lightness and darkness became tied to skin color. **TUFIAKWA!**

Therefore, it became humanly impossible for the followers of the religions of ISFET to practice what they preach for they have created a **double standard** on the justice of what it means to be human. What they preach to the Other, who is considered evil because of skin color differences, is whatever that can conceal their motive. **They are not interested in human brotherhood and sisterhood. What they are interested is power over the Other so that they can use and abuse the Other as they wish, from the standpoint of their passions and desires. They are very ignorant of EKUMEKU.**

*This **Double Standard**, which is based on skin color contraption, is the basis of their downfall, for they have proven their total disregard to the humanity of the Other.* What we must have is **One Humanity** according to the Divine Plan of AMUN in whom we trust, and also **One Standard** of judgment for the justice of what it means to be fully human. It is with One Humanity that we would have One Standard for the justice of what it means to be fully human.

Every human spirit can become an Ekwueme regardless of the human spirit's skin color. Whosoever is an Ekwueme in the Spirit of MAAT, regardless of skin color differences, ought to be justified to the Truth of what it means to be fully human.

The Sethians were very ignorant of EKUMEKU and were unable to comprehend the Truth of what it means to be fully human. Instead, they erroneously believed that low melanin pigmentation is the only relevant standard to the justice of what it means to be fully human. But they were totally wrong. **Nobody has the right to eternally condemn another human spirit to an inferior condition just because of the involuntary condition of being born in the world of Ekwensu with a particular skin color.**

The foolishness of *Sethianism* is the false notion which promotes the illusion of white supremacy against blackness. Sethianism is **Nzuzu** period. **There is nothing in Sethianism but absurdity.** Low melanin pigmentation has never and will never be morally superior to high melanin pigmentation. Sethianism is an absurd aberration in the history of human life. There is no moral conviction that can be used to justify Sethianism. Sethianism is evil because it lacks human morality.

The apparent contradiction in the words and deeds of the Sethianists can make one wonder whether they are capable of understanding the true meaning of justice. For, it is so apparent that it does not need the coming of the **Chosen One** for one to become disagreeable to it. If you tell the Sethians the Truth which insists that without the interdependent order of the universe that the independent nature of life would be meaningless. They would say *Yes* and *No* at the same time. The Sethians speak from both sides of their mouth.

It is very easy to say 'love your neighbor as you love yourself'. But what is said has always been diametrically opposed to what is practiced. So, the motive lies with the deeds and not with the words, the end justifying the means. **For their words represent nothing but their subterfuge to gain undue advantage against the Other.**

Human morality is what is important and not the institution of words and forms. That is why, Sethianism contradicts itself for the words and forms are not in harmony with the historical truth of their deeds and actions. It was very easy for the Sethians to make spurious claims of superiority during the historical time of **Oge Nzuzu** due to the ignorance of EKUMEKU. But in this time of **Nzoputa Uwa**, such self-inflated claims would be absurd without any impact on the Truth of the divine birth of EKUMEKU on the Second year of **Nzoputa Uwa**.

The Ekwueme Way of Life, from the First year of **Nzoputa Uwa**, has been the ultimate expression of human morality because the Creator of the universe is One. The One is AMUN and the Divine Plan is EKUMEKU. There is no other Creator of the universe but AMUN in whom we trust. There is no God in any form or shape that is worthy of worship because every God is the created image of the human mind. It is only one Universal Truth of life that matters in time and in eternity. This one Universal Truth of life is the Truth of the divine birth of EKUMEKU. It is the Truth of the One Creator of the universe that is the Universal Truth of **One Humanity**.

WHAT HINDERS THE SETHIAN IS NSI

Let it be known that what hinders the Sethian from becoming a full and completely realized human being is Nsi. The Sethian lives in agreement with Nsi in the dead end nature of the world of Ekwensu. Be it the **Alusism** of living in agreement with Nsi of racism, color-confrontation , genocide, murder, injustice, hypocrisy, wickedness, fornication, covetousness, envy, deception, lying, homosexuality, lesbianism, rebellion, maliciousness, malignity, gossiping, empty pride, backbiting, hatred of the Truth of the divine birth of EKUMEKU, boasting, disobedience, or any unrighteousness, every agreement with Nsi is evil. This agreement with Nsi is the hindrance, the barrier, that keeps the human spirit entangled with evil in the vicious circle of eternal death.

What then shall every Unbeliever do for the realization of the Truth of the divine birth of EKUMEKU, you may ask? Forsake the agreement with Nsi upon which you were born in the dead end nature of the world of Ekwensu and accept EKUMEKU as your eternal Savior and Redeemer.

Be Silent and Meditate on the timeless Truth of the divine birth of EKUMEKU. Believe that there is only One Humanity. Only One Universal Truth of Life! And also, only One hindrance to your life and salvation. Declare your **Nkwekolita** in fellowship with the living Haremakhet. Believe and act on the timeless Truth of the divine birth of EKUMEKU on the Second year of **Nzoputa Uwa.**

THE DOCTRINE OF ISFET

No doubt, *Sethianism* is anti-human. When a doctrine is anti-human, there is no way that it can speak to the heart of all humanity. When a doctrine eternally condemns the significant portion or section of humanity by degrading their humanity because of their level of melanin pigmentation, such a doctrine can never speak for the Truth of what it means to be fully human. The Path of ISFET is characterized and dominated by the condition of the Sethian processes of elemental life. The Sethians are the dominant people of ISFET.

All that burns and consumes echoes the basic principle of Sethianism. But the fundamental condition of Sethianism encourages the abuse of human morality through color confrontation, which has no moral basis for justification. However, what defiles a human spirit is neither the whiteness of the skin nor the blackness of the skin; but instead, it is the unrepentant life of living in agreement with Nsi. **There is no inherent opposition between black skin and white skin. Yet Sethianism created a color confrontation to justify itself because it has no truth within it.**

Without any shadow of doubt, the Sethians had tried very much to make blackness represent the symbol of inferiority and by association to make the Akwunakwuna to represent the incarnation of evil, the embodiment of evil. Without any regard to the humanity of the Akwunakwuna, a serious crime was instituted against the humanity of the Akwunakwuna. It has been done and now Deliverance has come for all humanity to be liberated from the dead end nature of the world of Ekwensu from the agreement with Nsi.

Now Deliverance has come to the Sethians to renounce ISFET and live MAAT through the devotion of purpose to the supreme principle of EKUMEKU. The Sethian ought to surrender unconditionally to the Divine Will of the One Creator of the universe. Whoever would ignore, falsify or deny the timeless Truth of the divine birth of EKUMEKU is an Unbeliever. Whosoever is an Unbeliever is an Ekwensi who is dead in Nsi.

The Truth of the divine birth of EKUMEKU is my life and my salvation and upon this everlasting Truth of the Revelation of EKUMEKU shall every Ekwensi be redeemed. The Sethian ought to wake up from the deep sleep of slumber in iniquity and unrighteousness and accept the timeless Truth of the One Creator of the universe. **The Sethian is not beyond redemption because the One Creator of the universe is the only Creator of life and death**. The All-Knowing AMUN in whom we trust is the One Creator of Being and Becoming, darkness and lightness, blackness and whiteness.

If you are born into the *Sethian* condition or process of elemental thinking and knowing, it is now time for you to wake up from your deep sleep and slumber. You must no longer divide humanity into a color-confrontation or skin color contraption of making a human spirit inferior just because of basic skin color differences. You may try to deny it; but it is embedded upon your conditioned bodily passions and desires. Since you were born in the world of Ekwensu, let it be known that the *Sethian* condition of living a life is not superior to either the *Akwunakwuna's* condition or the *Akwunaset's* condition because the whole world of Ekwensu lives in agreement with Nsi. Admit that low level of melanin pigmentation can never be morally or intellectually superior to high level of melanin pigmentation.

What every human spirit must accept is that there is only One Creator of the universe that all humanity ought to worship and serve. If you choose not to worship the One Creator of the universe, you must know that you are a wretched Unbeliever. At the same time, whosoever is an Unbeliever is in the need of EKUMEKU. As we have One Creator of the universe, so must we have **one standard** for the justice of what it means to be fully human. As you can see, we do not need a double standard of white against black.

Every human spirit regardless of skin color is born in the world of Ekwensu involuntarily with the potential essence that is necessary to become an Ekwueme. The symbol of the Ekwueme People of Truth is **THE HOLY ANKHUWA**--The Timeless Truth of the World of Life--and whosoever did not enter into the **World of Life** before the physical demise of the body has set humanity one step backward and would never realize life everlasting.

The Ekwueme People of Truth are the New People on the planet: The New Humanity. The Ekwueme is without any shadow of doubt The Universal Being.

Let it be known that whosoever is born on the involuntary conditioning of the Sethian process of elemental life ought to be born again in the image of EKUMEKU. Whosoever is not born again is entangled with evil in the vicious circle of eternal death.

If the Sethian without being born again in the image of EKUMEKU tries to claim that he or she believes in One Humanity. Ask such a blighted Unbeliever whether he or she knew that there was a double standard during the time of **Oge Nzuzu** to the justice of what it means to be human? But the Ekwueme should waste no time debating or arguing with the Unbelievers whenever it is not in the best interest of the mission of **Nzoputa Uwa**. The Truth of the divine birth of EKUMEKU does not need any elemental speculation of life. With divine guidance from AMUN in whom we trust, the Ekwueme would write the history of human life and the Unbelievers would sign it in their hearts.

What is fundamentally true is that every Unbeliever ought to repent from Nsi and accept the Almighty Spirit of EKUMEKU as the eternal Savior and Redeemer of all humanity. The Chosen One was chosen by the One Creator of the universe to serve the Holy Cause of Nzoputa Uwa. If you are a New Believer in the wholesome Truth of the divine birth of EKUMEKU, declare publicly the **Nkwekolita** of the Ekwueme Universal Life in fellowship with the living Haremakhet. Join or start (if there is none in your locality) an EKUMEKU Study Group in your locality in order to become a part of the experience of the **New Humanity**.

Let us all bear witness to the everlasting Truth of the divine birth of EKUMEKU on the Second year of Nzoputa Uwa. Let it be known that it is impossible for the Ekwensi to hold on to the Ekwensism of the world of Ekwensu while at the same time striving to enter into the **World of Life.** The Ekwensi must repent from Nsi, break its yoke and forsake its condition of life through the devotion of purpose to the supreme principle of EKUMEKU.

WHEREFORE, the Doctrine of ISFET reveals the sham of the claims of universal brotherhood erroneously made by the followers of the religions of ISFET, which are based on the make-believe doctrines about life.

THE CONCEPT OF ONE GOD IS A HOAX

The dominant forces of the Lower Self, the forces of ISFET or the Alusi forces represent the oppositional principle against the forces of MAAT who are the Ekwueme People of Truth. The Lower Self, the forces of ISFET and the Alusi forces are one and the same Ekwensu people who live in agreement with Nsi. The Ekwensu people worship the created images of the human mind instead of the One Creator of the universe.

Although the **Path of ISFET** manifests the Ekwensism of the Sethian people, The Doctrine of ISFET is the diametrical opposite to the ethos of MAAT. The Doctrine of ISFET has revealed the sham of the claims of universal brotherhood erroneously made by the religions of ISFET. The religions of ISFET, which are based on make-believe doctrines about life, preach universal brotherhood but practice the supremacy of whiteness against blackness, lightness against darkness. In the eternal struggle to determine what it means to be fully human, the Sethian people have managed to use and abuse the Akwunakwuna and the Akwunaset through ignorance, falsehood and deception to divide humanity in an erroneous schema of the supremacy of low melanin pigmentation against the high melanin pigmentation. Through this erroneous schema that is based on the involuntary condition of the human spirit, the Sethians propagated the illusion of white supremacy against blackness without any moral conviction.

The concept of one God became the whitening light used to deceive the human spirit into becoming partner in its own destruction. But the concept of one God is a hoax because it degraded blackness and elevated whiteness by making the whiteness of the skin superior to the blackness of skin. When one is tricked into believing or accepting as genuine something that is false, something that was established by fraud, such a person has been duped.

The concept of one God as a historic movement in time and space is a hoax because it is not universal in its awareness of what it means to be fully human, and had been built on an anti-black frame of reference. The concept of one God is a hoax because it created the illusion of lightness superseding darkness. The concept of one God is a hoax because it degraded the humanity of the human spirit with high melanin pigmentation and elevated the humanity of the human spirit with the low melanin pigmentation. The concept of one God is a hoax because it promotes the illusion of white supremacy against blackness. The concept of one God is a hoax because it is based on the make-believe doctrines of worshiping the created images of the human mind instead of the worship of the One Creator of the universe. The concept of one God is a hoax because it rejects the truth of the oneness of being. The concept of one God is a hoax because it is based on the separateness of being. The concept of one God is a hoax because it is opposed to the Divine Plan of AMUN in whom we trust. The concept of one God is a hoax because it is diametrically opposed to the Truth of the divine birth of EKUMEKU on the Second year of **Nzoputa Uwa.** The concept of one God is a hoax because it misuses the universal principles of lightness and darkness. The concept of one God is a hoax because it abuses human morality in its false notions of good and evil.

The concept of one God is a hoax because it is diametrically opposed to the Truth of the One Creator of the universe. The concept of one God is a hoax because it divides humanity based on skin color and promotes the illusion of one skin color being morally superior to other skin colors. The concept of one God is a hoax because it creates many forms of separation from the Divine Plan of the One Creator of the universe. The concept of one God is a hoax because the Ekwensu people who preach it do not practice what they preach. **The concept of one God is a hoax because it exists in agreement with Nsi.** The concept of one God is a hoax because it is based on ignorance, falsehood and deception. The concept of one God is a hoax because it is not based on the Truth of the renounciation of ISFET and the restoration of MAAT as the dominant consciousness in the universe of life.

The concept of one God is a hoax because it cannot liberate the human spirit from the dead end nature of the world of Ekwensu. The concept of one God is a hoax because it ignores, falsifies and denies the Truth of the divine birth of EKUMEKU on the Second year of **Nzoputa Uwa**. The concept of one God is a hoax because it can never save the individual Chi from the vicious circle of eternal death. The concept of one God is a hoax because it does not elevate the human spirit beyond and above the world of Ekwensu. The concept of one God is a hoax because it is opposed to the Living Truth of the **World of Life.** The concept of one God is a hoax because it is diametrically opposed to the Everlasting Truth of the One Creator of the universe.

THE TWO SERVANTS OF THE TRUTH

The Two Servants of the Truth of the divine birth of EKUMEKU are the faculty of ISFET and the faculty of MAAT. The faculty of ISFET represents the independent nature of life in the universe; while the faculty of MAAT represents the interdependent order of the universe. Although the continuous unfolding of life is impossible without the faculty of ISFET and the faculty of MAAT, whenever ISFET is not subordinated to

MAAT, the faculty of ISFET becomes the embodiment of disorder in the universe of life. Whenever MAAT is not the dominant consciousness, the faculty of ISFET would exist in a state of independence in the universe of life and would exist in a disunited opposition with the faculty of MAAT. In such an Ekwensi condition of living a life, the principle of ISFET would become an immoral principle, manifesting the separateness of being in opposition to the Truth of the oneness of being. It is humanly impossible to live MAAT without renouncing ISFET through the devotion of purpose to the supreme principle of EKUMEKU. That is why, the human spirit can never overcome evil by doing good without the repentance from Nsi.

The principle of MAAT when it exists in disunited opposition with the principle of ISFET becomes entangled with the forces of the Lower Self and would become immoral in principle without the devotion of purpose in EKUMEKU. Whenever the faculty of MAAT is incapable of subordinating the faculty of ISFET, the dominant consciousness would be dominated by the faculty of ISFET. It is only with the devotion of purpose to the supreme principle of EKUMEKU can the faculty of MAAT become morally capable of subordinating the faculty of ISFET.

In other words, the faculty of ISFET and the faculty of MAAT are the Two Servants of the Everlasting Truth of the divine birth of EKUMEKU. The fundamental principle of MAAT represents everything that is order in the universe of life; while the fundamental principle of ISFET represents everything that is disorder in the universe of life. Although neither ISFET nor MAAT can exist without the other, the moral imperative is to overcome evil by doing good through the devotion of purpose in EKUMEKU. As the human spirit renounces ISFET by living MAAT through the repentance from Nsi, MAAT becomes the dominant consciousness subordinating ISFET as the secondary force in life.

The meaning and purpose of life can neither be understood nor can it be realized without the unification of the faculties of MAAT and ISFET in consciousness. In mineral, vegetable, plant and animal, the faculty of ISFET predominates the faculty of

MAAT. On the contrary, in human life, the faculty of MAAT is ordained according to the Divine Plan of the One Creator of the universe to subordinate the faculty of ISFET when the human spirit has become a devoted follower of the Divine Plan of the One Creator of the universe.

THE CONCLUSION

The Ekwueme believes in the best Idea, in the truthfulness of life, in the moral struggle to conquer death, in the ethics of overcoming evil by doing good and in the devotion of purpose to the supreme principle of EKUMEKU. We owe it as a moral duty to ourselves, our ancestors and our Creator to become the devoted followers of the Divine Plan of AMUN in whom we must trust.

Therefore, the Doctrine of ISFET serves as an ideological, moral and ethical counterpoint to the ethos of MAAT. The fundamental principle of ISFET is the complementary opposite to the fundamental principle of MAAT. Since there is no absolute good in the faculty of MAAT, so also there is no absolute evil in the faculty of ISFET. The human moral struggle must be based first on identifying what is MAAT and what is ISFET according to the Divine Plan of the One Creator of the universe through the devotion of purpose in EKUMEKU. Second, through the identification and realization of what is MAAT and what is ISFET according to the Living Truth of **The Holy Ankhuwa**, then the moral struggle would be to displace ISFET and restore MAAT as the dominant consciousness in the universe of life.

The fundamental principle from the beginning of creation is the duality in the universe of life. Therefore, the displacement of ISFET and the restoration of MAAT as the dominant consciousness in the life of the human spirit would manifest the Living Truth of the divine birth of EKUMEKU on the Second year of Nzoputa Uwa.

But without the repentance from Nsi, the Sethian has no other way of attaining harmony and balance in the universe of life.

Thus, whatever the Sethians preach cannot be confirmed by their actions. It then becomes a moral gimmick rooted in the rhetoric of deceit used as a front to disarm and pacify the Other who is ignorant of EKUMEKU and is considered by the Sethians to be the embodiment of evil just because of the mere differences in skin color.

The forces of ISFET represent disorder in the Divine Order of EKUMEKU. To them, what is right is whatever can be conquered either by deceit or by brute force. The forces of ISFET understand no other language but that of disorder. This disorder feeds on the idea of the survival of the fittest where the end is made to justify the means. The forces of Alusi thus conceive what is right to be whatever that could satisfy their own vested interests. Indeed, they are characterized by their unjust passion and desire to satisfy their vested interests at the expense of the Other. So, they live life through strife and deception. They tend to employ the brute force of might as the character of their life. Hence, they owe their condition of living a life to brutish tendency and deception. **The forces of ISFET therefore conceive morality as make-believe, as a gimmick that is capable of concealing their unjust vested interests.**

The illusionary power of the forces of ISFET lies in the art of deception. The Alusi forces are the unrighteous monsters of deception because they can distort good to seem like evil and can project evil to seem like good. They preach what they cannot practice and practice what they do not preach. But since there can never be moral liberation without ethical salvation, the Sethians are entangled with evil in the vicious circle of eternal death. It is only through the **Path of Ekwueme** can the human spirit self-realize moral liberation through ethical salvation according to the Divine Plan of the One Creator of the universe. **WHEREFORE, the principle of ISFET when it exists in a state of independence from the supreme principle of EKUMEKU is an immoral principle because it would exist in a disunited opposition with the moral principle of MAAT.** OTUA-KA-ODI!

CHAPTER FIVE

THE NEW HUMAN PARADIGM

Celebrate every New Year of Nzoputa Uwa with your family and every Ekwueme throughout all the years of your lifetime. ....The Chosen One

To conquer and destroy the Other, who is considered evil because of mere skin color differences, for the sake of obstinate power is the underlying motive of Sethianism....The Chosen One

Whatever that is Nsi is opposed to the Truth of the divine birth of EKUMEKU and whatever is opposed to the Truth is death....THE HOLY ANKHUWA

Whoever is unrepentant in the belief of *Sethianism* is evil and whosoever is an unrepentant Sethian has never and would never make any positive contribution to the advancement of human morality. Since without human morality there can never be human civilization, every Unbeliever embodies the negation of human civilization. ...COM

Onye ndi ilo gbara gburugburu na eche ndu ya nche mgbe nile. Umunnem n'ime EKUMEKU, chetanu na ndi ilo no na aka ekpe ma nodukwa na aka nri. Nwenu okwukwe puru iche na Ozioma Eziokwu nke Chukwudi Onye Nzoputa Uwa wotara maka igbaputa ndu n'ime Uwa Ekwensu, ka olile anya ndu ebighebi we zukwa oke n'ime Chineke....Onye Nzoputa Uwa

PREAMBLE

The fantastic devotion to light and its transfiguration turned the high melanin pigmentation to become the embodiment of evil and the whole world of Ekwensu lived in agreement with this moral error. The low melanin pigmentation was erroneously made the paradigm of what it means to be fully human without any moral justification. By tying skin pigmentation to the universal principles of lightness and darkness and by associating evil exclusively with dark pigmentation, the whole world of Ekwensu was abusing human morality.

But skin color must never and can never be the basis of human morality. Since there must be human morality as opposed to skin color contraption, the New Human Paradigm of the Ekwueme has come into universal expression in order to exemplify what it means to be fully human. The religions of ISFET created the illusion of a struggle between the principle of lightness and the principle of darkness in their make-believe doctrines about life, and then made the Sethian error of tying them to skin color, because they bear witness to the foolish conspiracy to dishonor the black skin.

Without any regard to human morality, the Ekwensu people are very ignorant of EKUMEKU because they worship the created images of the human mind instead of the One Creator of the universe. **Let it be known that whosoever dishonors an Ekwueme because of the fantastic lie of skin color contraption of the Sethian people shall be punished in this life and in the life Hereafter.**

INTRODUCTION

During the time of **Oge Nzuzu**, the religions of ISFET created a skin color contraption in order to justify their existence because they lack the truth of human morality. With their skin color contraption, the black skin was condemned to eternal doom as the embodiment of evil and the white skin was elevated to eternal glory to become the embodiment of everything that is good. Let it be known that the followers of the religions of ISFET are abusing human morality whenever they associate evil with the black skin. It is their misapplication of the universal principles of darkness and lightness that had made the Unbelievers to associate everything evil that their Ekwensi mind could conceptualize with the dark skin. The dark skin was erroneously made to become the sole recipient of a fraudulent curse that is a fantastic lie. Thus, for example, the false belief of the Ekwensi that when the human face is darkened it shows an evil disposition or when the human body is dark it represents the embodiment of evil; and this fallacy was widely propagated by the Ekwensu people. This foolishness of the Ekwensu people became entrenched during the time of **Oge Nzuzu** and even the Akwunakwuna who could have known any better than the Sethian people, who originated this moral error, lived in agreement with this form of Nsi. In other words, the human paradigm which promotes the illusion that black is dishonorable and white is honorable must be abandoned forthwith.

As a result of the skin color contraption of the religions of ISFET, the Akwunakwuna was relegated to the bottom pit of human life, used and abused in the degradation of the human spirit. Without any regard to human morality, the views of the Akwunakwuna were condemned; the beliefs of the Akwunakwuna were dismissed as irrelevant; the traditional behaviors of the Akwunakwuna were discounted as childish; the history of the Akwunakwuna was reduced to nothingness; and above all, the humanity of the Akwunakwuna was disregarded. The Akwunakwuna was made to become the laughing stock in the world of Ekwensu. **But from this sheer force of snobbery and ridicule has the New Human Paradigm emerged in disagreement with Nsi to fulfill the Divine Plan of the One Creator of the universe.**

The Ekwueme is the New Human Paradigm because the Almighty Spirit of EKUMEKU has triumphed against Nsi. This Truth of the divine birth of EKUMEKU is without any shadow of doubt the Ultimate Reality of life in the universe. That is why, the Truth of the divine birth of EKUMEKU has convicted the whole world of Ekwensu with the evil of being in agreement with

Nsi. The Ekwensi is the Unbeliever who is dead in Nsi.

The Ekwensi is the Unbeliever who is dead in Nsi. The Ekwensi is the Unbeliever who is ignorant of EKUMEKU. The Ekwensi is the Unbeliever who worships the created images of the human mind. The Ekwensi is the Unbeliever who is not a devoted follower of the Divine Plan of the One Creator of the universe. The Ekwensi is the Unbeliever who does not follow in the footsteps of the Chosen One. The Ekwensi is anybody who does not follow the Divine Plan of AMUN in whom we trust.

THE EVOLUTION OF THE HUMAN PARADIGM OF THE EKWUEME

There are three universal principles that affect all things in the universe. They are the mind, time and space. Put together, they constitute what we should know as *Change*. When these three principles are brought into a state of harmony, at the point of equilibrium, the establishment of the delicate balance necessary for the unfolding of life becomes self-evident; and the true purpose of *Change* would be realized according to the Divine Plan of the One Creator of the universe. In other words, *Change* would no longer appear to be in conflict or in opposition to the Divine Plan of the One Creator of the universe.

As a result, order would displace disorder; truth and righteousness would be restored; falsehood and anarchy would be vanquished; the moral and ethical life of humanity would be dominated by the Ekwueme People of Truth, and the world of EKUMEKU would dominate the world of Ekwensu; while the Ekwensu people would find their true place in the universe; MAAT would be restored; ISFET would be displaced to become the secondary force in the universe of life. ISFET would cease to be the dominant force; instead, it would become the servant. This is the true cycle of the **Eternal Wheel of Nzoputa Uwa.**

As one of the three universal principles that affect all things in the universe, the mind helps human beings to locate themselves in time and space. If truth is the character of the universe, then mind, time and space are the primary agencies of truth. Given that human beings live by truth as opposed to fact, what makes one human becomes not just the biological aspect of being human, such as skin color, but also the values of what it means to be human which define the normative standard of the human being. True values do not exist in a vacuum; they must be the products of the mind, time and space. When values ceased to be the products of the mind, time and space, they can only be traditions, rituals, dogmas, useless rites or entertaining ceremonies that have lost their essential meaning and significance to Divine Thought, for Divine Thought is eternal, unchangeable and unalterable in consciousness. These types of values that have ceased to be the products of mind, time and space can be used to reflect the historical process of a people and can be the symbols of a potential strength of a people or symbols of a potential weakness of a people. Both depend on how they are used to interpret reality or celebrate life.

The celebration of life itself cannot be divorced from the experience gained from the knowledge of MAAT and ISFET. Without the experience of the eternal struggle between MAAT and ISFET, there can never be any true knowledge worthy of the name. Without the experience of MAAT being the dominant consciousness in the life of the human spirit, the realization of what it means to be fully human is unattainable.

Those who are the devoted followers of the Divine Plan of the One Creator of the universe, following in the footsteps of the Chosen One, are able to transcend and triumph against the eternal struggle that exists between MAAT and ISFET through the devotion of purpose to the supreme principle of EKUMEKU in Chineke Consciousness of life.

Therefore, it is the devotion of purpose to the supreme principle of EKUMEKU that is the Ultimate Reality of life Here and of Life in the Hereafter. Without the devotion of purpose to the supreme principle of EKUMEKU, there can never be true knowledge of the eternal struggle between MAAT and ISFET; and without the experience of the true knowledge of EKUMEKU, there can never be true repentance from Nsi.

Wherefore, it is in the freedom of consciousness can the human spirit be reborn in the image of EKUMEKU to gain the true knowledge of good and evil; and it is in the freedom of consciousness can an Ekwensi become an Ekwueme. **The Ekwueme is the devoted follower of the Divine Plan of AMUN in whom we trust whose individual Chi has been awakened to the eternal Truth of the divine birth of EKUMEKU on the Second year of Nzoputa Uwa.**

THE MEDITATIVE MIND OF THE EKWUEME

Let it be known that thought should serve as the guide of action and the function of the meditative mind is to serve as the crucible in which creative thought is generated and realized. The meditative mind of the Ekwueme ought to be universally understood.

The meditative mind of the Ekwueme is the mind that has repented from Nsi; the mind that has been liberated from all forms of agreement with Nsi; the mind that is free from every yoke of Nsi; the mind that is devoted to the Divine Plan of AMUN in whom we trust; the mind that has gained the true knowledge of good and evil; the mind that is disciplined to worship only the One Creator of the universe. The meditative mind of the Ekwueme is the mind that renounces ISFET by living MAAT as the human spirit follows in the footsteps of the Chosen One. The meditative mind of the Ekwueme is the universal mind that exists in disagreement with Nsi in the wholeness of eternity. The meditative mind of the Ekwueme is the universal mind that has transcended the skin color contraption of the Ekwensu people. The Universal Being is the Ekwueme who had transcended the skin color contraption of the Ekwensu people and has become the devoted follower of the Divine Plan of AMUN in whom we trust. Thus, the universal mind of the Ekwueme does not exist in a vacuum; rather, it is the ultimate expression of what has been the goodness of life during the time of **Oge Nzuzu** and the fulfillment of the Truth of the divine birth of EKUMEKU on what would be the goodness of life in this time of **Nzoputa Uwa**.

Let it be known that meditation through the devotion of purpose to the supreme principle of EKUMEKU is the only solution to the state of Chineke Consciousness in human life. Meditation is a discipline of the devotion of purpose in EKUMEKU whereby the mind is made to stay still. In short, meditation is a mental state or a state of the mind which manifests itself when the mind is not agitated, confused or restless, but instead devotional, peaceful or devoted. Thus, the meditative mind is the dynamic state of creative silence that has the moral capacity to manifest the ultimate reality of life in its most fundamental, powerful and universal character.

In other words, meditation is the transformation of consciousness through the devotion of purpose by the means of concentration, contemplation, detachment and/or deep reflection on the divine teachings of **The Holy Ankhuwa**. The process of meditation is the control of thought and control of action which help us to change the rate of our mental vibration from the lower laws to the higher laws of the universe. Because concentration helps us to direct our energy on the consciousness of the individual Chi, while contemplation helps us to turn the objective thoughts inward, meditation is the process of controlling the mind through the will power of *Biafranic* practice as opposed to the mind controlling the will involuntarily.

Every Ekwueme to one degree or another practices meditation unconsciously. But conscious meditation goes beyond the unconscious meditation. This is because conscious meditation is a principle that is used to train the mind to work for its owner as opposed to working against the owner.

Thus, the cultivation of the principle of meditation is applied for the sole purpose of developing the mind to serve the divine purpose of which it is intended by AMUN in whom we trust. The mind must be trained to serve the Ekwueme human being who has it and not to work against the individual consciousness of the

NZOPUTA UWA

Chi.

A trained mind is an asset to the ultimate reality of human morality and to the highest possibility of human development, whereas an untrained mind is a liability. An untrained mind acts involuntarily because it functions against the will of the Ekwensu people. That is why, the Ekwensi mind is the embodiment of evil because it is a corrupted mind, corrupted by its unrepentant agreement with Nsi. An untrained mind controls the will of the person who has it through the passions and desires of the bodily conditions. By controlling the will, it becomes the master of the will and is mostly out of control. Being out of control, the untrained mind is always out of focus. It is a restless mind because it does not stay still. An untrained mind can be a source of constant irritation because it cannot concentrate on an idea for a very long time. Every little thing can distract an untrained mind. Because it is easily distracted, an untrained mind is very unreliable. It is always reacting to things, instead of responding to things. It reacts without thinking because it is restless and out of control. Given that an untrained mind is a restless mind, it consumes more energy than it can generate. As a result, it creates stress, anxiety, pain, apathy, ignorance, headache, low morale, low self-esteem, mental retardation, conflict, confrontation, etc., on the human spirit whose low energy level makes him or her tired, depressed or bored about the problems of life.

The devotion of purpose to the supreme principle of EKUMEKU makes it possible for the human spirit to have power and control over its own thoughts. Those who can change the quality of their thoughts are capable of transforming their unwanted circumstance. The human spirit has the power of choice to either remain in slavery and bondage in the dead end nature of the world of Ekwensu or to be liberated from the vicious circle of eternal death. But without the training of the mind through the devotion of purpose in EKUMEKU to be obedient to the eternal will of its own consciousness, the will of the individual to overcome evil by doing good cannot become the dominant force in life.

It is through meditation that we can empower the will to control the mind when the individual Chi has been awakened to the everlasting Truth of the divine birth of EKUMEKU on the Second year of **Nzoputa Uwa**. All distractions must be eliminated in any genuine meditation and the mind should be concentrated for a single purpose, that is the devotion of purpose to the supreme principle of EKUMEKU. At the same time, contemplation is the capacity of the mind to reflect on its own thoughts when it has gained considerable control of its inner workings. The energy a restless mind wastes reacting to things can be utilized more effectively when we develop the moral capacity to control our thoughts and our actions.

When we begin to control our thoughts, we will begin to respond to things as opposed to reacting to them because we would have transformed our state of receptivity. The human spirit would experience the ultimate reality of the Almighty Spirit of EKUMEKU through meditation when the mind and its consciousness can exist in harmony with the Divine Plan of AMUN in whom we trust.

The Ekwueme Way of meditation is fundamentally different from every other type of meditation. Why? This is because true meditation can never exist without the attainment of the devotion of purpose to the supreme principle of EKUMEKU. Meditation is the quest to apprehend the divine inspiration of **The Holy Ankhuwa** in order to self-realize the supreme vision of **Nzoputa Uwa** through the devotion of purpose in EKUMEKU.

Thus, the basic principle of meditation is devotion of purpose to the supreme principle of EKUMEKU, manifesting the conscious regulation of mental energy which is used to crystallize in the mind the timeless Truth of the divine birth of EKUMEKU on the Second year of **Nzoputa Uwa** in order to attain our highest good. **Without the devotion of purpose to the supreme principle of EKUMEKU, all other meditative qualifications will have no value.**

Therefore, meditation is used by the Ekwueme to gain control of the lower forces of life by transcending them in the

mind and body. When the Chosen One teaches about meditation, we must be mindful and not be forgetful of the power of thought and how a devoted mind can aid in the healthy living of life. Human consciousness in its highest potentiality and possibility is the ultimate reality of the power of thought in its devotion of purpose to the supreme principle of EKUMEKU. Without any shadow of doubt, the human mind that has repented from Nsi and is being purified from Nsi has the devotional power to be the master of the body because it would exist in harmony with the supreme principle of EKUMEKU. There is no condition or circumstance in life that cannot yield itself to the devotional power of thought when the human spirit is a devoted follower of the Divine Plan of the One Creator of the universe. It is with the devotional power of thought can the Ekwueme gain dominion over the Lower Self in the Spirit of MAAT.

Wherefore, the character of the human spirit represents the quality of its thought about the meaning and purpose of human life and the Ekwueme character can be identified with the Almighty Spirit of EKUMEKU to the extent that the Believer is striving to follow in the footsteps of the Chosen One. It is through thought, word and deed that we can become the devoted followers of the Divine Plan of AMUN in whom we trust. Yet, it is through the purification of thought from Nsi that the Ekwueme is made in the image of EKUMEKU when the human spirit has devoted its life to the attainment of the ultimate state of EKUMEKU in this life.

In the Hidden Realm of thought, the Ekwueme is the good Biafranist who understands the importance of self-control and self-mastery. Through the devotion of purpose to the supreme principle of EKUMEKU, every Ekwueme has the moral capacity to realize the state of Chineke Consciousness in this universe of life. In other words, the mastership of the Ekwueme exists because of the Divine Thought of EKUMEKU, which guides and directs the character, condition and environment of those who are the devoted followers of the Divine Plan of AMUN in whom we trust.

No doubt, the principle of meditation is one of the transformative and regenerative agencies of life that can be used by the human spirit to empower the will in the self-realization of the true meaning and purpose of human life. Since a caterpillar shall one day transform itself into a butterfly, an elemental being can also transform himself or herself into an Ekwueme. If the larvae can overcome its cocoon and endowed with wings fly out, so can the mind of an elemental being transform itself to become an Ekwueme mind.

THE NAKEDNESS OF THE UNBELIEVERS

The moral values of good and evil must never be tied to skin color because skin color opposition can never be the basis of human morality. The Ekwensi is ignorant of EKUMEKU and as a result the Unbeliever is abusing human morality by associating everything evil with the black skin.

When the Unbelievers misconstrue evil to be embodied in the darkest members of the human family, they are associating evil with the black skin. When the Unbelievers claim that the dark side is the evil side, they are showing that they do not believe in human morality. When the Unbelievers misconstrue light to be the absolute good and dark to be the absolute evil, they are abusing human morality.

In this abuse of human morality, black and dark are synonymous which are associated with every conceivable notion of evil, such as horrible, frightening, obscure, ominous, wretched, ugly, gloomy, somber, impure, nasty, unclean, depressing, oppressive, detestable, sinister, adverse, dismal, funereal, bleak, dirty, or foolish. According to the Divine Plan of AMUN in whom we trust, all these terms can be used to describe the whole world of Ekwensu because of the condition of living in agreement with Nsi.

In other words, the Sethians created a skin color contraption without human morality. For, just as white skin can be horrible, frightening, obscure, ominous, wretched, ugly,

gloomy, somber, impure, nasty, unclean, depressing, detestable, sinister, adverse, dismal, funereal, bleak, dirty, or foolish, so also can black skin when the human spirit is not a devoted follower of the Divine Plan of the One Creator of the universe. Since that is the case, the root cause of such a condition has nothing to do with skin color; instead, whenever any of these conditions exist the cause is rather the agreement with Nsi that has entangled the human spirit with evil in the vicious circle of eternal death.

It is not the skin color of the human spirit that ought to cause such a condition to exist. To the contrary, it is the unrepentant life of living in agreement with Nsi. What is evil has nothing to do with the skin color of the human spirit. To the extent that the human spirit with black skin can be an Unbeliever, so also can the human spirit with white skin. Since every Unbeliever is entangled with evil in the dead end nature of the world of Ekwensu, it is morally a serious error for anybody or group to associate a particular skin color with the exclusive monopoly of being the embodiment of every conceivable notion of evil. The religions of ISFET lack human morality because they promote the illusion of white supremacy against blackness.

Let it be known that what defiles the human spirit is neither the whiteness of the skin nor the blackness of the skin. What defiles the human spirit is the unrepentant life of living in agreement with Nsi. Let it be known that Nsi is in opposition to life and whatever that is in opposition to life is death. Whatever that is Nsi is opposed to the Truth and whatsoever is opposed to the Truth is death.

Therefore, to ascribe and associate every conceivable evil that the human mind could conceptualize to the black skin is Nsi. It is the unjust wish or desire of death to the black skin; that is to say, the death-wish to the black skinned people. For if the black people are made to be the embodiment of evil, whatever that can be done to control them, to make them dependent and to destroy their capacity to think would appear justifiable. But the black people are not the embodiment of evil because the moral values of good and evil must never be tied to skin color.

People who look alike do not necessarily behave alike. When the human spirit has gained the true knowledge of good and evil, it becomes very clear that the Sethian's skin color contraption is delusional and morally a serious error. It is a serious error to attempt to kill the spirit of black people by associating every conceivable evil that the human mind could think of to the black skin. Since it is only Nsi that can kill the spirit, Nsi is the root of all evil because whatever that can kill the spirit is bound to destroy the body. **Whatever that seeks to kill life, that seeks to degrade the humanity of the Other, that fosters the supremacy of whiteness against blackness, that is obsessed in controlling the Other unjustly, that has no human morality and that is against the Divine Plan of the One Creator of the universe is Nsi.**

Agreement with Nsi is the condition of living a life in the world of Ekwensu without becoming a devoted follower of the Divine Plan of the One Creator of the universe. Agreement with Nsi is the condition of living a life in the world of Ekwensu without following in the footsteps of the Chosen One. Agreement with Nsi is the condition of living a life in the world of Ekwensu without renouncing ISFET by living MAAT according to the Divine Plan of AMUN in whom we trust. O Yes! Agreement with Nsi is the condition of living a life in the world of Ekwensu without striving to attain the devotion of purpose to the supreme principle of EKUMEKU.

THE CHOSEN PEOPLE OF NZOPUTA UWA

According to the Divine Plan of AMUN in whom we trust, it is the attainment of the devotion of purpose to the supreme principle of EKUMEKU that makes the mind to stay still whenever the Ekwueme is meditative on the moral struggle between the Higher Self and the Lower Self, or between the forces of MAAT and the forces of ISFET, or between the **World of Life** and the world of death or between good and evil. Thus, the Devotion of Purpose to the supreme principle of EKUMEKU is the act of worship. Being the act of worship to the One Creator of the universe, it implicitly and explicitly signifies the self-realization of the ultimate reality in human life. The act, thought or word that is lived according to the Divine Plan of AMUN in whom we trust for the blessings of all humanity and for the expansion of the knowledge of what it means to be fully human is the Truth of the divine birth of EKUMEKU.

Thus, worship must never be relegated to the simple function of going to the Haremakhet once a week for fellowship service and/or meditation with the living Haremakhet. Worship implies and demands the ultimate reality of life in the wholeness of eternity by the active devotional discipline of the Ekwueme. Therefore, the devotion of purpose to the supreme principle of EKUMEKU is the ultimate reality of life Here and also of the life Hereafter. It is only through the devotion of purpose to the supreme principle of EKUMEKU can the human spirit become an Ekwueme.

The devotional discipline of living MAAT by renouncing ISFET affirms itself as the ultimate value of the human life with its dynamism and wholesomeness in the act of giving and in the act of receiving in Chineke Consciousness of life. The devotion of purpose to the supreme principle of EKUMEKU is the act of worship that is based on the supreme vision of **Nzoputa Uwa** in the worship of the One Creator of the universe, with its universalism, dynamism and mechanism of meaning in the process of living a life of repentance from Nsi. No doubt, the devotion of purpose to the supreme principle of EKUMEKU is the master key to the Ekwueme Universal Life. Without the attainment of the devotion of purpose, the human spirit would be in bondage and slavery in the dead end nature of the world of Ekwensu.

The virgin birth of the Ekwueme life for the human spirit has been ordained by the One Creator of the universe in the sequence and disposition of the Revelation of EKUMEKU in the life of Chukwudi. In the Revelation of EKUMEKU in the life of

Chukwudi, the One Creator of the universe has made the ultimate reality of human life self-realizable to all humanity in the Spirit of MAAT. That is why, the Ekwueme bears witness to the Living Truth of the divine birth of EKUMEKU that the highest potentiality of human life is now actually manifest in the Ekwueme Universal Life.

Let it then be known that it is only the Truth of the divine birth of EKUMEKU that can reveal the past of the mighty struggle between the forces of MAAT and the forces of ISFET. It is only the Truth of the divine birth of EKUMEKU that can be used to examine the present moral struggle between the Ekwueme and the Ekwensi. And it is only the Truth of the divine birth of EKUMEKU that can foresee and disclose the future of the mighty struggle between the **World of Life** and the world of death, between the world of EKUMEKU and the world of Ekwensu.

Wherefore, it is only the eternal Truth of the divine birth of EKUMEKU that can manifest the ultimate reality of life in this universe of life. In other words, it is only the Truth of the divine birth of EKUMEKU that can transform and convert the Ekwensi to become a devoted follower of the Divine Plan of the One Creator of the universe. That is to say, without any shadow of doubt, that it is only the Truth of the divine birth of EKUMEKU on the Second year of Nzoputa Uwa that can transform the Ekwensi to become converted as an Ekwueme. Conversely, it is only the Truth of the divine birth of EKUMEKU that has the ultimate power of life and death because it transcends the limitations of mind, time and space.

Let it be known that the followers of the religions of ISFET can never be reconciled to the Truth of the divine birth of EKUMEKU without their repentance from Nsi. For without the repentance from Nsi, it is humanly impossible for the Unbeliever to be justified to the Living Truth of the divine birth of EKUMEKU. In their abuse of human morality, the followers of the religions of ISFET were unable to justify their false belief of good and evil and would never be able to reconcile what they preach with what they practice.

The followers of the religions of ISFET are very ignorant of EKUMEKU and would never be able to self-realize the everlasting Truth of what it means to be fully human without renouncing ISFET by living MAAT. No doubt, there is no human morality in the religions of ISFET because their flawed concept of evil is anti-human. The religions of ISFET can never be able to justify their false notion of good and evil since it is based on skin color contraption. **There has never been and there will never be any moral struggle between the lightness of the day and the darkness of the night. There has never been and there will never be any moral struggle between blackness of the skin and the whiteness of the skin.**

Without any doubt, the followers of the religions of ISFET orchestrated the struggle between high melanin pigmentation and low melanin pigmentation because they have no truth to justify their bodily passions and desires to control and/or to destroy the significant section of humanity in their obstinate lust for power.

During the time of **Oge Nzuzu**, we were held captive in Nsi, deceived by the skin color contraption of the religions of ISFET, were dead to all forms of Ekwensism of many kinds, were enslaved in the bondage of Nsi in the dead end nature of the world of Ekwensu and were indeed condemned to a life with neither meaning nor purpose. But now, our eternal Savior and Redeemer has come to redeem us from the bondage and slavery of the historical process of **Oge Nzuzu.**

SPIRITUAL BLESSINGS IN EKUMEKU

There is only One Creator of the universe. Everything else in the universe of life is the creation of the One Creator of the universe. The One Creator of the universe is **AMUN** in whom we trust. The Holy Name of AMUN is the descriptive reference to the location of the One Creator of the universe in relationship to life. The Holy Name of AMUN is the Truth of the **Hidden One** that is the One Creator of the universe. The One Creator of the universe is the **Hidden One**, AMUN in whom we trust, that is above and beyond everything in creation.

As the Ama Ama Amasi Amasi, beyond name and form, **AMUN**, in whom we trust, is the One Creator of the universe of Life. Before there was any opposition between MAAT and ISFET, before there was any Life or Death, before there was Darkness or Lightness, Blackness or Whiteness, there was **AMUN** in whom we trust All alone as the **Ama-Ama-Amasi-Amasi**. Without any doubt, the One Creator of the universe is **AMUN** in whom we trust, **THE HIDDEN ONE**, the Hidden Beginning of All Beginning. The **Greatest AMUN** in whom we trust is **The Hidden One** behind all creation and yet the Truth of the One Creator of the universe must be renewed through the mission of **Nzoputa Uwa** in every generation according to the Divine Plan of **AMUN** in whom All Truth Resides by following in the footsteps of the Chosen One for the mission of **Nzoputa Uwa**.

The Chosen One for the mission of **Nzoputa Uwa** was chosen by the One Creator of the universe for the mission of **Nzoputa Uwa**. Let it be known that the Chosen People for the mission of Nzoputa Uwa are the Ekwueme People of Truth. The Ekwueme People of Truth are the devoted followers of the Divine Plan of the One Creator of the universe. They are the People of Chineke who are against the worship of any God in whatever form or shape. They are my Beloved People because they follow in my footsteps through the devotion of purpose to the supreme principle of EKUMEKU. The Ekwueme People of Truth are the **New Humanity** who would exist in the wholeness of eternity to renounce ISFET by living MAAT according to the Divine Plan of AMUN in whom we trust.

If you are not a devoted follower of the Divine Plan of the One Creator of the universe, whatever you are, whether you are an Akwunakwuna, a Sethian or an Akwunaset, you are an Unbeliever, an Ekwensi who is agreeable to Nsi. Whomever is agreeable to Nsi is dead in Nsi and whosoever is dead in Nsi is opposed to the truthfulness of life and whomever is opposed to the Truth of the divine birth of EKUMEKU is mortal and perishable. The Ekwueme People of Truth shall act upon the

Unbelievers according to the Divine Plan of AMUN in whom we trust so that they may be redeemed from the dead end nature of the world of Ekwensu.

If you are an Unbeliever, you are doomed to perish, if you do not repent from Nsi and confess EKUMEKU as the eternal Savior and Redeemer of all humanity. As an Unbeliever, you cannot know the future of the Ekwueme People of Truth because you lack the supreme vision of Nzoputa Uwa; and yet the Ekwueme People of Truth know your future if you were not to repent from Nsi, for you are doomed to perish in the abyss of Ekwensism. We know who you are because we were once like you in the ignorance of EKUMEKU. So, we know your Ekwensi condition of living a life more than you can imagine.

Let it be known that the human spirit can never self-realize the wholesome Truth of what it means to be an Ekwueme without becoming a devoted follower of the Divine Plan of the One Creator of the universe. The elemental being can never self-realize the true meaning and purpose of human life without following in the footsteps of the Chosen One for the mission of Nzoputa Uwa. Without the repentance from Nsi, every Unbeliever is entangled with evil in the vicious circle of eternal death. Without renouncing ISFET and living MAAT through the devotion of purpose to the supreme principle of EKUMEKU, every Ekwensi is living for nothing in the dead end nature of the world of Ekwensu.

Without trusting only in AMUN in whom we trust, every Unbeliever can only worship the created images of the human mind. Without worshipping only the One Creator of the universe, every Unbeliever is dead in Nsi in ignorance, falsehood and deception. The divine birth of EKUMEKU on the Second year of Nzoputa Uwa is a blessing to all humanity. Why? Because once we repent from Nsi and accept EKUMEKU as our eternal Savior and Redeemer from the dead end nature of the world of Ekwensu, we would become partakers in the everlasting Truth of the divine birth of EKUMEKU on the Second year of **Nzoputa Uwa. The Ekwueme People of Truth would become**

your true brothers and true sisters in the Almighty Spirit of EKUMEKU when you repent from Nsi.

Let us all bear witness to the timeless Truth of the divine birth of EKUMEKU that we may become the living Haremakhet. Let us become the devoted followers of the Divine Plan of the One Creator of the universe. Let us believe in the eternal Truth of the One Creator of the universe. Let us renounce ISFET by living MAAT in the Almighty Spirit of EKUMEKU. **Let us become the Chosen People for the mission of Nzoputa Uwa by following in the footsteps of the Chosen One.** Let us become the missionaries of peace and justice in human life by fighting against all forms of Ekwensism of any kind. Let us become the Ekwueme People of Truth who are on the mission of Nzoputa Uwa. Let us overcome evil by doing good as we follow in the footsteps of the Chosen One for the mission of **Nzoputa uwa.**

My brothers and sisters in EKUMEKU, let us become the living testimony that there is the Higher Self battling against the Lower Self in this universe of life. Let us repent from Nsi and declare publicly the **Nkwekolita** of the Ekwueme Universal Life. Let us worship only the One Creator of the universe without any fear or favor. Let us become one in the Almighty Spirit of EKUMEKU in the eternal quest for universal brotherhood and sisterhood in the Spirit of MAAT. Let us renounce ISFET by living MAAT through the devotion of purpose to the supreme principle of EKUMEKU.

Hear! My Good People in EKUMEKU, let us bear witness to the everlasting Truth of the divine birth of EKUMEKU on the Second year of **Nzoputa Uwa.**

THE CONCLUSION

The human spirit who is encumbered by the skin color contraption of the Ekwensu people would entertain thoughts and make utterances that would have nothing to do with the ultimate reality of what it means to be an Ekwueme. Such an

Ekwensi mind would live in a make-believe world where everything dishonorable is tied to the black skinned people and everything honorable is tied to the white skinned people.

Let it be known that it is a confused mind that would purposely debase the black skin to eternal doom in order to elevate the white skin to eternal glory. Wherefore, the Ekwueme is not morally bound to recognize or respect the immorality of the Unbelievers. An Unbeliever has no moral rights which an Ekwueme Believer is morally bound to recognize. No doubt, the skin color contraption of the Ekwensu people is an immoral philosophy devised by the Sethian people. The Sethians built their philosophy of religion mostly based on skin color contraption. Also, the Sethian materialistic philosophy of race is wholly based on skin color. There is no truth in the philosophy of Sethianism. OTUA-KA-ODI!

CHAPTER SIX

WE ARE THE EKWUEME PEOPLE OF KEMET

DEDICATED TO:
The memory of **Chikwado Nwalimu**

(Chancellor Williams)
A true son of Kemet
A true fighter of the people of Kemet

He's one with a vision
One who fought for the people
One who lived his life for the people

The one that practiced what he preached
And died so that we may live
A true Ancestor!

I am the Chosen One for the divine mission of **Nzoputa Uwa**.
Before me, there was none and after me, there will be no other.
.....The Chosen One

Rejoice in the Holy Name of AMUN in whom we trust for the One Creator of the universe is the only One worthy of worship. Let us all bear witness to the Truth of the divine birth of EKUMEKU on the Second year of Nzoputa Uwa.
----The Chosen One

Ife na eme unu bu ndi Akwunakwuna si unu na aka. Onye ajulu

aju adighi aju onwe ya. Kedu ka unu si ju onwe unu ma n'eche na ndi madu ozo ga ekweta na unu bu madu? Maduaghozia obuluzie Maduno n'ime Chineke maka na Maduno Ka Ego, Chukwudi Ka Alusi, EKUMEKU Ka Ekwensu, AMUNEMHET!
.....Onye Nzoputa Uwa

The Absolute Good, the supreme moral Law and the unfailing Divine Will of the One Creator of the universe is the Divine Plan of AMUN in whom we trust. In other words, the Almighty Spirit of EKUMEKU is the Divine Plan of the One Creator of the universe that is within us and around us as it has been revealed and written in **The Holy Ankhuwa.**

Let it then be known that what was revealed and written in **The Holy Ankhuwa, Abstracts Vol.1 Version**, pages 60-61, has been fulfilled according to the Divine Plan of AMUN in whom we trust. In page 60, the Word of Truth states: "The New Afrikans are neither an ethnic group nor a national group; but instead, the New Afrikans represent a world group that transcends geographical boundaries". Also, in page 61, the Word of Truth states: "The name "Afrika" or "Africa" shall be changed when the time is right to exist in harmony with the mission of Nzoputa Uwa according to the Divine Plan of AMUN in whom we trust". The Word of Truth continues: "The Holy Land shall be given a new name when the time is right in the Spirit of MAAT."

As the Ekwueme People of Kemet, we have stood, as a single people, on our own feet, to define and to declare the originality of our humanity. Our ancestors, Chikwado Nwalimu, Chike Anta Diop and Nnamdi Azikiwe, can now rest in peace because what was ordained by the One Creator of the universe has been fulfilled. The Kemite's Historical Declaration of the **6th Tehuti 17 N.U.** has demolished on the one hand the Akwunkwuna's divisive notions of a tribal, ethnic or national patrimony; and on the other hand, it has fulfilled the transcendental matrimony of the new world culture that transcends tribal, ethnic and national boundaries. The Kemites both in the Homeland and in the Diaspora are one people championing the mission of **Nzoputa Uwa**. Following in the footsteps of the Chosen One, the Kemites would increasingly become the civilizing agents of historical change for the goodness of life, constantly emphasizing their unity of origin in the historical existence of the Chosen One.

The tribal, ethnic or national tendencies must be subordinated to the unified consciousness of what it means to be an Ekwueme as would be exemplified by the Kemites. With the emergence of the Kemites in the mighty struggle to displace ISFET and restore MAAT as the dominant consciousness of universal life, their historical mission would inevitably dominate and affect the tribal, ethnic and national forces of disunity among the people, becoming the social cement of historical change. Therefore, the world of the Kemite is inseparable from the Ekwueme World Order and yet not every Ekwueme is a Kemite. The Ekwueme is the Universal Being and of course every Kemite is an Ekwueme.

NDUMODU

My beloved people of Kemet, never doubt yourself for you are the Kemites and your Motherland is the Holy Land of KEMET. All of you who are my people are the Kemet-Nu. Let everybody know that you are the Kemite wherever you live, work or visit. Do not allow anybody to deceive you into answering any other name. Wherever you are, never fail to identify yourself as the Kemite. Let us leave that calumnious misrepresentation called Africa to those who are not with us in the Almighty Spirit of EKUMEKU.

Let it be known that you are not an African; instead, you are the Kemite. Never allow anybody to call you an African because you are more than an African. You are my people, Ndi Kemet. We are the Ekwueme People of Truth because we are the devoted followers of the Divine Plan of the One Creator of the universe. Our divine mission is **Nzoputa Uwa** because we exist in the wholeness of eternity in disagreement with Nsi. We disagree with the Ekwensu people in their agreement with Nsi.

Therefore, we exist to contradict their evil passions and desires as we become the embodiment of the Living Truth by renouncing their evil passions and as we fight against the Ekwensism of the world of Ekwensu for the sake of the truthfulness of EKUMEKU. **Thus, by rejecting the name Africa, we become disagreeable to the calumnious misrepresentation that it signifies. The negative self-image that goes with the name Africa has also created the negative self-concept of Africans as lesser beings. We have abandoned that name because it represents nothing but death to us.** The name Africa can only bring nothing to us but death and desolation. So, we have rejected it because it is not in harmony with the divine mission of **Nzoputa Uwa**. We have rejected it because we represent the New Human Paradigm. The name Africa is poison to us and we can no longer identify with whatever that is in agreement with Nsi. Oh, what a new Dawn! The Almighty Spirit of EKUMEKU is the only Truth. The Almighty Spirit of EKUMEKU is our only Comforter, Savior and Redeemer. Nothing else Matters!

INTRODUCTION

The Creator is One. The One is AMUN and the Divine Plan is EKUMEKU. There is no other Creator of the universe but AMUN in whom we trust. Wherefore, there is no God that is worthy of worship. Why? This is because every God is a created image of the human mind. Without any doubt, every God is dead in Nsi. Consequently, there is no God that can save an Unbeliever from Nsi. It is only the Almighty Spirit of EKUMEKU that can save an Unbeliever from Nsi.

In other words, it is a futile effort to pray to any God for protection from Nsi. It is a futile effort to live the life of an Ekwensi. Every Unbeliever is an Ekwensi who lives in agreement with Nsi. So, every Unbeliever is naked and immoral. Without repentance, the Unbeliever is doomed to perish. As long as the Unbeliever has not repented from Nsi, whatever the Unbeliever does, says or thinks would be in agreement with Nsi.

There can never be any bond of brotherhood or sisterhood between the Ekwueme People of Truth and the Ekwensu people, except that the agreement with Nsi upon which the Ekwensu people live must be acted upon.

REPENT AND BE SAVED

Never call yourself a **Kemite**, if you have not repented from Nsi. **Mother Kemet** does not want her children to come back to her as second class beings.

Let us have a basic understanding of the process that we must undergo to become repentant. Without the purification of thought, there cannot be the repentance from Nsi. **What then is the purification of thought?**

The purification of thought starts from our individual will to be free from the yoke of every agreement with Nsi from that moment of self-contrition in consciousness. It is to be free in thought from whatever that exists in opposition to the Truth of the divine birth of EKUMEKU. The purification of thought is the act or an instant awareness of being and becoming that is against every form of *Ekwensism* of any kind. It is to be disagreeable to Nsi by following in the footsteps of the Chosen One for the mission of **Nzoputa Uwa.**

Through the purification of thought, word and deed, we become repentant. **When we repent from Nsi, we would become pure in our thought that is necessary to realize Human Freedom in the Unity of Thought.** What we must know about repentance from Nsi is that it is to change our life from living in agreement with Nsi, to turn it around from living in agreement with Nsi, to become aware of Nsi as the root cause of all evil and to fight against all forms of agreement with Nsi through the devotion of purpose to the supreme principle of EKUMEKU.

The blessings of EKUMEKU cannot be self-realizable without the moral certitude that is the righteousness of the devotion of purpose to the Divine Plan of the One Creator of the universe.

NZOPUTA UWA

Because wherever nothing gathers all will disperse in the disintegration that would lead back to **Nzuzu,** the blessings of life would become manifest through **Nzuko**. But without the repentance from Nsi, what may appear as the blessings of life would have neither meaning nor purpose. That is why, it is only through the voluntary effort of the individual can the human spirit be redeemed from the vicious circle of eternal death; and yet it is only by the devotion of purpose in EKUMEKU can the human Spirit be Saved from Nsi.

O Mother Kemet!
Whence did the centuries gone by?
The good old days that are no more.
Your children thine cried.
But alas!
They had been taken away from you.
In your presence,
They were called half-human and half-monkey.

The mistakes of their fathers-
They paid with their blood, labor and sweat.
Enslaved and colonized,
They were treated as wild animals.
Wild beasts who were-
Incapable of being tamed and domesticated.
Lo!
They cried out to Mother Kemet.
Why have they forsaken us?

Brutalized and dehumanized,
They rejected thee.
And sought comfort in the created image of their oppression.
Behold, they lifted their face in sorrow.
And prayed to the created image for protection.
Nay!
The created image echoed back to them.
And it was like a dream.
Yet, it was a voice that was heard.

But then the voice was heard again and again.
What did the voice say?
Whiten thyself thru white magic.

Unu shall first lose thy mother's identity.
Reject the truthfulness of EKUMEKU.
Bleach thy skin, conk thy woolly hair.
Lest thou become the servants of my children.
In serving my children,
Thou shall be honored.
Honorary white I shall make thee.
Second class white in your deeds and thoughts,
Thou shall become.
The ego-trip and effigy of my children.

Mother Kemet is weeping!
She is crying-
And wailing-
For her children-
Stretching out her hands-
Begging them to come back to her-
In the Almighty Spirit of EKUMEKU.

AMUNEMHET, they heard!
The Voice came from the Chosen One
Calling upon them to repent from Nsi
And thereupon, the Chosen One was in their midst
Nkuzimatism
Biafranism
Ekwuemeism
Herukabakanism
Harembetism
Then, their voice of fellowship was heard.
What was heard is the Living Truth:

The Creator is One
The One is AMUN
And the Divine Plan is EKUMEKU.
OTUA-KA-ODI!

COMMENTARY

Many *Akwunakwuna* Unbelievers bleach their skin and conk their woolly hair because they really want to be considered human, from the standpoint of the old human paradigm. Since the old human paradigm is in agreement with Nsi, the Akwunakwuna who also lives in agreement with Nsi must conform to the Ekwensism of the world of Ekwensu in order to be accepted honorarily as white, which is the old human paradigm that had excluded the Black humanity from what it means to be fully human.

The old human paradigm erroneously project blackness as the absolute evil, as less than human, and whiteness as the absolute good. Although the pink skin is not white, it is made to become white through the very ab-stratification that is white magic. **This unattainable whiteness became fragmented and the process involved the vital symbolic negation of blackness with bizarre justifications for the intensified hatred against those who are caught in the web of its desolation.** Through its amoral definition of good and evil, the black skin became the root of all evil and by implication the black people became the embodiment of all conceivable evil.

It is a skin color contraption without human morality that is preoccupied with the degradation of blackness and the glorification of whiteness. But this whiteness that is being glorified is a magnified lie because the pink skin is far from being white. The created image that made the high melanin pigmentation the outcast within the human family is the embodiment of evil because of the contradiction and inconsistency that exists between the professed values of the religions of ISFET and the actual corruption of human morality that they validate. What they preach is not what they practice and what they practice has no human morality.

Even if skin whiteness is humanly attainable in its sense of the absence of color, colorlessness, it does not warrant the debasement of the humanity of those who do not want to be associated with the delusion of skin whiteness. Therefore, the moral values of good and evil must not be based on skin pigmentation because every human spirit is born in the world of Ekwensu in agreement with Nsi. **The old human paradigm condemned the black skin to eternal doom and elevated the white skin to eternal glory which has created the illusion of white supremacy.**

As a result, the human spirit whose skin color is very far from being white, in striving to this unattainable whiteness, is moving towards the abyss that is the dead end nature of the world of Ekwensu, in the vicious circle of eternal death, **without even knowing it. No doubt, the old human paradigm degraded blackness, and by association made the black skin to become something that is dishonorable, unworthy and ugly**. Yet it is a grave moral error to apply by misapplication, to unjustly impose and to arrogantly ascribe to skin color false values of good and evil. **It is a grave moral evil, illegal and criminal to split the universal relationship that exists between darkness and lightness and then by a misguided association tie everything that is conceived to be evil to the black skin and everything that is conceived to be good to the so-called white skin.**

Without any doubt, it is an abuse of human morality to condemn the dark skin to eternal doom and to elevate the pink skin to eternal glory for the absurdity of a whitened skin. This whitened skin delusion is nothing but a contraption that has been used to degrade the humanity of those who are ignorant of EKUMEKU by projecting them to be less than human and by condemnation and denunciation.

THE HEART OF OUR BELOVED KEMET

Righteousness cannot exist without the devotion of purpose to the supreme principle of EKUMEKU because without living

MAAT by renouncing ISFET whatever the human spirit thinks, says or does would be in agreement with Nsi. **What then is MAAT?**

According to the Divine Plan of the One Creator of the universe, MAAT is the interdependent order of the universe in its constantly unfolding of life. Without any shadow of doubt, MAAT is the divine challenge of time and space, cause and effect, spirit and matter, etc., that is necessary through the devotion of purpose to the supreme principle of EKUMEKU in establishing Truth, Justice, Balance, Harmony, Order, Reciprocity and Propriety. In other words, whatever that is not MAAT is ISFET. Whatever that is diametrically opposed to the ethos of MAAT can only express the ethos of ISFET. Whatever that is not ORDER is Disorder. Therefore, the Universal Aim of the Ekwueme Life in its divine sanction is to strive for harmony, balance or complementarity between the world of EKUMEKU and the world of Ekwensu. For, nothing can exist independently without the constant interaction of its pair of opposite.

Wherefore, the heart of our beloved Kemet is the heart of righteousness. It is the heart of human morality. It is the heart of the Truth of the One Creator of the universe. The heart of our Motherland Kemet is the heart of the **Ozioma of Truth**. It is the heart of AMUN in whom we trust. The heart of our Motherland Kemet is the heart of the devotion of purpose to the Divine Plan of AMUN in whom we trust. It is the heart of the supreme principle of EKUMEKU. The heart of our beloved Kemet is the heart of the Truth of the divine birth of EKUMEKU on the Second year of Nzoputa Uwa. It is the heart of the mission of Nzoputa Uwa. The heart of our Motherland Kemet is the heart of the Chosen One for the mission of Nzoputa Uwa. It is the heart of Chukwudi Onye Nzoputa Uwa. The heart of our Motherland Kemet is the heart of the Ekwueme People of Truth. It is the heart of the Kemites, Ndi-Kemet. The heart of our Motherland Kemet is the heart of the Living Truth. It is the heart of the righteousness of living MAAT by renouncing ISFET.

Let it be universally realized that the human spirit who lives in agreement with Nsi can never be righteous. There is no way that the human spirit who lives in opposition to the Divine Plan of the One Creator of the universe can be a righteous human spirit. Without any doubt, the Ekwensi lives in agreement with Nsi because of the ignorance of EKUMEKU. Any body, spirit or entity that lives in agreement with Nsi is in opposition to the Divine Will of AMUN in whom we trust, and thereby is unrighteous according to the Divine Plan of AMUN in whom we trust.

Righteousness cannot exist without the devotion of purpose to the supreme principle of EKUMEKU because without living MAAT by renouncing ISFET whatever the human spirit thinks, says or does would be in agreement with Nsi. Righteousness cannot exist without the true knowledge of good and evil. It is the knowledge of good and evil that enables the human spirit to attain the devotion of purpose in EKUMEKU. Without the devotion of purpose in EKUMEKU, there cannot be true righteousness in human life.

Righteous is the human spirit who believes in the Truth of the One Creator of the universe; who renounces ISFET by living MAAT; who worships only AMUN in whom we trust; who overcomes evil by doing good; who is disagreeable with Nsi; who follows in the footsteps of the Chosen One. Let it be known that righteousness is not kneeling down, prostrating or praying to a created image from morning until night without human morality. Righteousness is the devotion of purpose in EKUMEKU whereby the Higher Self is made manifest in human life. **Righteous is the one who gathers to help the needy, to give hope to the hopeless, food to the hungry, comfort to the comfortless, water to the thirsty, cloth to the naked, in order to save the individual Chi of the human spirit for EKUMEKU.** Righteousness is not taking without giving, preaching without practice, practice without preaching, knowledge without location, materialism without spirituality, spiritualism without materialism, theory without practice, practice without theory.

Righteousness is the attainment of the devotion of purpose to the supreme principle of EKUMEKU that enables the human spirit to live in disagreement with Nsi. In order to cross the threshold that separates the Ekwueme from the Ekwensi, the human spirit must repent from Nsi. Righteousness is not the proclivity to substitute words for actions, to confuse word with deed or to mistake preaching with practice. Righteous is not the one who institutes words and forms, but instead is the one who is the manifest expression of human morality in word and in deed.
Righteousness is not in the worship of any created image of the human mind. Righteous is the one who has realized that what defiles the human spirit is neither the whiteness of the skin nor the blackness of the skin; but instead unrighteousness is the unrepentant life of living in agreement with Nsi. Righteous is the one who is a devoted follower of the Divine Plan of AMUN in whom we trust who is the manifest expression of the Living Truth. Righteous is the Ekwueme who is the living Haremakhet in the eternal struggle between MAAT and ISFET. Righteous is the Universal Being who fights against the skin color contraption of the Ekwensu people. Righteous is the Kemite who wages Biafra against the Unbelievers without fear or favor. The Ekwensi who steps across the threshold to join the Movement of **Nzoputa Uwa** shall be redeemed from the dead end nature of the world of Ekwensu. Righteous is the Ekwueme who is Chineke Conscious in the midst of the mighty struggle between the Higher Self and the Lower Self. Righteous is the Ekwueme who does not surrender to the evil passions and desires of the Lower Self.

CONCLUSION

Let it be known that the heart of our beloved Kemet is in the New Human Paradigm. Without any doubt, the heart of our Motherland Kemet is not in the old human paradigm. As a result, the New Human Paradigm has superseded the old human paradigm. This new dispensation would restore human dignity and wipe out the illusion of white supremacy, human morality would be restored, and skin color contraption would be vanquished. The Truth of the divine birth of EKUMEKU would become the ruling principle and the Unbelievers must either step out from their deluded *whiteness* or be superseded by the supreme principle of EKUMEKU. No doubt, the only salvation for the Ekwensi is the repentance from Nsi. Without repentance, the Unbeliever is doomed to perish.

The old human paradigm was based on skin color contraption without human morality. It was based on the false notion of a struggle between the forces of darkness and the forces of lightness. But from the beginning of creation, there has never been an inherent moral struggle between darkness and lightness. The religions of ISFET created the illusion of a struggle between darkness and lightness because they lack the truth of human morality.

The One Creator of the universe is AMUN in whom we trust. The creation of the universe began with the Divine Plan of AMUN in whom we trust. It is from the Almighty Spirit of EKUMEKU that all things were created and are being created. **Before creation began, there was neither darkness nor lightness. Darkness and lightness came into being as the result of creation according to the Divine Plan of AMUN in whom we trust. Thus, the notion that lightness superseded darkness is fundamentally flawed. This is because darkness and lightness are identical in creation. One cannot exist without the other. Darkness and lightness are only gradation of energy in the universe, neither can be used in any moral sense to exclusively represent good nor evil except in the corrupt minds of the followers of the religions of ISFET.**

In other words, it is a grave moral error to split the universal principles of darkness and lightness from each other and then by a misguided association relate this unwholesome division to skin color. Let it be known that lightness can never supersede darkness for without darkness there can never be lightness. The notion that promotes the flawed idea of lightness acting upon darkness is patently false. At the same time, the low melanin pigmentation that associates itself with lightness is delusional.

Why? Because the high melanin pigmentation that is erroneously associated with darkness is in truth the direct absorber of light. It is the heat that comes from the lightness of the sun which made life possible and melanin pigmentation serves as the absorber of the energy from the sun. Lightness = High Melanin Pigmentation (HMP). Darkness = Low Melanin Pigmentation (LMP).

Therefore, it is the relative absence of lightness that is the cause of low melanin pigmentation and it is the perfect absorption of lightness that is the cause of high melanin pigmentation. Dark skin is directly related to the energy of lightness and the pink skin is directly related to the energy of darkness. The pink skin can be called the true skin of darkness; while the black skin can be called the skin of lightness in the true sense of the word. The dark skin has direct relationship with the energy of light which is the trigger of the high melanin pigmentation; whereas the pink skin is the result of the relative absence of the energy of light which creates the low melanin pigmentation. This is the interdependent order of life in the universe. **Thus, the pink skin does not have any greater monopoly to light than the darker skin.** It is only in the abstraction of white magic that the darker skin is erroneously tied to darkness.

But the dark skin is not synonymous with darkness because the high melanin pigmentation can only exist because of its direct access to light; while the pink skin is not synonymous with light because the low melanin pigmentation can only exist because of the relative absence of light. It is the process of darkness that caused the existence of the low melanin pigmentation. In other words, the true meaning of darkness is the absence of lightness and the true meaning of lightness is the absence of darkness. Since darkness is the absence of lightness, its direct reflection is the low melanin pigmentation; and since lightness is the absence of darkness, its direct reflection is the high melanin pigmentation. Lightness = Dark Skin. Darkness = Pink Skin. Because of the interdependent order of the universe, the dark pigmentation is the skin of lightness and the pink pigmentation is the skin of darkness. Yet due to ignorance, falsehood and deception, the dark skin was erroneously tied to darkness and the pink skin was erroneously tied to lightness.

Associating lightness to absolute good and darkness to absolute evil, the religions of ISFET built their make-believe doctrines about life on the false supposition of tying the black skin to darkness and transfiguring the pink skin to become white. They then created the illusion of a struggle between darkness and lightness from where they began to associate themselves with lightness. As they made lightness the absolute good, darkness became the absolute evil. **By this skin color contraption, the black skin became the sole target of their fantastic devotion to lightness through which the black skinned people were projected to become the embodiment of evil without any moral justification.**

Nevertheless, the moral values of good and evil must never be tied to skin color and have nothing to do with the universal principles of darkness and lightness. **Since without the lightness of the sun, there can never be the darker skin and since without the darkness that is the absence of the lightness of the sun, there can never be the pink skin, it is an abuse of human morality to tie the dark skin to darkness.** The dark skin which is light made manifest in the human body has been abused to become the absence of light in the human body. There can never be the dark skin without light. The pink skin when it is exposed to light for a reasonable time tends to become darker than it was before. To the extent that the dark skin exists because of the lightness of the sun, it is to the same extent that the pink skin exists because of the relative absence of light from the sun. The pink skin can never be the reflection of light more than the black skin.

The black skin exists because it is the direct reflection of the energy of light in the human body. Without any doubt, there is no inherent moral struggle between darkness and lightness because the dark skin is produced by lightness and the pink skin is produced by darkness. Wherefore, there can never be any dichotomy or polarization between darkness and lightness. In other words, there is no moral justification for the orchestrated struggle between darkness and lightness. **That is why, the Ekwueme would never condemn anybody just because of skin color differences.** The Ekwueme has condemned the Unbelievers to eternal doom because of the evil that they do. It is the agreement with Nsi of the Ekwensu people that the Ekwueme would always act upon and not their skin color. Skin color can never be the basis of any true moral struggle.

The moral struggle between good and evil is the eternal struggle between MAAT and ISFET, between the Higher Self and the Lower Self, between the forces of Chi-Ukwu and the forces of Alusi, between the world of EKUMEKU and the world of Ekwensu and between the Ekwueme and the Ekwensi. There has never been and there will never be any moral struggle between darkness and lightness. Wherefore, the Truth of the divine birth of EKUMEKU has displaced ISFET and restored MAAT as the dominant consciousness in the universe of life.

Repent from Nsi and accept EKUMEKU as your eternal Savior and Redeemer from the dead end nature of the world of Ekwensu. Whether you are black or pink it does not matter, so long as you have repented from Nsi and have confessed EKUMEKU as your eternal Savior and Redeemer in the Holy Name of AMUN in whom we trust. Then, you declare publicly the **Nkwekolita** of the Ekwueme Universal Life in fellowship with the living Haremakhet that you may be Harembetized as the follower of the Divine Plan of the One Creator of the universe. OTUA-KA-ODI!

CHAPTER SEVEN

THE CHRONOLOGY OF THE LIFE OF CHUKWUDI

Before the time of **Nzoputa Uwa**, we were doomed, condemned to perish in our agreement with Nsi. But now our eternal Savior has come to save us from the yoke of living in agreement with Nsi.

As we celebrate the Seventeenth Year of **Nzoputa Uwa**, a historical chronology of the life of Chukwudi *Onye Nzoputa Uwa* from the beginning to the present is necessary for a comprehensive understanding of the historical life of the Chosen One. Although this present chronology is selective and yet to be final, it would serve as the basic framework upon which future chronologies would be developed.

We celebrate the Seventeenth Year of **Nzoputa Uwa** because it is the year of the Historical Declaration of the Kemites and the Rebirth of the People of Kemet, both at home and abroad. The rise of the Kemites would be championed by those who are directly inspired by the dispensation of Chukwudi, either from the Holy Land or from the Diaspora with a somatic norm image that would contrast with the skin color contraption of the religions of ISFET. The transcendent beauty of life in disagreement with Nsi is the diametrical opposite of the skin color contraption of the religions of ISFET. The codes of conduct, beliefs and institutions must conform to the Truth of the divine birth of EKUMEKU on the Second year of Nzoputa Uwa. In the same vein, it is the Truth of the divine birth of EKUMEKU that is the indispensable guide to human thought and behavior.

The world of the Ekwueme is without boundary in space and yet the Kemite must be rooted in historical space and time. In other words, it is only the unfettered free mind of the Ekwueme that can experience the ultimate reality and indeed the ontogeny of the Kemite is inseparable from the New World Order of EKUMEKU. Since during the time of Oge Nzuzu we were dehumanized and our humanity denied through the skin color contraption of the religions of ISFET, it is imperative that we must restore our collective humanity by exercising our human freedom for self-definition. By defining ourselves as the Kemites, we are exercising our human freedom in self-definition. We can no longer recognize the humanity of anyone who does not recognize our humanity. If we are denied the right to be human, then nobody else should have that right to be human. **We are human beings and the exercise of our human freedom is inseparable from our humanity. We are the Ekwueme People of Kemet. Without any doubt, we the Kemites are a people, one people indeed.**

THE BASELINE OF THE EKWUEME CALENDAR

The baseline against which to measure change/time between the time of **Oge Nzuzu** and the time of **Nzoputa Uwa** is the key to the Ekwueme Calendar.

Let it be known that **Oge Nzuzu** was the time before the time of **Nzoputa Uwa**. **Oge Nzuzu** is the time when we were ignorant of EKUMEKU and as a result, it is the time of foolishness. **Oge Nzuzu** was the time of hopelessness and despair because we lacked the true knowledge of good and evil. **Oge Nzuzu** is the time when we lived in agreement with Nsi. **Oge Nzuzu** is the time when we were the living dead, living for nothing in ignorance, falsehood and deception. **Oge Nzuzu** is the time of the living dead, living for nothing in ignorance, falsehood and deception. It is the time of ignorance, the time of bondage and slavery, the time when everybody lived in agreement with Nsi.

Nzoputa Uwa is the time of the struggle between good and evil, between MAAT and ISFET, between the world of EKUMEKU and the world of Ekwensu. It is the time of the mighty struggle to overcome evil by doing good. **Nzoputa Uwa** is the historical time of the divine birth of EKUMEKU. It is the time of the dispensation of Chukwudi for the self-realization of Chi-Ukwu-Di in us. This dispensation of **Nzoputa Uwa** is not by prayers, not by kneeling down or prostrating. Instead, it is by Chineke Consciousness. It is by the devotion of purpose to the supreme principle of EKUMEKU can the Truth of this dispensation be self-realizable by the human spirit. That is to say, it is by the repentance from Nsi can the human spirit be liberated from the vicious circle of eternal death. It is by renouncing ISFET and living MAAT can we become partakers of the Living Truth. Yes, it is through the struggle to overcome evil by doing good can we follow in the footsteps of the Chosen One for the mission of **Nzoputa Uwa**.

To work out the dates of events in your own life according to the Ekwueme Calendar, our point of departure is 1993 of the Ekwensu Calendar(EC). Subtract 1993 to the date, then you will arrive at the Ekwueme Calendar Reckoning. For example, an event that happened in 2010 (EC) is reckoned to be on the 17 NU. When you subtract 1993 from 2010, it will give you 17. That is 17 NU. Convert all important dates in your life to the Ekwueme system of reckoning time. Also, what happened in 1970 (EC) would be 1993 minus 1970 = 23 ON. Moreover any date Before the EC Calendar began, for example, 30 BEC, add 30 to 1993 and you get our date 2023 ON. There is an almost three months differences between our New Year and their New Year. Our New Year begins on the Spring Equinox according to the reckoning of the Ekwueme Calendar System.

A CHRONOLOGY OF IMPORTANT EVENTS IN THE LIFE OF CHUKWUDI

ON = OGE NZUZU

NU = NZOPUTA UWA

ON 72 = Chukwudi's father, Maduaghozia Okeke, was born in Oba

ON 60 = Chukwudi's mother, Ntupuanya Motuanya, was born in Oba.

ON 58 = The death of Chukwudi's grandfather, *Nze* Okeke Ugonwanne Adebe, in Oba.

ON 55 = The death of Chukwudi's paternal grandmother, Gwamniru Adebe, in Oba.

ON 42 = Maduaghozia Okeke married Miss Ntupuanya Motuanya in Oba

ON 29 = Chukwudi Okeke Maduno was born in Kaduna

ON 27 = Escaped from the tyranny of death. Chukwudi escaped death in Kaduna. He was taken to a hide out, a Bunker in Oba, because the enemy was out to overcome the birth of Chukwudi, to exterminate the new life. He was hidden inside a Bunker in Oba until the war ended.

ON 26 = The Declaration of Biafra and the subsequent war. The seed of the Biafran ethic was planted.
ON 24 = The Ahiara Declaration
ON 23 = The Biafran war ended with the popular slogan, "No Victor, No Vanquished". Evidently, the Proto-Biafrans won the moral battle, despite the pogrom perpetrated against them because of the unholy alliance of the enemy forces. The End of the war thus was a compromise between the Truth of MAAT and the might of ISFET.

ON 12 = Chukwudi graduated from Merchants of Light School Oba.

ON 11 = Chukwudi started work at the Nigerian Breweries PLC Kaduna. He resigned when father died in the year 09 **Oge Nzuzu**. After his father's burial, he became an importer of electronics parts, buying Japanese made products from Singapore and marketing them wholesale in Lagos. Chukwudi made enough money and with support from brothers, Uche and P. Ikenna

Maduno , started thinking seriously about the problems of the Afrikan humanity. This is because wherever he had traveled then through his business ventures outside the Continent he had noticed that there is an evil tendency to dishonor the black skinned people. However, the reason for this evil was unknown to him then. The need to know more planted in his mind the idea of going back to school abroad.

ON 09 = The death of Chukwudi's father, G. Maduaghozia Okeke.

ON 08 = Chukwudi went to Singapore on a business trip. He sat in a bus beside a native who became outwardly hostile and verbally abusive as he left his seat. Who did this to us, he asked himself. That experience helped to open his eyes to the evil of white magic. He decided to visit Old Kemet. It was the turning point of his life.

Chukwudi spent seven days in the ruins of Old Kemet, contemplating about his future. Chukwudi decided to go to Mbadiegwu to gain more experience.

ON 07 = Chukwudi sojourned to Mbadiegwu {USA}, Atlanta Georgia to be precise. Enrolled at the then Clark College in the old Atlanta University Center.

ON 06 = Chukwudi enrolled at Atlanta Metropolitan College.

ON 04 = Chukwudi graduated from Atlanta Metropolitan College. Also, he enrolled at Kennesaw State University, Marietta Georgia.

ON 03 = Chukwudi was elected to the Student Union Government as Major Events Chairman in Kennesaw State University. (Then it was called Kennesaw State College.)

ON 02 = Chukwudi graduated from Kennesaw State University. He enrolled at Clark Atlanta University to study African and African American History.

NZOPUTA UWA

ON 01 = This is 1993 of the popular Ekwensu Calendar(EC). This is the Year Before Separation. Chukwudi finished coursework on his Graduate Program and put final research ideas to his Theory of White Magic. This year is the Last Year of **Oge Nzuzu.**

....
....

01 NU = This is the 1994 of the Ekwensu Calendar(EC). <u>*THE POINT OF ORIGIN OF THE EKWUEME SYNTHESIS. This*</u> First Year of **Nzoputa Uwa** marked the End of **Oge Nzuzu** and the beginning of the time of **Nzoputa Uwa.** The text, **WHITE MAGIC: The Origins and Ideas of Black Mental & Cultural Colonialism,** was published in this First Year of **Nzoputa Uwa.**

The creative principle of Unity and Guidance came into being through the divine intervention of the One Creator of the universe.

02 NU = Through the divine intervention of the One Creator of the universe, the divine birth of EKUMEKU on the Second year of **Nzoputa Uwa** was realized as the Ultimate Reality. As a result, The EKUMEKU Universal Declaration was born in Atlanta. The Chosen One was chosen by the One Creator of the universe for the mission of Nzoputa Uwa to serve as the perfect witness of the Truth of the divine birth of EKUMEKU and to embody its ultimate reality. The Chosen One became the Perfect Witness of Divine Justice. The reckoning of the Ekwueme Calendar began from the Second Year of NU. Chukwudi began to teach and preach. The Revelation of EKUMEKU in the life of Chukwudi is realized as the divine ordinance of the One Creator of the universe. The Ankhuwa came into universal expression. "The Ankhuwa" means "The World of Life". Thus, "The Holy Ankhuwa" means "The Living Truth of the World of Life".

Ohacracy: The Undercurrent of Africa-Centered Nationalism was published.

03 NU = EKUMEKU Study Groups began to be organized.

04 NU = The Chosen One began to gather his companions & disciples. Letters were sent to many people in the world of Ekwensu. Open letters sent out to the media houses.
The African Herald Newspaper edited and published by Dr. R.O. Nwachukwu in Dallas Texas published some of the early letters. The Chosen One was challenged by an Unbeliever in **The African Herald Vol. 8 No.06,** Sebek 04 N.U.(June 1997 EC), with anti-Ekwueme polemic write up, **"I Wish Maduno Well"**. The letter was so much humbug without any basis in the ultimate reality of **Nzoputa Uwa**. The Akwunakwuna intended to turn back the water of life when it should flow. However, he was challenged in the subsequent editions of the same publication by two men who wrote rejoinders to rebuke his evil aspersions. Dr. **B. Nwabueze Umez** and Alphonse Riley-James recorded their names in history in support of the Truth. (Alphonse Riley-James after his **Harembetism** changed his name to **Chike Kamau Maduka**.) The intention of the letter was aborted as good overcame evil in that early beginning.

05 NU = Mazi Chike Kamau Maduka became the right hand man of the Chosen One along with other devoted Ekwuemenu. Every Unbeliever is at the left hand of the Chosen One. Chibuzo Ezeani, Chizor El-Sun Arah, Chima Emeka Chidinma, Abiodun Adekunle, Chika Ekwueme and many more others declared publicly the **Nkwekolita** of the Ekwueme Universal Life and became part of the original foundation of the Ekwueme World Order. Although our growth has been gradual and developmental, it is consistent. Many more have become the Ekwueme in their hearts and sooner than later would make their public declaration of **Nkwekolita**.

06 NU = Successful missionary journey to New York in Brooklyn and Harlem initiated by Dr.Jack Felder. **The Daily Challenge** Newspaper gave prominent center coverage with pictures titled **"Maduno 'White Magic' Shakes Up Black New Yorkers"** written by Nolan Jones, 3rd Nekhebet 06 NU, (July 21

1999) Final Edition. The Movement of **Nzoputa Uwa** began to gain momentum in New York area, in the prisons and else where as the message of **Nzoputa Uwa** gives hope to the hopeless. The Chosen One taught at Soul Source Bookstore & Cafe opposite R.W. Woodruff Library in Clark Atlanta University Center. Many of those who came were amazed by the single-mindedness of the Truth of **Nzoputa Uwa**.

07 NU = The Atlanta Encounter with the enemy forces. The Chosen One defeated his enemies with the hammer of the Truth.

The first website of the Movement of **Nzoputa Uwa** was designed by Tunde D. Lowo.

08 NU = The Chosen One returned to the Motherland after many years in Mbadiegwu.

09 NU = The development of the IMHOTEP Haremakhet began. Akhenaten Haremakhet began its organization in Oba.

Teaching and preaching at Rumuokoro Roundabout, confrontation with police who wanted to deny the Master Teacher the right to teach the people.

10 NU = Chukwudi married former Miss Nneka Ugboma

13 NU = The death of Chukwudi's Mother.

14 NU = Chukwudi's son, Chukwuka Maduno, was born on 28th Sekhmet 14 N.U.

The Holy Ankhuwa, Abstracts Vol. 1 Version, was published and in print.

17 NU = Chukwudi's daughter, Ifeoma Maduno was born 19th Sekhmet 17 NU

Chukwudi's brother, Amaechi Maduno died on the 6th Ausar 17 NU.

THE HISTORICAL DECLARATION on the 6th Tehuti 17 NU and the Rebirth of the People of Kemet. The Kemites are one people and their character is derived from their common origin and common destiny. The Kemites derive their common origin in the historical existence of the Chosen One for the mission of **Nzoputa Uwa.**

18 NU = Nzoputa Uwa: The Holy Ankhuwa Abstracts Vol . 2 was published.

.......to be continued

CHAPTER EIGHT

THE CHOSEN ONE HAS COME FOR HUMAN FREEDOM

Whatsoever is agreeable to Nsi must be acted upon for the sake of the Truth because everything that is agreeable to Nsi is in opposition to the Divine Plan of AMUN in whom we trust.....THE HOLY ANKHUWA

Let it be known that the old human paradigm is agreeable to Nsi; **while the New Human Paradigm is disagreeable to Nsi. With the divine birth of EKUMEKU on the Second year of Nzoputa Uwa**, the battle line has been drawn between the immorality of living in agreement with Nsi and the morality of existing in disagreement with Nsi from where the history of human life should henceforth be explained and understood. It is either one is agreeable to Nsi or one is disagreeable to Nsi. There are no two ways about it. If you are agreeable to Nsi, you are no other than an Ekwensi who is ignorant of EKUMEKU. If you are disagreeable to Nsi through the devotion of purpose to the supreme principle of EKUMEKU, you are no other than an Ekwueme. Whosoever is not an Ekwueme is an Ekwensi without any doubt whatsoever.. ...The Chosen One.

Let it be known that whosoever does not repent from Nsi is against me and my mission. Thus, whosoever is against me and the mission of Nzoputa Uwa is equally against the Divine Will of the One Creator of the universe of life.....The Chosen One.

Chukwudi, **The Chosen One of Nzoputa Uwa,** is also the founding father of the New Afrikan World. The everlasting mission of Nzoputa Uwa would be unfulfilled without the Ascent of the Haremakhet towards unity and guidance. Thus, the mission of **Nzoputa Uwa** is the Holy Cause for every bona fide Ekwueme and yet it is the mission of the New Afrikans par excellence.. ...The Ekwueme People of Truth.

MADUKA

The transitions from the condition of the Old African to the condition of the Renascent African and then to the more complete form of human life of the New Afrikan are motivated by the quest for Human Freedom. Without moral liberation and ethical salvation, the New Afrikan could not have come into universal being.

The mission of **Nzoputa Uwa** was ordained by the One Creator of the universe since the beginning of creation. The time period before the Supreme Idea of **Nzoputa Uwa** was brought into manifest expression does not mean that this Supreme Idea did not exist before it came into universal manifestation. What it means is that the One Creator of the universe did not yet actualize the Supreme Idea of **Nzoputa Uwa** through the special human vehicle to bring it into material existence in order to exist in time and space during the time of **Oge Nzuzu**. We cannot guess just why the One Creator of the universe actualized the Holy Cause of **Nzoputa Uwa** when it was done; but we do know that before an Idea of substantial magnitude is revealed and manifested there must have been sufficient preparation. Why the One Creator of the universe chose the Chosen One to receive the divine revelation of **Nzoputa Uwa** from the First year of **Nzoputa Uwa** is an answer that lies with **The Greatest AMUN in whom we must trust.**

INTRODUCTION

The world of EKUMEKU stands on its own Truth, standing over and against the world of Ekwensu, comparable to nothing except its universal character. The absurdity of a life without the spiritual aim, a life without human morality, a life devoid of the Spirit of Truth, a life that worships the created instead of the One Creator of the universe, a life that lives in agreement with Nsi, is the slavery and bondage of the Ekwensi condition of living a life.

Let it be known that underlying all creation, is the **Hidden One**, the self-created AMUN in whom we trust, that is the One Creator of the universe. In every generation, there would always be my people, *the Ekwueme People of Truth,* that shall be sent forth by the One Creator of the universe in the Almighty Spirit of EKUMEKU to champion the Holy Mission of **Nzoputa Uwa** through the devotion of purpose to the supreme principle of EKUMEKU. The attainment of the devotion of purpose to the supreme principle of EKUMEKU enables the human spirit to comprehend and contend against the monstrosity of living in agreement with Nsi.

Wherefore, I say unto you, as I bear witness to the Truth of the divine birth of EKUMEKU, that you must no longer behave as the Ekwensu people behave, in their evil of unbelief, in their whitened delusions, in their absurd skin color contraption, in their abuse of human morality, in their violation of the universal principles of darkness and lightness, in their life of living in agreement with Nsi because of their ignorance of EKUMEKU and in their nakedness and immorality. You must never yield to those who live in agreement with Nsi, to their evil passions and desires, for they can only lead you astray. Let it be known that there can never be the purity of thought without the repentance from Nsi.

THE MASTER TEACHER HAS COME FOR HUMAN FREEDOM

Let it be known that the Fall of the Old African was the inevitable transition by which the New Afrikan could come into world historical existence. The transition from the Old African to the New Afrikan is the Renascent African. The Renascent African lacks human morality; and as a result, the Renascent

African is without any moral conscience and is incapable of self-reflection in the true sense of the word.

In order to self-realize the essential being of the New Afrikan, that is, **The Kemet-Nu or Ndi Kemet,** the Renascent African must become disagreeable with Nsi, which can only start with the reflection of thought within itself and a cultivated consciousness of becoming an Ekwueme in thought, word and deed. Individual self-reflection on the eternal struggle between MAAT and ISFET manifests an inward moral conscience that is necessary for the human spirit to become born again in the image of EKUMEKU.

Historical change from the Old African and the Renascent African to the New Afrikan is impossible without the **Movement of Nzoputa Uwa.** Whenever there is historical change, it must have its supreme cause, for historical change does not occur in a vacuum. The actual succession of phases from the Old African to the Renascent African and from the Renascent African to the New Afrikan is the functional relationship between the sequence and the disposition which brought the change from bondage and slavery to the Freedom in the **Unity of Thought**.

The cordinated spacial system begins with the originality of **Ndi Kemet**. Thus, the **Kemetic world** would gain new and critical relevance in the Living Truth as the name Africa gradually becomes a thing of the time of **Oge Nzuzu,** which is a thing of the past before the time of **Nzoputa Uwa**. The Ekwueme would fight to extend the bounds of **Nzuko** by humbling the Unbelievers and by propagating the mission of **Nzoputa Uwa**. Essentially, this is the Holy Cause and the eternal reward is the everlasting life in Chineke Consciousness.

Without any doubt, the Ekwueme came into universal being when nothing else was universal in its being and becoming. The Ekwueme bears witness that the skin color contraption of the Ekwensu people is devoid of human morality and is very far from being universal. Evidently, its false claim of universal validity is a sham because skin color contraption can never be the basis of human morality.

It is at the point of equilibrium, which is the center of the creative forces of life, that the **Universal Being** emerged in the image of EKUMEKU in order to live MAAT by renouncing ISFET. The struggle between the Ekwueme and the Ekwensi therefore exists in the wholeness of eternity to displace ISFET and restore MAAT as the dominant consciousness in the universe of life. Thus, the ultimate reality that expresses the Almighty Spirit of EKUMEKU is unrealizable without the manifest realization of the divine authority of the Chosen One who has been chosen by the One Creator of the universe for the mission of **Nzoputa Uwa**. From the divine authority, came the knowledge of good and evil, the reckoning of time, the struggle to overcome evil by doing good, the morality to repent from Nsi and the Human Freedom to become disagreeable to Nsi.

The Master Teacher of the divine message of **Nzoputa Uwa** is **Chukwudi Okeke Maduno. The Master Teacher Said: I have come with the Living Truth to set unu FREE and apart from the historical process of Oge Nzuzu.**

Let it be known that the Chosen One for the mission of **Nzoputa Uwa, Chukwudi, Onye-Nzoputa-Uwa** has come for the Deliverance of the human spirit from the dead end nature of the world of Ekwensu. No doubt, the Chosen One has come for Human Freedom. The Master Teacher is known to have developed the universal consciousness to know the mind and heart of every human spirit that lives in agreement with Nsi. The Chosen One is the Great Judge of every individual Chi.

The mind of the human spirit who lives in agreement with Nsi is unreflected and underdeveloped because it is yet to be free and is entangled with evil in the vicious circle of eternal death. Thus, the liberation of the human spirit from the dead end nature of the world of Ekwensu is the mission of the Master Teacher. The Master Teacher points the Way for the salvation of the individual Chi from Nsi and the human spirit who follows in his footsteps realizes the eternal Truth of Salvation of the CHI through the devotion of purpose to the supreme principle of EKUMEKU.

In other words, true Human Freedom can never be realized so long as the human spirit lives in agreement with Nsi. The morality of repentance is necessary which would make the human spirit to become aware of the existence of Nsi as the root of all evil. The struggle to overcome evil by doing good would have neither meaning nor purpose as long as the human spirit lives in agreement with Nsi. It is when the human spirit has become disagreeable with all forms of **Ekwensism** of any kind that true Human Freedom is realized. The Master Teacher has come for Human Freedom in the Almighty Spirit of EKUMEKU. Those who follow in his footsteps have come to realize the true consciousness of what it means to be fully human.

The Freedom of the human spirit from the bondage and slavery in the dead end nature of the world of Ekwensu is the world historical character of the Ekwueme People of Truth. The Human Freedom to live in disagreement with Nsi is the fundamental principle of the New Human Paradigm. This Human Freedom that has been realized in the wholeness of eternity, evolved from the cultural universes of the Old African and the Renascent African, and it is destined to transform the meaning of what it is to be fully human.

HUMAN FREEDOM AT LAST

Let it be known that whosoever follows in the footsteps of the Chosen One is destined to be Free. The Chosen One has come to make us all Free. **Free at last**. Yes, in thought, word and deed!

Free from all forms of Ekwensism of any kind. Free from the bondage and slavery in the dead end nature of the world of Ekwensu. Free from ignorance, falsehood and deception. Free with the perfection of the spirit to be saved from Nsi. **Free at Last.**

The human spirit having gained the consciousness of its Freedom, through the devotion of purpose to the supreme principle of EKUMEKU, becomes the Universal Being who is the devoted follower of the Divine Plan of the One Creator of the universe. Since every human spirit is born in the world of

Ekwensu in agreement with Nsi, it is only through the transforming process of becoming disagreeable with Nsi can the human spirit arrive at the Truth of Human Freedom.

FREEDOM IN THE UNITY OF THOUGHT

The Human Freedom of the Ekwueme is realized when the Spirit of Truth has taken possession of the mind of the human spirit, finding a dwelling place in the individual consciousness of the Chi. The Truth of the divine birth of EKUMEKU is then realized once the human spirit has surrendered unconditionally to the Divine Will of the One Creator of the universe in exchange for the Freedom of the Living Truth that becomes manifest, which is attained through the devotion of purpose. Consequently, the human spirit becomes liberated in the Living Truth, becomes an Ekwueme who would exist in the wholeness of eternity to renounce ISFET and to live MAAT by following in the footsteps of the Chosen One for the mission of **Nzoputa Uwa.**

Thus, Human Freedom is self-realized and the **Unity of Thought** is the substantial Truth that animates it. The unification of the human spirit in Freedom of the **Unity of Thought**, of the Life that is characterized, inspired and made manifest by the eternal Truth of the divine birth of EKUMEKU on the Second year of **Nzoputa Uwa,** is the Spirit of Truth that is in and out of itself the **Universal Being**.

In other words, there can never be the true **Unity of Thought** or the Spiritual Union of the human spirit without the attainment of the devotion of purpose to the supreme principle of EKUMEKU. The Ekwensi does not know what it means to self-realize the Human Freedom in the **Unity of Thought**. It is thought that is fundamental in the Freedom of the human life. Without the human ability to realize Freedom in the **Unity of Thought**, the human spirit would not be fundamentally different from many animals that can be often more united in their action than the human spirit.

The human spirit ought to develop true moral conscience in order to be liberated from the eternal struggle that would always exist between the forces of MAAT and the forces of ISFET. For, it is the knowledge of good and evil that awakens the human spirit to strive in the realization of the Human Freedom that exists in the **Unity of Thought**.

There can never be neither **Human Freedom** nor **Unity of Thought in the unreflected life of the Ekwensu people which is based on the evil passions and desires of the Lower Self. Since all evil passions and desires of the Lower Self are opposed to Human Freedom, it is the devotion of purpose to the supreme principle of EKUMEKU, that is the master key to the Unity of Thought.** No doubt, the essential principle of EKUMEKU is Human Freedom and its manifestation is realized in the **Unity Thought** within the core substance of the universal Truth of Life.

The supreme principle of EKUMEKU is the eternal Truth whereby the worship of the One Creator of the universe is the beginning and the final aim of human existence. The divine birth of EKUMEKU is the only Truth in which the whole is capable of uniting in thought, word and deed, where all distinctions are extinguished through the devotion of purpose as the divinely substantial power of being and becoming. Being in disagreement with Nsi, is the consciousness of this Unity and the universal experience of this **Unity of Thought** is the revelation of EKUMEKU in the life of Chukwudi. Its universal realization would be the rise of a world historical people who are self-conscious of their world historical mission, who are not limited in mind, time and space, who are Free in their **Unity of Thought**, who embrace all that genuinely convert to the Truth of their world historical mission to become the devoted followers of the Divine Plan of AMUN in whom we trust and whose morality is based on the true knowledge of good and evil as opposed to the skin color contraption of the Ekwensu People.

When there is no human morality, there can never be human dignity. Human Freedom would be unknown. Without

human morality, what can only rule are the evil passions and desires of the Lower Self.

The whole world of Ekwensu lives in agreement with Nsi. As a result, there is no human morality in the world of Ekwensu. **Anybody who lives in agreement with Nsi has no human morality and therefore can never be free.** There can never be human freedom without the repentance from Nsi. Wherefore, Human Freedom exists in the **Unity of Thought** and it is realized when the human spirit has become an **Ekwueme** in thought, word and deed.

WHAT DOES THE NAME AFRICA MEAN TO YOU?

My brothers and sisters in EKUMEKU, we must abandon the name Africa or Afrika for the sake of the Truth of the divine birth of EKUMEKU on the Second year of **Nzoputa Uwa**. We must do it for our own supreme good. Indeed, we have already done it.

My brothers and sisters in the Diaspora, this is where your role can be decisive. If there is any of you who does not understand what is at stake, the Humble Servant of EKUMEKU is here to serve you in humility and truth. Let it be known that we are the Kemites, The Kemet-Nu, without any doubt whatsoever. We are the **Kemites, The Kemet-Nu,** by descent and we are the Ekwueme People of Truth by moral conviction. **Our mission is Nzoputa Uwa because we are the devoted followers of the Divine Plan of the One Creator of the universe**. Therefore, our Holy Land is the beloved Continent of Kemet. Whenever there is an opportunity to spread our message let us ask the Unbeliever: *Do you know the continent that is called Kemet?*

Our brothers and sisters in the Holy Land have a lot of work to do as well. We must do what our people in the Diaspora ought to do as well, if not more. With the change of name, the true history of our beloved continent would begin to unfold. Whatever you can do, just do it for my sake, if not for your own sake. Sooner than later, you shall be blessed with the means to spread the message of **Nzoputa Uwa** in the Holy Name of AMUN in whom we trust. But do not wait until that time. Start with the means at your disposal presently.

We are the world historical people of Kemet and the Chosen One has been chosen by AMUN in whom we trust to deliver humanity from every agreement with Nsi through the Almighty Spirit of EKUMEKU. The Chosen One has come for Human Freedom.

For the doubting Unbelievers, meditate on what I have to say to you as follows: We must recognize the Freedom that we have to identify with our Essential Being. **The Kemet-Nu** cannot identify with the name Africa. We do not recognize its origin and it does not have its origin within the continent. Since we cannot trace its positive beginning with the history of our beloved continent, we cannot identify with it as a world historical people. We know how the name came about because it was imposed from without; and what was called Africa originally was a conquered territory that excluded Old Kemet. *Thus, the name Africa is an arbitrary invention that the Kemet-Nu, Ndi Kemet, will never accept.*

It is unacceptable to us that our continent would be identified with nothing from its glorious past that can inspire the future. **What does the name Africa mean to you?** How can such a name unify the consciousness of her people? We must reject that name since we are fully awake. We must identify with our past by calling ourselves the People of Kemet and our continent, the Land of Kemet. We are **Ndi Kemet, The Kemet-Nu**, being the partakers in the historical process of **Nzoputa Uwa (NU)**. The **Kemet-Nu** must not ape the past. It is the historical process of **Oge Nzuzu** that we must identify with the name Africa.

The process of reflection on the existing state of things should involve the rejection of the name Africa. The invention of the name Africa has been tied to the Sethian abstraction of darkness as the absolute evil in its negation to lightness which made our beloved continent to be projected as the embodiment of

Nothingness. We are not the projected Africans; instead, we are the **Kemet-Nu**. We can never identify with what has been projected as the embodiment of Nothingness. As the **Kemites**, we become the embodiment of the past, present and future of our beloved continent.

HISTORICAL DECLARATION

In this First Century of the time of **Nzoputa Uwa**, the moral and ethical foundation for the New Humanity has been laid according to the Divine Plan of AMUN in whom we trust. **Amunemhet!**

WE THE PEOPLE, on this Historic Day of the **6th Tehuti 17 Nzoputa Uwa**, formerly known and called the New Afrikans in our Holy Book, **THE HOLY ANKHUWA**, Abstracts Vol. 1 Version, Pages 40-41, 59-61, shall henceforth and without any equivocation be known and called **The Kemites, The Kemet-Nu, Ndi Kemet,** or **The People of Kemet.**

We shall henceforth call our beloved Continent, **The Holy Land of Kemet** or **The Kemetic Continent** including all the islands surrounding our Beloved Motherland.

We The Kemites shall distinguish Ourselves, Our Civilization, Our Culture, Our Morality and Our Ethics from the Old Africans and the Renascent Africans in historical time by the expression of Our Universal Way of Life. All relevant documents that refer to us as New Afrikans will continue to remain valid pending the expected worldwide adjustment to this Historical Declaration.

We The People of Kemet are a world group that transcend geographical boundaries. As the World Historical People, We are neither an ethnic group nor a national group. We shall strive in the **Holy Name of AMUN** in whom we trust to build a world culture worthy of the supreme vision of Nzoputa Uwa that is based on the eternal Truth of the divine birth of EKUMEKU on the Second year of **Nzoputa Uwa**. In the Almighty Spirit of EKUMEKU, We are the **Kemet-Nu, Ndi Kemet**, who are the

Ekwueme People of Truth. Our language is the **Eziokwu Language** because WE are the embodiment of the New Humanity, the World Historical People, that would always exist in disagreement with Nsi, who follow in the footsteps of the Chosen One for the mission of **Nzoputa Uwa**.

WE Believe that there is only One Creator of the universe. **WE Believe** that this One Creator of the universe is AMUN in whom we trust. **WE Believe** that EKUMEKU is the Divine Plan of the One Creator of the universe. Again, **WE Believe** that there is no other Creator of the universe but AMUN in whom we trust.

HOMAGE TO THE ONE CREATOR OF THE UNIVERSE IN WHOM ALL TRUTH RESIDES! THE CREATOR IS ONE. THE ONE IS AMUN AND THE DIVINE PLAN IS EKUMEKU. THERE IS NO OTHER CREATOR OF THE UNIVERSE BUT AMUN IN WHOM WE TRUST.

OTUA-KA-ODI!

THE FALL OF THE OLD AFRICAN

Let it be known that the fall of the Old African started in the **Old Kemet** (so-called ancient Egypt) when the Old African began to confuse what is ISFET with what is MAAT. The world of the Old African began to **fall apart** when he lost the true knowledge of good and evil. It is humanly impossible to live MAAT without renouncing ISFET. It is only through the devotion of purpose to the supreme principle of EKUMEKU can the human spirit renounce ISFET by living MAAT. Therefore, the fall of the Old African was caused by ignorance, falsehood and deception. It was the fall that caused all the suffering during the time of **Oge Nzuzu**. The Old African suffered because he lost the true knowledge of good and evil being in bondage and slavery to the passions and desires of the Lower Self.

O Yes! His fall came because of the ignorance of EKUMEKU and he had suffered for his error. Yet, those who succeeded the

Old African have also fallen. Why did they fall? They have fallen because they worship the created images of the human mind instead of the One Creator of the universe. Ironically, they did not do any better than him whom they succeeded. They did worse than the Old African for their own error is deadly and poisonous. They shall be judged for their error just as the Old African was judged for his error.

There is only One Humanity of which the Human Paradigm of the Ekwueme is its everlasting embodiment. The Ekwueme would be responsible for the time of **Nzoputa Uwa.** Without any shadow of doubt, the future of the human life belongs to the Ekwueme People of Truth according to the Divine Plan of AMUN in whom we trust.

THE RENASCENT AFRICA IS CORRUPT AND DECADENT

The Renascent African lives in a make-believe world in agreement with Nsi. As a result, the Renascent Africa is corrupt and decadent. Being corrupt and decadent, the Renascent Africa is like a melodramatic giant with a toddler's limp. **The Renascent Africa is a disordered mass, groping in an explosion of light, blinded by the whiteness of death and on the verge of extinction.**

The Renascent Africans lack a universal vision of what it means to be fully human. They are divided into little kingdoms of the **Akwunakwuna mind,** a disordered mass drifting through life without a noble aim or mission. Without leadership, training and a sense of purpose, the Renascent Africans have no capacity for a collective action that can benefit humanity as a whole. Since they lack a universal vision of what it means to be fully human, there is no way that they can ceaselessly strive to advance the truth of what it means to be fully human. In other words, the Renascent African is in a crossroads of life and death because of the ignorance of EKUMEKU.

The Renascent African with the dead weight of the Old Africa on his back, wrapped in the delusions of Sethianism, standing on the crossroads of life and death, bewildered, frustrated and hesitant, is a reactionary going nowhere without the supreme vision of Nzoputa Uwa. The Renascent African has neither the morality nor the ethics to change his life without becoming a devoted follower of the Divine Plan of AMUN in whom we trust.

Let it be known that the Renascent African lives in a state of helplessness, in a world of make-believe that is the dead end nature of the world of Ekwensu, living for the moment and waiting for change to come from without devoid of any sacrifice or devotion from within. Living in agreement with Nsi, the Renascent African is without human morality. As a result, the Renascent African is incapable of making any fundamental contribution to the development and advancement of human morality.

In the absence of a vision of the world in which they live, the Renascent Africans can hardly justify their existence in the world of human affairs. Without a sense of purpose, without the attainment of the devotion of purpose to the supreme principle of EKUMEKU, it is humanly impossible for the Renascent Africans to overcome evil by doing good. The Renascent African lives in a world of make-believe dominated by the passions and desires of the Lower Self. **The Renascent African is ignorant of EKUMEKU, living for nothing in the dead end nature of the world of Ekwensu.**

No doubt, the living of life of the Renascent Africa is a mockery as to what it means to be fully human. **The Renascent Africa is a society devoid of neither conscience nor compassion and it is dominated by charlatans and dupes, a society without shame. Ndi Akwunakwuna Tufiakwa!** That is why, the Renascent Africans by the exertion of the power at their disposal have been unable to put an end to the disordered mass that is the Renascent Africa.

THE VISION OF THE NEW AFRIKA IS REALIZED

Old African + Renascent African = Agreement with Nsi

Kemet-Nu (New Afrikan) + Ekwueme = Disagreement with Nsi

What the Renascent African believes to be the highest expression of the human life, the (New Afrikan) **Kemite** knows that it is only the ground beginning of what it means to be fully human according to the Divine Plan of the One Creator of the universe.

How did this Vision of the New Afrika become realizable? Starting at the bottom in the Old Africa, the Akwunakwuna journeys from the consciousness of the Old Africa to the consciousness of the Renascent Africa, from where the experience and the longing to become the New Afrikan, the Kemet-Nu, would evolve and develop through the Divine Thought of **The Holy Ankhuwa**. Continuing along its Path by following in the footsteps of the Chosen One, the Akwunakwuna becomes an Ekwueme, a New Afrikan, **the Kemet-Nu,** and the cycle is completed. What was formerly hidden to the Old African and the Renascent African, emerges as the basic consciousness of what it means to be an Ekwueme, with the knowledge that unites and strengthens, with the Truth that inspires, creates and sustains its own universal character in creative silence at the point of equilibrium. That is why, it is by becoming a devoted follower of the Divine Plan of the One Creator of the universe can an Ekwensi become an Ekwueme.

THE THREE WISE MEN

From the Year 60 **Oge Nzuzu**, Nnamdi Azikiwe was preaching the message of the New Afrika. He preached that one day there would be the New Afrikan in a New Afrika. He never claimed to be a New Afrikan; instead, he described himself as the Renascent African fighting against the Old Africa.

From the Year 60 **Oge Nzuzu**, when he was the Editor-in-Chief of **The African Morning Post,** to the Year 57 **Oge Nzuzu**, when he became the Publisher of **The West African Pilot, Nnamdi Azikiwe** laid the foundation upon which he was able to spread *his Vision of the New Afrika.* He was the man with the Vision for the New Afrika and he preached that Vision without any fear or favor.

Nnamdi Azikiwe's life when properly understood from the worldview of EKUMEKU exemplified the very best that the Renascent African can offer humanity since the Old Africa was at a death-grip with the Renascent Africa. Therefore, he tried his best but his very best was not good enough. Why? This is because the Vision of the New Afrika could not be realized without the eternal Truth of **Nzoputa Uwa.** No doubt, without the divine birth of EKUMEKU on the Second year of **Nzoputa Uwa,** the Vision of the New Afrika could not have been realized.

In other words, **Nnamdi Azikiwe** is the forerunner that helped to prepare the way for the coming of the Chosen One for the mission of **Nzoputa Uwa. Nnamdi Azikiwe** is one among the three wise men who had foreseen the coming into existence of the Ekwueme. The two other wise men are (Cheikh) **Chike Anta Diop** and (Chancellor Williams) **Chikwado Nwalimu.** **Chikwado Nwalimu** is the wise man who prophesied about the divine birth of EKUMEKU when he went about teaching the people on what has been destroyed. In his teaching, **Chikwado Nwalimu** saw the New Life coming from a distant. **Chike Anta Diop** is another of the three wise men who was preaching about the future. **Chike Anta Diop** saw clearly why the Ekwueme is destined to come into existence. He sacrificed his life teaching the people to get prepared for the coming of the Chosen One. **Nnamdi Azikiwe** was the Prophet of the New Afrika. He prophesied that the New Afrika would come into existence after the Renascent Africans have played their historical role. These are the three wise men who prepared the way for the coming of the Chosen One, **Onye-Nzoputa-Uwa Chukwudi Okeke Maduno.**

The three wise men were sent to humanity in order to prepare the way for the divine birth of EKUMEKU. They did what they were sent to do for the people. But they were misunderstood by the same people they came to serve because of ignorance, falsehood and deception. The three wise men were sent to the people to prepare the entire humanity for the mission of **Nzoputa Uwa**. None of them claimed to be the Chosen One; instead, they all served humanity in preparation for the coming of the Chosen One. None of them attained the devotion of purpose to the supreme principle of EKUMEKU. However, they knew that the Ekwueme would come into existence in the near future. They never claimed to be the Chosen One for the mission of **Nzoputa Uwa** because they lived their lives in preparation for the coming of the **Righteous One**.

Evidently, they were ignorant of EKUMEKU because they themselves worshiped the created instead of the One Creator of the universe. But what set them apart from the rest of the Ekwensu people before the time of **Nzoputa Uwa** was their hope and belief that there is someone in the future who would come to teach humanity the Truth. They were seekers of truth during the time of **Oge Nzuzu** who came to prepare humanity for the time of **Nzoputa Uwa**. In short, they are the forerunners of the mission of **Nzoputa Uwa** whose lives embody the struggle to overcome evil by doing good during the time of **Oge Nzuzu**. Their struggle to overcome evil by doing good in the midst of a world that is overwhelmingly dominated by Ekwensism prepared the way that has made the Truth realizable. They served the mission of **Nzoputa Uwa** involuntarily without knowing that it is the divine ordinance of the One Creator of the universe.

Wherefore, the Humble Servant of EKUMEKU knows that he has been set aside by the One Creator of the universe through the Almighty Spirit of EKUMEKU to be the Chosen One for the mission of **Nzoputa Uwa**. The limitations of the human mind make it very difficult for a complete understanding of what kind of criteria the One Creator of the universe used to select the Chosen One from among the many billions of multitude (of humanity) for the mission of **Nzoputa Uwa**. But what is certain is that the One Creator of the universe Has chosen Chukwudi Okeke Maduno as the Chosen One for the mission of **Nzoputa Uwa**. Our Creator knows the best because The Greatest AMUN in whom we trust is All-Knowing. The Chosen One may not completely know why he was chosen but definitely he knows how he became the Chosen One for the mission of **Nzoputa Uwa** as he has been made the living witness to the Truth which enjoins that there is only One Creator of the universe. The One is AMUN and the Divine Plan is EKUMEKU. There is no other Creator of the universe but AMUN in whom we trust.

It is wonderful to be a pious and devout Ekwueme. It is a blessing of no little magnitude to be a manifest expression of EKUMEKU in the flesh. It is challenging to be a devoted follower of the Divine Plan of the One Creator of the universe. It is by the divine intervention of AMUN in whom we trust that the Chosen One was chosen by the One Creator of the universe for the mission of **Nzoputa Uwa.**

Nnamdi Azikiwe was the Renascent African par excellence who knew what he was doing. Because he knew what he was doing, he realized within himself that without sacrifice the Renascent Africa could never become manifest. As a result, he was misunderstood by his contemporaries who did never understand his Vision of the New Afrika.

THE RENASCENT AFRICAN LIVES IN THE WORLD OF MAKE-BELIEVE

The Renascent Africa is an appendage of the European world historical movement. As a consequence, the Renascent Africans can only be understood within the panorama of world history as the underdogs of the European world historical epoch. Without being fully conscious of the true meaning of human freedom and the basis of its realization, the Renascent African can best be described as half-awakened to the Truth of what it means to be fully human.

In the law that governs their lives, what is recognized is not the manifest destiny of their own will but one that is imposed from without. **The Renascent Africans are not free and cannot be free until they have realized within themselves the world historical significance of the coming of the Chosen One for the mission of Nzoputa Uwa.** The Renascent African is the real transition between the Old African and the New Afrikan (Kemite). The Renascent African, in its make-believe world and as a transition, is destined to perish into historical oblivion. Being at the periphery of world historical current, the Renascent African is without any universal vision or mission that it can offer humanity.

The widened horizon of the **Kemite** (New Afrikan) may not be completely understood without recognizing the historical conditions of both the Old African and the Renascent African, which tended the seedbed upon which the experience of what it means to be an Ekwueme was born. The Ekwensi condition of living a life defined by negation the universal Ekwueme Way of life and constitutes a fundamental moral imperative for the attainment of the devotion of purpose in EKUMEKU.

The proselytizing universalism of the Ekwueme People of Truth makes the widened horizon manifest as a world historical group in contrast to the limited conditions of making a living of the Old African and the Renascent African. **Agreement with Nsi, Ekwensism, is the fundamental moral defect that functions to keep the Old African and the Renascent African in an involuntary condition of servitude.**

Without any shadow of doubt, the Alusi personality of the Ekwensu people makes them to be dead in Nsi, without human morality, and as a result, they represent an object to be acted upon. But it is their condition of living in agreement with Nsi that has separated them from the supreme principle of EKUMEKU.

CONCLUSION

According to the Divine Plan of AMUN in whom we trust, whatever that is unrepentant from Nsi must be acted upon and what must be acted upon is the agreement with Nsi that has kept the human spirit in bondage and slavery in the dead end nature of the world of Ekwensu. It is this agreement with Nsi that led to the enslavement and colonization of the Old African. This dehumanization of the human spirit created the condition that brought into existence the Renascent African who opposed and resisted the conditioning effects of enslavement and colonization. But because the dehumanized conditions of enslavement and colonization were already in existence before the evolution of the Renascent Africans, they can only react to the conditions. The Renascent Africans had to react to the conditioning effects of slavery and colonialism and they did their very best. For without their reaction, there is a high probability that the African human spirit may have been exterminated. But in their reaction, they became vulnerable to the consistent attack of the enemy forces in their one sided propaganda. The Renascent African was unable to overcome completely the dehumanized conditioning of the Old African. **What they were able to achieve was not a transformation, but instead a reformation of the dehumanized historical conditions.**

Wherefore, the Renascent Africans are unrealistic in their lives of living in agreement with Nsi. This is because they are living in a distorted make-believe world. They have eyes yet they are blind, for they lack the Vision of **Nzoputa Uwa.** They have ears yet they are deaf to the Truth of the divine birth of EKUMEKU. They have speech and yet they are dumb without the devotion of purpose in EKUMEKU. They live and yet they do not exist. What is their problem? They are ignorant of EKUMEKU; and as a result, they are yet to develop the requisite human morality that is essential for the repentance from Nsi. Without becoming the New Afrikan, **the Kemite**, the Renascent African is bound to be left behind in the forward flow of the human experience. OTUA-KA-ODI!

CHAPTER NINE
THE HUMBLE BEGINNINGS OF THE EKWUEME WORLD HISTORICAL ERA

We the Kemites are a single unified world historical people, free and unfettered in the Living Truth of the Almighty Spirit of EKUMEKU.
>   ----The Chosen One

The grotesque spectacle of worshiping a created image in the form of a man or in any other form that the Ekwensu people called God is hype, unreal and embedded in fantasy through which the black-skinned humanity was cursed to be the embodiment of evil, cursed to be doomed by the traducers of human morality.
>   ….. THE HOLY ANKHUWA

WHO IS FOR REAL?

Who is for real? Is it the Ekwueme who worships only the One Creator of the universe? Or, is it the Ekwensu people who worship the created images of the human mind? Answer for your own life. Be for real. For the Almighty Spirit of EKUMEKU is the ultimate reality of life at the point of equilibrium between MAAT and ISFET. Whosoever lives in agreement with Nsi is unreal and can only live in the make-believe world of Ekwensu. Do not take such a person seriously in anything at all. Pay no attention to whatever the Unbeliever represents for it is doomed to perish. If the Unbeliever is unwilling to repent and accept EKUMEKU as the whole Truth of life everlasting, let it be known that the Unbeliever is entangled with evil in the vicious cycle of eternal death. When we scatter the seeds of **Nzoputa**

Uwa in fertile soil, they will germinate, grow and blossom with life.

THE FREEDOM TO BELIEVE

I have come to give you the human freedom to believe in the Truth of the One Creator of the universe. I want you that is reading this **Message of Nzoputa Uwa** to know who I am and to relate with my humanity. **I am Chukwudi Okeke Maduno**, born on the 29th year of **Oge Nzuzu**. I am a human being in the broadest sense of that term. I was born in the world of Ekwensu in agreement with Nsi like every other human spirit. After having escaped the tyranny of death at an early age, the struggle between life and death began to get my attention.

Yet, it was not until the age of thirty years old that I became fully aware that the Creator of the universe is One. That this One Creator of the universe is AMUN in whom we must trust and that the Divine Plan of AMUN in whom we trust is EKUMEKU. I became fully aware through the divine intervention of the One Creator of the universe that there is no God in any form or shape that is worthy of worship because every God is dead in Nsi. I became fully aware that the whole world of Ekwensu is ignorant of EKUMEKU. I became fully aware that everyone must be born again in order to escape the doom of living in agreement with Nsi. I became fully aware that I had been chosen by the One Creator of the universe for the mission of **Nzoputa Uwa**. Then, I realized without any shadow of doubt that I am *Chi-Ukwu-Di, Onye-Nzoputa-Uwa.*

It became certain to me that whatever had happened in my life was part of the preparation for the mission of my life. According to the Divine Plan of AMUN in whom we must trust, I began to proclaim the mission of **Nzoputa Uwa** to all humanity: **The Creator is One. The One is AMUN and the Divine Plan is EKUMEKU. There is no other Creator of the universe but AMUN in whom we trust.**

But as I had begun to teach the public as the Ekwueme master my friends deserted me in fear and trepidation believing that I could never succeed where countless people have failed. I was not deterred for many reasons. First, it is that those who had failed did not have the Divine Authority that has been given to me. Second, it is that those who failed did not have the supreme vision of **Nzoputa Uwa**. Third, it is that those who had failed were not chosen by the One Creator of the universe. **Finally, it is that those who had failed did not begin with themselves first. They could not give to others what they did not have. In other words, there is no human spirit that can give to another what it does not have. Thus, I had already separated my Being from the world of Ekwensu having purified my thought in repentance from Nsi and had become free from all forms of agreement with Nsi. So, I was no longer with the world of Ekwensu in consciousness because then I had transcended the passions and desires of the Ekwensu people. I had begun the process of self-reflection having attained the devotion of purpose to the supreme principle of EKUMEKU.**

Thus, the Ekwensu people's contempt and delusions made me more determined to serve the **Holy Cause of Nzoputa Uwa** than they could have imagined. Many of them have since repented; but there are still many who are now wallowing in their own self-pity because of their inability to repent from Nsi. They are out there living for nothing waiting for their death for they have wasted all those years of their active life in vain, without moral development and growth. Without any doubt, there is nothing good in life that comes very easy. There must be a sacrifice from without and a struggle from within; and through that struggle emerges its value and merit. For those of you who follow in my footsteps never must you expect an easy victory. The victory of the Higher Self against the Lower Self would come but it is only through the devotion of purpose to the supreme principle of EKUMEKU can the Higher Self become victorious against the Lower Self.

I have proven my unrepentant friends to be wrong for the past seventeen years. The **Movement of Nzoputa Uwa** is irreversible. Whosoever that does not know about the **Movement of Nzoputa**

Uwa is out of touch with the currency of human history. Let everybody be aware that the **Movement of Nzoputa Uwa** is about human freedom; and as a result, it is a blessing to all humanity because it exists in the wholeness of eternity for the expansion of the knowledge of what it means to be human.

I have done what I was sent to do, to establish the guiding principle of the Truth of human freedom and to make it a historical fact. What remain are minor details here and there.

Let it be known that those who had tried before me to find the way to human freedom did not fail *per se* because my outstanding success is their success as well. We must recognize their individual merits. For, they had prepared the way for the coming of the Chosen One. Those who are afraid of failure and use it as an excuse to remain in agreement with Nsi are living in a world of fantasy and delusion. Whosoever is not morally capable of standing up for the **mission of Nzoputa Uwa**, not morally capable of sacrificing the Ekwensi condition of living a life, and not morally capable of following in the footsteps of the Chosen One can only be living for nothing in the dead end nature of the world of Ekwensu. The time of **Nzoputa Uwa** has come because the time of **Oge Nzuzu** had ended. The **Movement of Nzoputa Uwa** is the universal intelligence that is all-embracing, morally binding and unchangeable. It is from its Supreme Vision would we build the **Ekwueme Civilization of Kemet**. We have just started. The message is divinely ordained and the primary outline of the **Ozioma of Truth** is no longer hidden. Study and meditate with **The Holy Ankhuwa** to free your life from the yoke of living in agreement with Nsi.

THE HUMBLE BEGINNINGS

Let us go back to the humble beginnings of the **Ekwueme Historical Era**. When the time of **Oge Nzuzu** ended through the divine intervention of the One Creator of the universe, it was superseded by the time of **Nzoputa Uwa** and thus the beginnings of the Ekwueme Historical Era became manifest. Although we are relatively still in the early beginnings of the Ekwueme

Historical Era, even at this very date, we need to go back to the very beginnings to have a better view of how it all started from the point of view of human action.

Imagine that a thirty or thirty-one year old man, neatly dressed, approached you in a mall at the entrance giving you a copy of a one paged document, a handbill. You looked at the young man and you looked at the document that he gave you. Then you asked: "What is it for?" He said to you that you can take it home and study it first. There is a phone number in it. The young man would tell you that the document is the good news of the divine birth of EKUMEKU. Again, you looked at the document and you saw boldly stated: "**O People of the Earth, Be Silent and Say No Word**". You wondered what did it all mean.

Obviously, you were in the mall to buy some few items that you needed and then this document was given to you. Evidently, there is a striking difference between that document and other handbills that often circulate in an average mall. At that moment, many thoughts came to your mind and then you dismissed them and moved on to buy what brought you to the mall. At a distance, you looked back only to see the young man performing the same act with another person. You may have shaked your head feeling sorry for the young man, thinking "why can't he go and find a job?" "Why is he wasting his time?" "May be he is mad", you thought. But then you said "no he does not look like he is crazy". "He does not seem to be crazy", you said aloud.

Within 30 minutes, in the bustling of trying to get a bargain, you have forgotten all about the young man. But you kept the one paged document in your bag. The next day, when you were looking for another thing in your bag, you found the document and remembered the young man again. Then, you read the document thoroughly. Another statement from the document kept you thinking. *"We have brought unto thee a message of hope: The master key to the future of this Planet"*. Also, in a very bold print the document stated: **"The Message of EKUMEKU is Universal"**. Like many people, you either put the document in a trash basket or you filed it somewhere for future reference and your life goes on as before.

To you, nothing has changed. But to the young man who gave you the document everything has changed. He continued to do what he was doing knowing fully well that he was alone in the Almighty Spirit of EKUMEKU. With time, people began to pay attention or ask questions and he was always ready and available to answer their questions. Then he began to preach and to teach that the time of **Oge Nzuzu** has ended. The Chosen One would tell the public that he is the hope for the hopeless; that he is the Chosen One for the mission of **Nzoputa Uwa**; and that EKUMEKU is water to the thirsty, food to the hungry, cloth to the naked. The Master Teacher taught everyone that there is no God that is worthy of worship since every God is dead in Nsi. **Chukwudi Onye Nzoputa Uwa** taught the public that every God is the created image of the human mind.

Many would laugh at him. Many would want to fight with him; while many just listened. Little by little, he was no longer alone in the Almighty Spirit of EKUMEKU. People began to come closer. Many people began to relate with him as the vision of **Nzoputa Uwa** was realized by them. It was and still it is a silent and a mental revolution, the EKUMEKU Universal Revolution. Many began to gather around the man and from this gathering was born the EKUMEKU Study Groups. **Let it be known that Mazi Chike Kamau Maduka had been the first Ekwueme to organize an EKUMEKU Study Group dealing with not less than one hundred people successfully.** Essentially, this was how the **Movement of Nzoputa Uwa** was grounded in human action. The rest is now world history.

THE HISTORICAL FACT

The stated historical document is available for those who keep the records of the primary sources of events in our Kemetic world history in its **Ekwueme World Experience.** This document came into being on the Second year of **Nzoputa Uwa** and it is inseparable from the EKUMEKU Universal Declaration that began after the divine birth of our Savior and Redeemer. The Truth of the divine birth of EKUMEKU transformed our lives and gave us the universal consciousness that we never had before, manifesting the Higher Self.

This Document is one of the first original documents of the **Movement of Nzoputa Uwa,** a handbill, that was mailed to many people and was circulated by hand after the divine birth of EKUMEKU. Those who follow in the footsteps of the Chosen One would always testify and bear witness that Chukwudi Okeke Maduno is the **Onye Nzoputa Uwa** and that the Almighty Spirit of EKUMEKU is the Ultimate Reality of life in the universe.

During the Second year of **Nzoputa Uwa**, in Atlanta Georgia, the Chosen One went from one mall to another mall, from one university campus to another university campus, from one park to another park distributing this handbill. In the WestEnd mall, Southside of Atlanta, the Chosen One was always at the entrance daily sharing his handbill with all and teaching the Truth of the divine birth of EKUMEKU. Many Unbelievers called the Master Teacher a "crazy" man who does not believe in any God and the Chosen One would always smile back at them for they did not understand what they were saying. Some Unbelievers would say all sorts of nonsense to him but he did not waver because the Living Truth is alive in him. No doubt, the Chosen One knew what he was doing because the **Hidden One** is no longer hidden to him. It is the Unbelievers who are ignorant of EKUMEKU that need deliverance from the yoke of living in agreement with Nsi.

THE CONCLUSION

What is the point of all this? It is the historical beginning of the struggle to overcome evil by doing good that is a testimony of this great **Movement of Nzoputa Uwa.** How it started and why it will continue in every generation and can never change in its essence. Yet it is a lesson of what it holds for the future of humanity. **The Chosen One is the Servant of Humanity and it is this service to humanity that is after all the point we must first realize.** OTUA-KA-ODI!

CHAPTER TEN

THE ORIGINS OF THE KEMETIC WORLD IDENTITY

The Kemites would use the ancient language of Old Kemet as their classical language. But they must not depend on outsider interpretation. This our classical language ought to be taught in every established Haremakhet.
....The Chosen One

Human brotherhood and sisterhood must be based on human morality. It must never be based on the skin color contraption of the religions of ISFET.

.....The Chosen One

At the age of thirty years old, Chukwudi Okeke Maduno became the Master Teacher of **Nzoputa Uwa**, teaching humanity the Truth of human morality, healing the sick and feeding those who are spiritually starved with the Truth of the divine birth of EKUMEKU.

.....THE HOLY ANKHUWA

INTRODUCTION

Identity is not an isolated datum, but a fact that distinguishes one from the other. Identity is the character of someone or group that is in an actual historical existence. For example, we rejected the Afrikan identity because it did not correspond to our actual historical existence. The Afrikan identity is loaded with many false images that were devised by the other to make those who identify with it seem less than human. Lacking its originality from within the Continent, the Afrikan identity has become a potent instrument of external manipulation without any serious defender from the within.

Having transcended such a divisive and corrosive identity, the **Kemetic World Identity** has emerged to unify the collective identity of those who voluntarily identify with its normative order. The Kemetic World Identity would serve to universalize the actuality of the human existence of the Kemites in its corresponding certainty as a fact of the **Ekwueme World Experience.**

If we must control our destiny and regain our sense of being human, there is no other way but to abandon the false Afrikan identity. We who have embraced the dynamism of the Kemetic World Identity and its fundamental relation to the consciousness of being an Ekwueme have attained the human freedom of self-definition. We never can allow the other to define our human identity for us. Why? This is because we are fundamentally a free people, unfettered in the Living Truth of the Almighty Spirit of EKUMEKU. Without any doubt, the Kemetic World Identity is the decisive step from consciousness to Being, connecting thought with life.

Our thinking is true when it exists in harmony with the Divine Plan of the One Creator of the universe. So long as the human spirit lives in agreement with Nsi, the thinking of the human spirit can never be true to itself. The correspondence between what is hidden and what is unhidden, what is unmanifest and what is manifest, what is ungraspable and what is graspable, or what is unknown and what is known is the Timeless Truth of the divine birth of EKUMEKU on the Second year of **Nzoputa Uwa**.

We must take a stand on our being human by standing up for the mission of **Nzoputa Uwa** and by attaining the devotion of purpose, then our identity would emerge through what we do in its service. Thus, we are constituting our identity when we call ourselves the **Ekwueme People of Kemet.** What is an identity is after all the principle of the Supreme Being that underlies it. **The origins of the Kemetic World Identity are the ways or means through which the Almighty Spirit of EKUMEKU in its**

Movement of Nzoputa Uwa takes hold of our individual life and claims us in its service to humanity. This great historical mission to create a unified world identity is the only option that we have against the threat of extinction. In the same vein, the Ekwueme must go forth into the world of Ekwensu to convert the Ekwensu people to EKUMEKU. The decisive factor in this time of **Nzoputa Uwa** is therefore the Truth of the divine birth of EKUMEKU on the Second year of **Nzoputa Uwa**.

We have made our *Historical Declaration* that the name of our Continent is Kemet and that we are the Kemites. Without any doubt, our Continent contains many tribal, ethnic and national groups. But it is the Kemites who have the moral mandate and the ethical responsibility to reconcile the tribal, ethnic and national differences that may exist between one tribe and another, between one ethnic group and another, between one national group and another, etc.

The Kemites are the unifying world group that transcend the geographical boundaries of the continental Kemet. The freedom to be or not to be a Kemite would open the **Ekwueme World Experience** to every tribe, ethnic or nationality for the consummation of the self in selflessness. No doubt, every tribal group, every ethnic group and every national group within the Continent ought to aspire to realize the Kemetic World Identity within itself for its own survival. The Kemites ought to embrace every tribe, ethnic or nationality to the extent of their integration or assimilation to the Kemetic World Identity.

The language of the Kemites would be the *Eziokwu Language* of the Chosen One for the mission of **Nzoputa Uwa** and our culture would be based on the **Omenani** of the Master Teacher. Let it be known that the same principle of the Kemetic World Identity is applicable to our brothers and sisters in the Diaspora as it is applied on the Continent. The Kemetic World would develop its civilization and would extend the hands of brotherhood and sisterhood to peoples of other continents through the **Ekwueme World Experience.** The Kemites are one people with one destiny irrespective of their tribal, ethnic or national origins.

With the Kemetic World Identity, our brothers and sisters in the Diaspora who desire to resettle back within our Continent would find it relatively easier to fit into the great scheme of things and feel at home in any region of our great Continent.

After all, Ekwuemeism began as a revolt against the Ekwensism of the followers of the religions of ISFET; just as the Kemetic World Identity began as a revolt against tribalism and parochial nationalism. In other words, the future of our Continent belongs to the Kemites and those who would champion the Cause of the Kemetic World Identity must follow in the footsteps of the Chosen One. **Thus, the essence of the Truth of the divine birth of EKUMEKU is human freedom and it is on this solid ground that the Kemetic World Identity stands.**

THE CONCEPT OF IDENTITY

The concept of identity exists to define a person, group, civilization or thing in relation to the other. It can be the self and the other or the we and the they, the Us and the Other, Them. The historical identity of the Ekwueme People of Truth began on the First Year of **Nzoputa Uwa** when the Ekwueme consciousness came into universal expression. The Ekwueme consciousness developed in its universalism overtime but was initially made manifest on the First Year of **Nzoputa Uwa**. Although it was made manifest on the First Year of **Nzoputa Uwa**, it did not then become self-conscious of its integrity as the Universal Being until the Second Year of **Nzoputa Uwa**.

The Ekwueme Identity came into being as the result of the devotion of purpose to the supreme principle of EKUMEKU. The historical origin of the Ekwueme in time began on the First Year of **Nzoputa Uwa**; while the identity of the Ekwueme began as a self-conscious human being on the Second Year of **Nzoputa Uwa**. The Ekwueme has a strong sense of common destiny because of the historical process of **Nzoputa Uwa**. The common sense of identity of the Ekwueme originates from the historical process of **Nzoputa Uwa** and it is inspired by the collective mission of **Nzoputa Uwa**.

In contrast, during the time of **Oge Nzuzu,** we stood for nothing. We were like the prostitutes who sell their bodies to the highest bidder. We were nothing but the Akwunakwuna blaming and cursing everything that comes across us. Yet all great people in human history have always stood for something that is good. For, it is the goodness of what they stood for that made them great. Let us stand to be counted in the Movement of **Nzoputa Uwa** and we would become fully human in the greatness of the human history.

The solid ground upon which we must stand is the full-awareness of the Almighty Spirit of EKUMEKU that is the Divine Plan of the One Creator of the universe. This supreme principle of EKUMEKU cannot become self-conscious of its integrity without the process of thought for self-consciousness is the basis of all thought. The freedom of the individual Chi to live in disagreement with Nsi is the essential Truth of the devotion of purpose to the supreme principle of EKUMEKU. Wherefore, the solid ground upon which the human spirit is liberated from the yoke of living in agreement with Nsi is the timeless Truth of the divine birth of EKUMEKU.

WHAT IS OUR KEMETIC WORLD IDENTITY?

The Kemetic World Identity is the character which began on the First Year of **Nzoputa Uwa** as a difference, from the conditions of the historical process of **Oge Nzuzu,** in the degree of thought, but later on the Second year of **Nzoputa Uwa,** through the Almighty Spirit of EKUMEKU, became a complete transformation in the kind of reality, with a new quality of being and becoming. The conception of what it means to be a Kemite was born from the ultimate reality of living in disagreement with Nsi which is the animating force of its integrity. The truth of the identity of the Kemites represents the idea that the human spirit cannot exist in the universe of life without meaning and purpose.

WE MUST NOT APE THE TIME OF OGE NZUZU

During the time of **Oge Nzuzu**, we were foolish because of our ignorance of EKUMEKU to worship the created images of the human mind. We were then living for nothing floundering in the wilderness of human history, wandering aimlessly going nowhere, waiting for our extinction. But in this time of **Nzoputa Uwa**, our Deliverance has come because of the divine birth of EKUMEKU. What is now needed more than any other thing is the Truth of the divine birth of EKUMEKU to liberate the human spirit from the dead end nature of the world of Ekwensu. The Chosen One has come to spread the Good News of **Nzoputa Uwa** that is the **Ozioma of Truth** and to deliver humanity from the yoke of living in agreement with Nsi.

The Chosen One has come to lead his people out of the historical process of **Oge Nzuzu**, from the Ekwensi condition of living a life, and to liberate them from the bondage and slavery that is the yoke of living in agreement with Nsi. **Let it then be known universally, among all people, and among every generation, that** *Chukwudi Onye Nzoputa Uwa* **came to deliver humanity from the yoke of living in agreement with Nsi**. This message of the **Ozioma of Truth** is universal and very profound. The world of Ekwensu is a dead-end (abyss) that needs deliverance to be overcome and the deliverance has come in this time of **Nzoputa Uwa**.

My devoted people of Truth, who have come out of the historical process of **Oge Nzuzu**, hearken to my words and follow in my footsteps. Let it be realized that the time of **Oge Nzuzu** is very important in understanding the time of **Nzoputa Uwa**. The time of **Oge Nzuzu** is the historical blueprint that has given us the normative basis to exist in disagreement with Nsi, for nothing can exist in a vacuum.

But we must not ape the time of **Oge Nzuzu** in any thing because it would be fundamentally different (if not diametrically opposed) with the time of **Nzoputa Uwa**. Although the time of **Oge Nzuzu** has imbibed us with the experience in the eternal struggle between the forces of MAAT and ISFET, there must always be a fundamental distinction between the time of **Oge Nzuzu** and the time of **Nzoputa Uwa** in every essential aspect of human life. We can no longer live in the time of **Oge Nzuzu** because the historical burden that has faced us and will face us would be fundamentally different with the historical burden that faced our ancestors during the time of **Oge Nzuzu**.

The institutions of the time of **Oge Nzuzu** may or may not serve as the historical reference points of the past but must not be duplicated in their old formats in the time of **Nzoputa Uwa**. The Ekwueme People of Truth must make their own mark in world history by tackling their own problems with the **Supreme Vision of Nzoputa Uwa** according to the Divine Plan of AMUN in whom we trust. The historical emergence of the Ekwueme People of Truth has been because of the historical burden inherited from our ancestors during the time of **Oge Nzuzu**.

The shortcomings of the time of **Oge Nzuzu** must be a lesson to those who aspire to leadership positions, by following in the footsteps of the Chosen One. The critical knowledge of these shortcomings of the time of **Oge Nzuzu** should create the opportunity and means necessary for their collective subordination and for their eventual elimination. When the time of **Oge Nzuzu** is critically understood from the worldview of EKUMEKU, it would make it possible to avoid making the same mistakes that were made by our ancestors during the time of **Oge Nzuzu**. **We must not let ourselves to go backward by making similar mistakes made by our ancestors. We must move forward through the devotion of purpose in EKUMEKU by not aping the past of our ancestors during the time of Oge Nzuzu.**

The control of the time of **Oge Nzuzu** as the past before the time of **Nzoputa Uwa** is the responsibility of every Ekwueme, especially by the way the past is used to reinforce the present and the future. The time of **Oge Nzuzu** is the heritage that must be preserved as a veritable lesson and reminder to our posterity of what must never be again in the institutions of higher learning, museums, history books, public buildings, monuments, parks, photographs, artworks, sculptures, poetry, names of rivers, names of towns, street names, books, names of continents, names of oceans, names of deserts, names of animals, names of significant landmarks, symbols and the symbolic.

The Ekwueme People of Truth have emerged in the center stage of world history as the *New Humanity* who are capable of tackling the problems of the time of Oge Nzuzu. The Ekwueme People of Kemet must distinguish ourselves from the past during the time of **Oge Nzuzu** by not aping the time of **Oge Nzuzu**. The Ekwueme must confront Ekwensism with the set goal of converting the Ekwensi to become a follower of the Divine Plan of the One Creator of the universe.

The historical process of **Oge Nzuzu** holds one of the fundamental challenges that the human spirit must overcome in order to become an Ekwueme. The time of **Oge Nzuzu** is the past because human experience has transcended it. The weaknesses of the time of **Oge Nzuzu** must be transcended. **The human spirit must come out of the historical process of Oge Nzuzu in order to enter into the historical process of Nzoputa Uwa.** We must not ape the time of **Oge Nzuzu** because we are the embodiment of the **New Human Paradigm.**

Therefore, the Ekwueme is the human spirit who strives to overcome evil by doing good. **The Ekwueme is the master of the World of Life who follows in the footsteps of the Chosen One for the mission of Nzoputa Uwa.** The Ekwueme is the devoted follower of the Divine Plan of the One Creator of the universe. The etymology of the term *Ekwueme* thus means *the master of life*. The Ekwueme is the master of the World of Life. The Ekwueme is the Universal Being who has attained the devotion of purpose to the supreme principle of EKUMEKU. In short, the Ekwueme is the Man and the Woman in the Almighty Spirit of EKUMEKU.

THE BLACK SKIN AS A CURSE BELIEF IS NZUZU

Imagine the evil of Ekwensism and its belief in black skin as a curse to humanity that you may understand why every agreement with Nsi is doomed to be vanquished. The false doctrine that propagated the Ekwensi belief of the black skin as a curse to the human family must be judged according to the Divine Plan of AMUN in whom we trust

The black skin as a curse belief is absurd and yet it is fundamental in grasping the normative premises of the religions of ISFET. One might ask, cursed by who and for what? Definitely, an answer can be: Cursed by the created images of the religions of ISFET.

The One Creator of the universe can never curse the black skinned people. Why? Because the Chosen One was chosen by the One Creator of the universe for the mission of **Nzoputa Uwa** and the Chosen One is a black skinned man, a Kemite. Therefore, it is not the One Creator of the universe that cursed the black skinned people to eternal doom. Without any doubt, it is the followers of the religions of ISFET that have cursed the black skinned people to eternal doom by their agreement with Nsi and in their belief of black skin being a sign of curse to humanity. The Chosen One is the Perfect Black skinned man and he is the perfect proof of black skin as being a blessing from the One Creator of the universe. Indeed, it is a blessing of no little magnitude to be a black skinned human being

The religions of ISFET created the fabulous belief or doctrine that the black skin is a curse to the human family. The religions of ISFET developed the fabulous doctrine or belief that the black skin is a curse to humanity that is doomed to perish. Do you agree that the black skin is a curse as to what it means to be human? Let us know. The religions of ISFET propagated the fabulous doctrine or belief that the black skin is a curse to humanity which made the black skin morally inferior to the pink skin. Do you agree? Let us know. The followers of the religions of ISFET made the dark skin synonymous with darkness and yet the dark skin is the perfect manifestation of the light from our sun in the human body. Do you agree that the dark skin is synonymous with darkness? Let us know. Without any doubt, the followers of the religions of ISFET are ignorant of the Truth which insists that the dark skin is Light made manifest in the human body. The Kemites must never be separated from the Ekwueme People of Truth. The Kemites are the People of Light, the people of the lightness of the sun. **The horrible skin color contraption by the religions of ISFET is a foolish criminality that is absurd in its immorality, human degradation and human deprivation.**

The Judgment of the Truth is upon the Unbelievers who developed, advanced and propagated the false belief or doctrine of the black skin as a curse to humanity. The Judgment of the Truth is against the Unbelievers who live in agreement with the false belief or doctrine of the black skin as a curse as to what it means to be human. The Judgment of the Truth of the divine birth of EKUMEKU is already upon the followers of the religions of ISFET for they would reap what they have sowed. For their foolish criminality is an abuse of human morality. They must repent or perish.

The followers of the religions of ISFET must confess every form of Nsi that they committed against the humanity of the black skinned people because of their false belief in a created image of the human mind. Whatever it is that has been used to propagate the false doctrine of the black skin as a curse to humanity must never be the same again. If it is the mind, that human mind must never be the same again. OTUA-KA-ODI. If it is a God that has been used to propagate the false belief of the black skin as a curse to humanity, that created image of the human mind must never be the same again. OTUA-KA-ODI. If it is a physical body or entity that has been used to advance the false doctrine of the black skin as a curse to the human family, that being must never be the same again. OTUA-KA-ODI. If it is a spirit that has been used to corrupt the human mind to the belief that the black skin is a curse to the human family, that spirit must die and can never be the same again. OTUA-KA-ODI. Whatever it is that was used to propagate the false belief of the black skin as a curse to the human family should henceforth become the servant of the mission of **Nzoputa Uwa** in its unconditional surrender to the Divine Will of AMUN in whom we trust.

If there is anybody, spirit or entity that has the knowledge, power or truth to defend the false doctrine of the black skin as a curse to the human family, let it show its Ekwensi form and it shall come to pass that it would no longer exist. We do not need any apology from the Unbelievers. What we must have is the repentance from Nsi. What have the black skinned people done that you Unbelievers did everything that you could do to remove them from the human family? You must come with your proofs and not your fables. If you cannot prove yourself to be right, then we would prove you to be wrong and guilty. This is our Judgment and it is the Final Judgment here.

Wherefore, the black skin as a curse belief is Nzuzu and it is the legacy of the time of Oge Nzuzu which has now been superseded by the time of Nzoputa Uwa.

THE PROCESS OF SELF-IDENTIFICATION

In the mighty struggle between the forces of MAAT and the forces of ISFET to dominate the consciousness of what it means to be fully human, the forces of ISFET devised a skin color contraption which made high melanin pigmentation the embodiment of evil. This has been a grave moral error because skin color must never be the basis of human morality. **The religions of ISFET in their doctrine of black moral inferiority developed various immoral dogmas that were used to deny the humanity of the black skinned people without moral justification.** As a consequence, the victimized and the victimizer, the traduced and the traducer became trapped in the dead end nature of the world of Ekwensu. Humanity as a whole was held at the ransom of Ekwensism during the time of **Oge Nzuzu** without any future. There could not be liberation for neither the victimizer nor the victimized until the divine birth of EKUMEKU on the Second year of **Nzoputa Uwa**.

Wherefore, let it be known that the problem of the Afrikan humanity must be fundamentally understood as the yoke of living in agreement with Nsi. Since this is the matter at stake, what is the solution to this complex problem of all humanity? Let it be known that the solution to the yoke of living in agreement with Nsi for all humanity is the repentance from Nsi. Once the human spirit repents from Nsi, the individual would attain the devotion of purpose to the supreme principle of EKUMEKU. As a result, the human spirit would become disagreeable to every form of agreement with Nsi. In consequence, the human spirit would become an Ekwueme in thought, word and deed. Becoming an Ekwueme would also warrant that the human spirit abandons the false Afrikan (Ekwensi) identity and would get on to the scaffold of the Kemetic World Identity.

This is what the Afrikan must do in order to realize the human potentiality that has been ordained by the Truth of the divine birth of EKUMEKU. The Afrikan in the Homeland and the Afrikan in the Diaspora cannot realize the collective potentiality of their humanity until they can exist in disagreement with Nsi, in thought, word and deed. At the same time, the Afrikan cannot become a Kemite, that is to say a New Afrikan, without following in the footsteps of the Chosen One for the mission of **Nzoputa Uwa**.

The Kemites must develop the Eziokwu Language to be the most potent instrument of knowledge, building upon the past while looking forward in the future. **The Eziokwu Language must be understood in its transcendental universalism as the Language of languages.** Without any doubt, the Eziokwu Language is destined to become the most potent language of thought yet devised in human history.

Let it then be known that the process of self-definition is the historical fact of human freedom. As the Kemites, the process of our self-definition would influence the development of the Eziokwu Language of the Ekwueme. For example, what the world of Ekwensu called the Atlantic Ocean would be known to us as the **Kemetic Ocean**. As we change all the Ekwensu names, so shall we begin the process of influencing others to accept the names as we would know them.

Our identity as the people of Kemet must be understood from its originality, character and quality of being to be the vital expression of our humanity. During the time of **Oge Nzuzu**, we were deceived through ignorance and falsehood to live in agreement with Nsi. But through the divine intervention of the One Creator of the universe, the divine birth of EKUMEKU was realized as the ultimate reality. As a result, the Ekwueme came into universal existence to live MAAT by renouncing ISFET

Through the devotion of purpose to the supreme principle of EKUMEKU, the human spirit would repent from Nsi. Having repented from Nsi, the human spirit would exist in disagreement with Nsi by following in the footsteps of the Chosen One for the mission of **Nzoputa Uwa**. When the human spirit has made the public declaration of **Nkwekolita** in fellowship with the living Haremakhet, the struggle to overcome evil by doing good would manifest the Ekwueme Universal Life. **Harembetism** becomes the methodology of socially cementing the forces of MAAT against the forces of ISFET. Indeed, the redemption of the human spirit from the dead end nature of the world of Ekwensu would elevate the human spirit above and beyond the Ekwensi condition of living in agreement with Nsi.

The Truth of the divine birth of EKUMEKU on the Second year of **Nzoputa Uwa** has freed us from all forms of agreement with Nsi, giving us the power of self-definition. Thus, the power of self-definition is a fact of human freedom. It is this Truth of self-definition that is at the heart of the Ekwueme Universal Life. This process of self-definition is a moral imperative in our struggle to renounce ISFET by living MAAT.

For example, when we defined ourselves as the People of Kemet, the Kemites, we were exercising the human freedom of self-definition. The human freedom to define ourselves as the Kemites and to call our beloved Continent The Land of Kemet brings with it a new awareness of self, a new sense of dignity and a new sense of identity. As we are transformed through the devotion of purpose to the supreme principle of EKUMEKU, so everything within us and around us is transformed. It is through the devotion of purpose to the supreme principle of EKUMEKU that the conviction of the necessity for the struggle is realized by the individual as indispensable in the being and becoming of the Kemite.

In other words, our identity as the Kemites cannot be given to us by anyone else; instead, it is our conviction that has made us to become the Kemet-Nu or would make us to become Ndi Kemet. It must be understood that once the individual has the conviction to undergo the process of becoming a Kemite, the human spirit must also accept the responsibility for the struggle of the Kemites to champion the mission of **Nzoputa Uwa**.

As the Kemite emerges, what is at stake becomes very clear: **The complete transformation of the structural pattern of thought and behavior in the old human paradigm must be the aim because the future lies neither in its reformation nor in its acceptance. The ontological vocation of the Kemites does not reside neither in the old human paradigm nor in its contradiction; but instead it involves the developmental process of the new human paradigm of the Ekwueme.**

It is the devotion of purpose to the supreme principle of EKUMEKU that enables the Ekwueme to act upon every agreement with Nsi. Without any doubt, the ontological and historical vocation of the Kemite is a reality in this process of becoming fully human. The Kemites as the world historical people championing the **Movement of Nzoputa Uwa**, which engages the human spirit to become aware of the existence of Nsi, are historical beings in fellowship with every bonafide Ekwueme. **Therefore, to become a Kemite is to exercise the power of self-definition, to change the world by transforming oneself, to become actively engaged in the Ekwueme World Experience, to become disagreeable with Nsi and to reclaim the right of self-definition in order to prevent the** continuation of the denial of the right of self-definition. By self-definition, the Kemite has begun the process of self-reflection in the act of partaking and manifesting the Truth of the divine birth of EKUMEKU on the Second year of Nzoputa Uwa.

THE CONCLUSION

To follow in the footsteps of the Chosen One, stand firmly on your own feet and declare publicly that you are an Ekwueme, in repentance from Nsi. The Ekwueme is the Universal Being. Any human spirit can become an Ekwueme regardless of ancestry and would be free to join the *Universal Brotherhood and Sisterhood in EKUMEKU*. We the Kemites are the foundation upon which this *NEW HUMAN PARADIGM* has come into universal expression.

The Kemites who constitute a world group, as opposed to tribal, ethnic and national bounded groups, are historical people who stress unity of origin in the mighty struggle to renounce ISFET by living MAAT. **This self-defined Kemetic world culture that has begun to emerge even though rooted in the continental Kemet transcends continental boundaries and must be understood as a world of its own.** It identifies with all who share its unity of origin and who participate in its world outlook as the term *Kemet* signifies in its etymological meaning.

In order to realize the universal dimension of the Ekwueme Way of life, the human spirit must discard the Ekwensi condition of living a life and thenceforth become identified with the Ekwueme humanity. The morality for life would become the devotion of purpose to the supreme principle of EKUMEKU, moving the human spirit to progressively discard whatever that is not in harmony with the Living Truth. **Because through our names, we are identified with history, what we call ourselves become fundamentally important to us as the world historical people. We must distinguish ourselves from the Ekwensu people by realizing the Truth of the divine birth of EKUMEKU in our individual lives.** For, to live a worthy life, we ought to believe wholeheartedly in the Truth that gives our lives meaning and purpose. We must define who we are with our names, our morality and ethics, our culture and civilization, our somatic norm image, our aesthetics and arts, our architecture, our dress codes, etc. We must shift our individual self-identification from the narrow confines of tribe, ethnicity, and nationality to the widened horizon of the world historical people of Kemet. **We are the Kemites not because of our tribal, ethnic or national origins, but instead we are the Kemites because of the wider and new horizon of possibilities that lie open to us.** OTUA-KA-ODI!

CHAPTER ELEVEN
THE REVOLUTION OF THE EKWUEME CIVILIZATION OF KEMET

THE HOLY ANKHUWA is the Living Truth of the World of Life, inspired in the Almighty Spirit of EKUMEKU as it has been revealed by the One Creator of the universe for the divine mission of **Nzoputa Uwa** according to the Divine Plan of AMUN in whom we trust.

.....The Chosen One

Those who work and labor for their salvation without truly attaining the devotion of purpose to the supreme principle of EKUMEKU are working and laboring in vain for whatever they do would be in agreement with Nsi.
.....THE HOLY ANKHUWA

What we must have is justice and not revenge. The Chosen One is the Perfect Witness of Divine Justice. The exercise of the legitimate force of Biafranism is to make the Unbeliever bear witness to the Truth of the divine birth of EKUMEKU on the Second year of Nzoputa Uwa.
....The Chosen One

TO WHOM DOES THE WORLD OF LIFE BELONG TO?

The World of Life belongs to those who follow in the footsteps of the Chosen One for the mission of **Nzoputa Uwa**. If you think that the World of Life belongs to you, declare publicly your **Nkwekolita** with the Holy Cause of **Nzoputa Uwa**. Opportunity comes but once to those who hearken to the Living Truth in repentance from Nsi. Declare publicly the **Nkwekolita** in the Spirit of MAAT and you will self-realize the **inner** meaning of the Truth of the divine birth of EKUMEKU on the Second year of **Nzoputa Uwa**.

Confess EKUMEKU as the whole Truth of Life Everlasting, as follows:

"I BELIEVE IN THE TRUTH OF THE ONE CREATOR OF THE UNIVERSE. I BELIEVE THAT THE ONE CREATOR OF THE UNIVERSE IS AMUN IN WHOM I MUST TRUST. I BELIEVE THAT EKUMEKU IS THE DIVINE PLAN OF THE ONE CREATOR OF THE UNIVERSE. OTUA-KA-ODI!"

WHAT IS IN THE NAME, KEMET?

Every world historical people must always come to the historic stage with its own self-definition according to its own stamp of distinction in order to identify their civilization in the forward flow of human history. A conscious historical people must bind themselves with a name that is rooted in the correct interpretation of their historical existence to express their collective identity and destiny.

The historical significance of the name *Kemet* is that its process would contribute in the spiritual unification of the dispersed and scattered Black humanity and would also minimize the divisive tendency within the continent by binding the West and East, North and South together as a whole in the mission of **Nzoputa Uwa. The name, Kemet, is indigenous to our great continent and it is perhaps the only name that all indigenous people of our continent would easily identify with. The name, Kemet, has its originality in the classical civilization of our beloved continent that had helped to humanize the planet. The name, Kemet, when it is applied to the continent means the Land of the Black people or the Black Land. It is a name that we must use to distinguish our continent from other continents on the planet and also to honor our ancestors who left an indelible legacy in human development.**

It is unacceptable for a people from another continent to determine the name and identity of our beloved continent. **The** continent of Kemet is the Land of the Black people and we the people of Kemet are the Kemites, the People of the Black Land. When we identify ourselves as the Black people, we are following in the footsteps of our ancestors who had defined themselves in the beginning of history as the Black People. We are the Black people not just because we identify with our ancestors who were the first people to define themselves as the Black people in human history; but also for the purpose of distinguishing ourselves from others. **When we call ourselves the Black people, we are associating ourselves with the Light of the Sun using the concept of blackness as a positive metaphor in relation to its essence in being a fundamental color in life**. Recognizing the artificiality of skin color designation, our identity as the Kemites ought to be understood as an ancestral heritage that cannot be separated from the devotion of purpose to the supreme principle of EKUMEKU. In addition, the name, Kemet, transcends whatever differences that may exist contemporaneously between one tribe and another, one ethnic group and another, one nationality and another, because it underlies the unifying principle for the whole continent.

Therefore, the name, Kemet, is a term that designates our continental landmass, our collective history, culture and civilization, a new image for our beloved continent. It is a positive self-image and group identity that goes beyond color designation because it is rooted in the continental landmass of the Holy Land, in the collective history and culture of our beloved continent. Without any doubt, the name Kemet is a valid historical, geographical and cultural heritage that would give a collective identification to us, our children and to the yet unborn without regards to tribe, ethnicity or nationality. Let us embrace it in the Almighty Spirit of EKUMEKU according to the Divine Plan of AMUN in whom we must trust.

Unlike the name Kemet, the name Africa or Afrika is a misnomer that was wrongfully imposed on our entire continent during the time of Oge Nzuzu, which has given the Afrikans a false sense of history. As the Kemites, our history goes back to the antiquity of human development and we must cease to identify with the distorted image that is called Africa or Afrika.

The evil that is the skin color contraption of the followers of the religions of ISFET was devised to brand the African as an outcast to be degraded, oppressed and exploited. As a consequence, the African has been projected in the world of Ekwensu to seem less than human (subhuman creature) and to be the embodiment of evil. As far as the Kemites are concerned, it is only a person who is insane that would accept and live in agreement with such an abuse of human morality and its total disregard to the humanity of the Unbelieving Afrikans. The Ekwueme People of Truth are on the mission of **Nzoputa Uwa** to convert the Ekwensu people to EKUMEKU by liberating the human spirit from the dead end nature of the world of Ekwensu.

INTRODUCTION

Whatever is its connotation and denotation, the term, *Africa* or *Afrika*, is no longer the name of our beloved continent as far as we are concerned. This ill-fated name has been changed for the goodness of our great continent and its people both at home and abroad. What the name represents now to us is the false identity of a grievous era when our people lacked the human freedom of self-definition. It is a name that we must identify with the horrible time of **Oge Nzuzu**. Our memory of this name may continue for an indefinite period in books and other historical records but it would be as the memory of a previous epoch that had already passed away. We must no longer use that name without qualifying the context upon which we are using it.

As we identify with our beloved *Kemet*, so would the **Black Continent, The Black Land**, identify with us in world history. If there are those who would insist on identifying the entire people of our continent with that false identity, what they would be telling us is that they do not recognize our human freedom of self-definition. We would equally treat them as those who do not deserve their own human freedom of self-definition. We must work hard to teach our people that the false Afrikan identity was based on ignorance, falsehood and deception; and that it is for their own good that they cease to relate with it any more. We are neither the Africans nor Afrikans; or are we the Afrikaners? Instead, **we are the Kemites**. The Kemites are in control of their destiny because they are rooted in the historical process of **Nzoputa Uwa**. Whosoever would continue to identify our continent with any name that we have rejected is contending with the false notion that our continent is a conquered territory and such an unbelieving bigot we will deal with as an enemy.

THE BIRTH OF THE NEW HUMANITY

The birth of the new human paradigm of the *Ekwueme* did not evolve in a vacuum. In the womb of time, the *Ekwueme* was conceived through the Immaculate Conception, emerging from the old humanity with an originality that has never been seen before. Standing on its own Truth and comparable to no other, the human paradigm of the *Ekwueme* grows and develops according to the Divine Plan of AMUN in whom we trust.

The Immaculate Conception of the new humanity was realized on the First year of **Nzoputa Uwa** through the divine intervention of the One Creator of the universe. But with the divine birth of EKUMEKU on the Second year of **Nzoputa Uwa**, the Truth of the One Creator of the universe became the Ultimate Reality of the human life. Wherefore, every *Ekwensi* must be born again before the human spirit can become an *Ekwueme*. To have access to the Truth of the divine birth of EKUMEKU is to break out of the bondage and slavery of the historical process of **Oge Nzuzu**. That is why, the historical process of **Nzoputa Uwa** is the reversal of the horrible yoke of living in agreement with Nsi.

THE KEMITES AND OUR WORLDVIEW

The term *Kemet* from its etymological origin means **The Land of The Black people or The Black Land** and in our *Kemetic* usage it would also mean the **Black Continent**. The "Dark Continent" euphemism of the Ekwensu people has no historical relationship with our concept of the Black Continent. We must never allow the Unbelievers to give us the definition of what our continent is to us. Self-respect is inseparable from the human freedom of self-definition. We must never allow outsiders to fool us into not recognizing the historical prototype of our identity. The historical prototype of the Kemetic World Identity is the Old Kemet and as the world historical Kemites of the time of **Nzoputa Uwa**, the identity of the Old Kemet is not open to self-doubt but a certainty that underlies our positive self-definition in the historical process of **Nzoputa Uwa**.

No doubt, we are not the **Old Kemite** and yet the Old Kemite is the ancestor of the **New Kemite**. The Old Kemite is the ancestral predecessor of the New Kemite; while the New Kemite is the cultural progeny of the Old Kemite. Clearly, there is a positive historical relationship between the Old Kemite and the New Kemite in culture and worldview. The Old Kemet constituted a particular geographical boundary, whereas the New Kemet transcends geographical boundaries even though rooted in the continental space that we call the **Continent of Kemet.**

Therefore, my brothers and sisters in EKUMEKU, now is the time to come home and stop the aimless wandering in the wilderness of human history that is fraught with confusion and conflict. The three wise men foresaw it that sooner than later the **Onye Nzoputa Uwa** would come to lead his people out of the aimless wandering in the wilderness of the historical process of **Oge Nzuzu**. With the divine birth of EKUMEKU comes the social dynamic of the **Kemetic World Identity**, manifesting the *Ekwueme World Experience* that is devoid of aimlessness and confusion. Let us henceforth leave the unrepentant African, Afrikan or Afrikaner wanderers in the wilderness of the historical process of **Oge Nzuzu** for they would no longer bear the name of our continent. **The name is KEMET.**

To every African or Afrikan both at home and abroad, meditate on the message of the **Ozioma of Truth** to overcome the evil of unbelief: Put an end to your aimless wandering and accept the Truth of the One Creator of the universe by following in the footsteps of the Chosen One. Repent from Nsi and confess EKUMEKU as the eternal Savior and Redeemer of all humanity. Renounce the worship of any God and accept that it is only the One Creator of the universe that is worthy of worship. Reject the false African identity and accept the dynamic reality of the **Kemetic World Identity**.

THE LIVING TRUTH

The Creator is One. The One is AMUN and the Divine Plan is EKUMEKU. There is no other Creator of the universe but AMUN in whom we trust.

By the Living Truth of ***THE HOLY ANKHUWA*** is the mission of **Nzoputa Uwa** that has been divinely ordained by the One Creator of the universe in the eternal struggle to overcome evil by doing good.

Every human spirit is born in the world of Ekwensu in agreement with Nsi. The human spirit is born again in the world of EKUMEKU in repentance from Nsi. When the human spirit has been born again, it will exist in disagreement with Nsi.

The attainment of the devotion of purpose to the supreme principle of EKUMEKU is the process wherein the Living Truth is made manifest in human life.

Chineke Consciousness is the union or harmonious relation whereby the individual Chi of the human spirit becomes attuned to the oneness of the Almighty Spirit of EKUMEKU wherein the Living Truth continuously recreates itself.

The actual aim of human freedom is to attain the state of Chineke Consciousness on this planet. Therefore, the ultimate human freedom is Chineke Consciousness. This ultimate source of human freedom is transcendental and it is beyond any form, condition or circumstance. When there is no Chineke Consciousness as the unifying principle of eternal life, there would be no everlasting life.

THE RESURRECTION OF THE DEAD

Every human spirit is born in the world of Ekwensu in order to be born again in the world of EKUMEKU. In order for the human spirit to be born again, there must be the resurrection of the individual Chi from the vicious circle of eternal death. Therefore, the resurrection of the dead from the dead end nature of the world of Ekwensu has been ordained from the beginning of creation, according to the Divine Plan of AMUN in whom we trust.

The resurrection of the dead is not for those who have died in agreement with Nsi. Those who have died in agreement with Nsi are dead in Nsi for eternity. **There is no resurrection of the dead for any human spirit who had died in agreement with Nsi.** The resurrection of the dead is for the living dead who lives in agreement with Nsi in the dead end nature of the world of Ekwensu. The living dead is the Ekwensi who is ignorant of EKUMEKU. The resurrection of the dead is without any doubt a reality of the Living Truth when the Unbeliever has repented from Nsi through the devotion of purpose in EKUMEKU. However, the Ekwensi cannot repent from Nsi without confessing EKUMEKU as the eternal Savior and Redeemer of all humanity from the dead end nature of the world of Ekwensu.

WHO WE ARE

We are the **Ekwueme People of Kemet** who are on the mission of **Nzoputa Uwa**. We are the devoted followers of the Divine Plan of the One Creator of the universe who follow in the footsteps of the Chosen One for the mission of **Nzoputa Uwa**. We are the devoted followers of the Divine Plan of AMUN in whom we trust. We are the Ekwueme People of the Black Continent, the people of the lightness of the sun. Wherefore, we are the Ekwueme People of Truth who strive everyday to renounce ISFET by living MAAT through the devotion of purpose to the supreme principle of EKUMEKU.

WHAT WE FIGHT FOR

We are fighting against the agreement with Nsi, **Ekwensism**, of the Ekwensu people. We are fighting against the conditions of living in agreement with Nsi. No doubt, we are fighting against the worship of the created image of the human mind that the Ekwensu people called God. Again, we are fighting against the ignorance, falsehood and deception of the religions of ISFET.

That is why, we are fighting for human morality as we battle against the skin color contraption of the followers of the religions of ISFET. It is a blasphemy against the Truth of the One Creator of the universe for anybody to accept the skin color contraption of the religions of ISFET. The Chosen One came to displace the **Ekwensism** of the world of Ekwensu in order to restore the interdependent order of the universe as he stands in judgment against every agreement with Nsi.

This time of **Nzoputa Uwa** would deliver us from the undue and horrible abuse of human morality during the time of **Oge Nzuzu**, from the degradation and the abuse of human morality, from the tyranny of the environment of ignorance, falsehood and deception. In pre-Ekwueme times, the followers of the religions of ISFET devised a skin color contraption which made the black skinned humanity the embodiment of evil. **This was a grave moral error because skin color must never be the basis of human morality.**

THE MESSAGE OF THE CHOSEN ONE

I have come with the Living Truth for the sake of human freedom, to everyone that is weighed down by the yoke of living in agreement with Nsi, to save the individual Chi of the Ekwensu people for EKUMEKU. I have come with the Living Truth of the divine birth of EKUMEKU that those who follow in my footsteps shall not perish but instead would realize life everlasting. I have come with the Living Truth to set unu apart from the historical process of **Oge Nzuzu** that all may be redeemed from the tyranny of the historical process of **Oge Nzuzu**. Because without the Living Truth there could never be human freedom, the Living Truth is inseparable from human freedom. We are fighting against the abuse of human morality of the religions of ISFET. Their dispensation had been superseded by the divine birth of EKUMEKU as a result. Wherefore, the whole world of Ekwensu is ignorant of EKUMEKU. The Ekwensu people worship the created images of the human mind instead of the One Creator of the universe. **The Ekwensi is the embodiment of evil**. In other words, let every Ekwensi repent from Nsi and confess EKUMEKU as the eternal Savior and Redeemer of all humanity.

The Chosen One explains further: I have come with a special mission to teach humanity the Truth of the divine birth of EKUMEKU. I have come with a special mission to lead humanity out of the dead end nature of the world of Ekwensu. I have come with a special mission to lead humanity out of the dead end nature of the world of Ekwensu.

I have come with the divine mission of **Nzoputa Uwa** to show you the Way to human freedom that you may be liberated from the yoke of living in agreement with Nsi. I have come with a special mission to give you the gift of salvation of your individual Chi.

When you become an *Ekwueme*, you would become the master of the destiny of your own life. You would no longer be deceived to live in agreement with Nsi. Everyday would become a blessing in your own life for you would no longer live in ignorance, falsehood and deception.

The ethic of the **Ozioma of Truth** is the human freedom to overcome evil by doing good. It does not rest on the fear of punishment and the hope of reward after the physical demise of the body. **It is the life here and not the life of the hereafter that needs human freedom.** Let there be neither compulsion nor violence in the Truth of human freedom. Preach to the Unbeliever, teach the Unbeliever the Truth of the divine birth of EKUMEKU, let the Unbeliever to know that it is only through

EKUMEKU can the human spirit worship the One Creator of the universe. But if the Ekwensi rejects the Truth of human freedom, let there be no compulsion or violence. Every unrepentant Unbeliever is entangled with evil and is in bondage and slavery without even knowing it. The redemption of the Unbeliever is only through the repentance from Nsi. An unrepentant human spirit needs deliverance and it is only the Almighty Spirit of EKUMEKU that can redeem the human spirit from the dead end nature of the world of Ekwensu.

The force of **Biafra** may be used against the unrepentant Unbeliever. Whenever there is an active opposition to the Truth of the One Creator of the universe, the force of *Biafra* may be waged against the unrepentant Unbeliever. Fight for the Truth of the divine birth of EKUMEKU, exercise the active force of Biafra against those who fight against you. But do not fight for the sake of fighting for the judgment of the Truth of the divine birth of EKUMEKU would be against you. Human freedom to believe or not to believe ought to be exercised so long as the Ekwensu people are not in an active opposition to the mission of **Nzoputa Uwa.**

DEVOTION OF PURPOSE

Let it be known that the devotion of purpose to the supreme principle of EKUMEKU is the life and the salvation of the human spirit on this planet. The devotion of purpose in EKUMEKU does not have its moral origins in bloodshed. The devotion of purpose to the supreme principle of EKUMEKU did not have its moral and ethical origins neither in blood covenant nor in blood testament. The devotion of purpose in EKUMEKU is not rooted in the shedding of neither the human blood nor the animal blood. The devotion of purpose in EKUMEKU does not require any form of blood sacrifice. There is no need to shed the blood of a human spirit or the blood of an animal for anyone to attain the devotion of purpose to the supreme principle of EKUMEKU.

In the world of Ekwensu, living in agreement with Nsi which constitutes the state of rebellion or opposition to the Divine Plan of the One Creator of the universe, the Ekwensi can only live in bondage and slavery. The devotion of purpose in EKUMEKU alone is what can redeem the human spirit from the dead end nature of the world of Ekwensu. Without the attainment of the devotion of purpose, whatever the human spirit does would be in agreement with Nsi. When we have become strengthened in our devotion of purpose, whatever we do in the Spirit of MAAT would be good. **Since it is not just good works that make the human spirit an** *Ekwueme*, **it is only through the devotion of purpose alone can any work be good**. It is only our devotion of purpose alone that can save us and yet everyone that is devoted does good works.

Without any doubt, there is no salvation outside of the devotion of purpose to the supreme principle of EKUMEKU. Those who work and labor for their salvation without truly attaining the devotion of purpose in EKUMEKU are working and laboring in vain for whatever they do would be in agreement with Nsi. It is only through the devotion of purpose in EKUMEKU can the human spirit be saved from Nsi.

To exist in disagreement with Nsi without the attainment of the devotion of purpose, is humanly impossible. Why? Because the divine birth of EKUMEKU has convicted the whole world of Ekwensu with the evil of being in agreement with Nsi. So long as the human spirit lives in agreement with Nsi, the work and labor of the human spirit for redemption from the dead end nature of the world of Ekwensu is futile. **Without the redeeming victory and triumph of the divine birth of EKUMEKU against Nsi, there could be no salvation from Nsi**. Wherefore, the salvation of the individual Chi from Nsi is truly realizable only through the devotion of purpose to the supreme principle of EKUMEKU. Devotion is by the free will and must never be something that can be forced upon anybody. **Nobody must be compelled to become a devoted follower of the Divine Plan of AMUN in whom we trust and yet no one must be allowed to live in an** active opposition to the Living Truth.

THE ALMIGHTY SPIRIT OF EKUMEKU

The Almighty Spirit of EKUMEKU is the Ultimate Reality of the human life and the cause of all generations, the substance of every seed and the definitive Truth of life and death. This Almighty Spirit of EKUMEKU is the Divine Plan of the One Creator of the universe. The Truth of the divine birth of EKUMEKU on the Second year of **Nzoputa Uwa** is the highest power of life in the universe. The Almighty Spirit of EKUMEKU is the Supreme Being/Force/Energy of life that is the highest power in the universe because it is the Divine Plan of the One Creator of the universe.

THE MOVEMENT OF NZOPUTA UWA

Through the divine intervention of the One Creator of the universe, the Chosen One was chosen for the mission of **Nzoputa Uwa**. Therefore, the mission of **Nzoputa Uwa** has been ordained for the displacement of ISFET and the restoration of MAAT as the dominant consciousness in the universe of life.

In the battlefield of life, there is an eternal struggle between the forces of MAAT and the forces of ISFET, between the Higher Self and the Lower Self, between the world of EKUMEKU and the world of Ekwensu, between what is good and what is evil and between what is freedom and what is bondage.

The mission of **Nzoputa Uwa** exists in the wholeness of eternity to displace the forces of ISFET and restore the forces of MAAT as the dominant consciousness in the universe of life. Without any doubt, the mission of **Nzoputa Uwa** exists in the wholeness of eternity to subordinate the Lower Self against the Higher Self and to make the world of EKUMEKU dominant against the world of Ekwensu. In other words, the mission of **Nzoputa Uwa** exists in the wholeness of eternity for the eternal struggle to overcome evil by doing good. Wherefore, what is unrepentant from Nsi must be acted upon and what is acted upon is the condition of living in agreement with Nsi.

The world of Ekwensu, which constitutes the state of rebellion or opposition against the Divine Plan of the One Creator of the universe, is destroying the equilibrium of life in the universe because of the ignorance of EKUMEKU.

Considering that the world of Ekwensu cannot fulfill the Divine Plan of AMUN in whom we trust without the world of EKUMEKU, it becomes clearly certain that life which is lived in agreement with Nsi can only create an imbalance in the universe of life. No doubt, this imbalance manifests itself not only in all life forms but also in the ecology of the planet. We see this in the abuse of human morality, in the destruction of the ecology of the planet, in the consequences of pollution, in the destructive potential of living in agreement with Nsi, in the extinction of many life forms, in the internal strife and arrogance of power of the Ekwensu people, etc. But out of this disequilibrium comes the divine birth of EKUMEKU which would ultimately restore the delicate balance that is needed between the World of Life and the world of death.

THE STRUGGLE FOR THE TRUTH

The struggle for the Truth of the divine birth of EKUMEKU is against all forms of **Ekwensism** of any kind. It is every form of agreement with Nsi that we would always fight and struggle against. That is why, the mission of **Nzoputa Uwa** is an everlasting blessing to every human spirit who has repented from Nsi.

Let it be known that our proto-Kemite ancestors were made captives and enslaved by the forces of ISFET during the time of **Oge Nzuzu** because they were divided against themselves. But as your proto-Kemite ancestors were conquered by being divided, so would you conquer the Unbelievers by being united. The interpenetration of the Kemites across territorial boundaries as settlers and missionaries would be inevitable, traversing the whole Black Continent strengthening trans-continental, intracontinental and inter-continental communication and mutual penetration. For my sake, let the Kemites strive to avoid unnecessary bloodshed and yet the Kemites must be firm and uncompromising as we spread the Almighty Spirit of EKUMEKU. But if an Unbeliever attacks a Believer, that is another matter altogether. The devoted follower of the Divine Plan of the One Creator of the universe would be justified to exercise the legitimate force of Biafranism in self-defense until complete victory is won against the Unbeliever. **The Unbeliever must surrender totally and unconditionally to the Divine Will of AMUN in whom we trust.** The devotion of purpose to the supreme principle of EKUMEKU is the master key that would always make all things possible according to the Divine Plan of AMUN in whom we trust. With devotion of purpose and missionary persistence, the Ekwueme People of Kemet, would supplant the religions of ISFET and destroy their superstitious rituals.

Every Unbeliever ought to believe that there is only One Creator in this universe of life. Every Unbeliever ought to believe that the One Creator of the universe is AMUN in whom we trust. Every Unbeliever ought to believe that the Divine Plan of the One Creator of the universe is EKUMEKU. But if an Unbeliever refuses to believe in the Truth of the One Creator of the universe, you do not have to annihilate the Unbeliever for that would defeat the Truth of your message of **Nzoputa Uwa**. If you annihilate the Unbeliever because the Ekwensi is unrepentant, the message of human freedom that you brought to the Unbeliever would have a question mark. The Ekwensi in death would have defeated you for you have become like the followers of the religions of ISFET who are known to kill those who reject their mythologies (faiths) without any moral justification.

LET EVERYONE KNOW THE TRUTH

We must strive to destroy the evil of unbelief; while we must be devoted to convert the Ekwensu people to the Truth of the divine birth of EKUMEKU. The followers of the religions of ISFET did not understand that there must never be any compulsion in the

Truth of human freedom. They had often killed those who rejected what they preached in their dispensation during the time of **Oge Nzuzu**. The time of **Oge Nzuzu** was the time of the dispensation of the religions of ISFET; while the time of **Nzoputa Uwa** is the time of human freedom that is the dispensation of the Living Truth in the Spirit of MAAT. The followers of the religions of ISFET were blood thirsty during the time of **Oge Nzuzu**; while the devoted followers of the Divine Plan of AMUN in whom we trust would be Truth thirsty in this time of **Nzoputa Uwa**. The followers of the religions of ISFET abused human morality through their skin color contraption that made the black-skinned humanity the embodiment of evil; whereas the followers of the Divine Plan of the One Creator of the universe would uphold human morality by not degrading and dehumanizing any particular skin color. The followers of the religions of ISFET believed in blood sacrifice; while the devoted followers of the Truth of the One Creator of the universe believe in the sacrifice of the Lower Self. The followers of the religions of ISFET believe in the make-believe life of ignorance, falsehood and deception; while the devoted followers of the Divine Plan of the One Creator of the universe believe in the Living Truth of the World of Life.

The followers of the religions of ISFET believe in the separateness of being; while the devoted followers of the Divine Plan of AMUN in whom we trust believe in the Oneness of Being. The followers of the religions of ISFET built their movements based on fear; while the devoted followers of the Divine Plan of the One Creator of the universe are building the Movement of **Nzoputa Uwa** based on human freedom. The followers of the religions of ISFET had committed abominations against humanity; while the devoted followers of the Divine Plan of AMUN in whom we trust have committed no abomination against humanity. The followers of the religions of ISFET preach one thing and practice another thing; while the devoted followers of the Divine Plan of the One Creator of the universe preach what they practice in the Spirit of MAAT. **The followers of the religions of ISFET believe in the Word of God; while the devoted followers of the Divine Plan of AMUN in whom we**

trust believe in the Truth of the One Creator of the universe.

The followers of the religions of ISFET are ignorant of EKUMEKU; while the devoted followers of the Divine Plan of the One Creator of the universe are the partakers in the Living Truth of the Almighty Spirit of EKUMEKU. The followers of the religions of ISFET live in agreement with Nsi; while the devoted followers of the Divine Plan of AMUN in whom we trust exist in disagreement with Nsi. The followers of the religions of ISFET are the Ekwensu people; while the devoted followers of the Divine Plan of the One Creator of the universe are the Ekwueme People of Truth.

Let it be known that the difference is very clear. You must ask yourself a very simple question: Where do I ought to belong? Another question that you must ask yourself is: Do I want to remain in the historical process of **Oge Nzuzu** entangled with evil or can I struggle to become conscious of the historical process of **Nzoputa Uwa**? Whatever you decide is your own future destiny. Make that decision for your own life. Your destiny is in your own hands. Use it wisely for there is no longer any future in the time of **Oge Nzuzu**. The time of **Nzoputa Uwa** is the future of human life. The future indeed is now.

THE TIME OF NZOPUTA UWA

The line of demarcation between the time of **Oge Nzuzu** and the time of **Nzoputa Uwa** is crossed when the human spirit ceases to live in agreement with Nsi and becomes consciously aware of Nsi as the root of all evil. Thus, the struggle to overcome evil by doing good truly begins from that moment of conviction when the lessons of the life that was lived in agreement with Nsi are carried forward into the life of the future that would be lived in disagreement with Nsi. It is then that the future becomes the present as the past and the future merge in the ultimate reality of the historical process of **Nzoputa Uwa**. We must have the sense of the time of **Oge Nzuzu** as the diametrical opposite of the time of **Nzoputa Uwa** and yet they both function in complementarity.

When this demarcation is understood in the life of the human spirit, it is then can the sense and discipline of the time of **Nzoputa Uwa** begin to develop and grow. For example, when or if human freedom is used as the framework for understanding the time of **Nzoputa Uwa**, then human bondage and slavery may be used as the framework of understanding the time of **Oge Nzuzu**.

The animating and controlling Idea of the **Ekwueme World Experience** is the Living Truth of being in disagreement with Nsi. **That is why, what separates the Ekwueme from the Ekwensi is that the Ekwensi lives in agreement with Nsi; whereas the Ekwueme exists in the wholeness of eternity in disagreement with Nsi.** The awakening of consciousness caused by the attainment of the devotion of purpose to the supreme principle of EKUMEKU makes the human spirit to become disagreeable with Nsi.

THE HISTORICAL PROCESS OF NZOPUTA UWA

On the First year of **Nzoputa Uwa,** the historical process of **Nzoputa Uwa** came into existence as the result of the divine intervention of the One Creator of the universe. It was the end of the time of **Oge Nzuzu** that made the realization of the historical process of **Nzoputa Uwa** possible. That is why, the historical process of **Nzoputa Uwa** could not have come into existence without the conscious intelligent action of the Ekwueme which made the Divine Will of the One Creator of the universe manifest. With its infinite power as the creative principle of life in its full consciousness, the divine birth of EKUMEKU became the Ultimate Reality on the Second year of **Nzoputa Uwa** as the result of its redeeming victory against Nsi.

Consequently, the Unity of Existence could not be realizeable without the attainment of the devotion of purpose to the supreme principle of EKUMEKU. Without any doubt, the Oneness of being an Ekwueme as opposed to the separateness of being an Ekwensi is the timeless Truth of the divine birth of EKUMEKU. In other words, the essential meaning of the historical process of

Nzoputa Uwa is the unification of human consciousness or the Oneness of being an Ekwueme. This collective consciousness of what it means to be an Ekwueme recognizes unity as a fundamental principle of life and does not see the differences in skin color as an insurmantable barrier to the Oneness of being an Ekwueme. The devotion of purpose to the supreme principle of EKUMEKU is the underlying unity that makes the Ekwueme fundamentally different from the Ekwensi.

As **The Holy Ankhuwa** teaches us, that all different manifestations exist to underlie the purpose of unification or unity, which is to go beyond all differentiations in order to realize our transcendental destiny. The historical process of **Nzoputa Uwa** is particular to the individual human spirit and yet it is universal in its ultimate reality to the human life. The One Creator of the universe is in every life and yet there is no life that is the One Creator of the universe. In order to attain the state of equilibrium that can exist between MAAT and ISFET, the forces of ISFET must be displaced and the forces of MAAT restored as the dominant consciousness of life in the universe. This state of equilibrium that is the Divine Plan of AMUN in whom we trust would establish MAAT as the dominant consciousness by the subordination of the faculty of ISFET.

In other words, the supreme principle of EKUMEKU is the state of equilibrium between the faculty of MAAT and the faculty of ISFET. Through the devotion of purpose to the supreme principle of EKUMEKU the will of the individual human spirit is aligned with the Divine Will of the One Creator of the universe and then the particular human spirit becomes the Universal Being. When the Lower Self is subordinated with the Higher Self, the creative energy of life would exist at the point of equilibrium through the devotion of purpose in EKUMEKU. This union of the Higher Self with the Lower Self is what ultimately makes the Ekwueme the devoted follower of the Divine Plan of the One Creator of the universe. Wherefore, the Chosen One was chosen by the One Creator of the universe for the mission of **Nzoputa Uwa** to bring together the warring worlds of Life and Death according to the Divine Plan of AMUN in whom we trust.

OUR CIVILIZATION

I am **Chukwudi, Onye-Nzoputa-Uwa.** There will not be another Chosen One after me. If you are unrepentant in being agreeable with Nsi and in worshipping a created image of the human mind, hoping against hope that you needed more time to repent from Nsi, meditate on your life for the time of judgment is at hand. Now is the time for human freedom, now is the time to leave the dead past alone.

The civilization of the Kemites has emerged with its vision of **Nzoputa Uwa** and it is based on the **Ekwueme World Experience**. Our civilization has already begun from the First year of **Nzoputa Uwa**. Our civilization has come to redeem the Ekwensi and to reconcile the world of Ekwensu with the World of EKUMEKU according to the Divine Plan of AMUN in whom we trust.

This Ekwueme civilization holds the master key for the future of human life. This Ekwueme civilization would destroy and make mockery the skin color contraption of the religions of ISFET. This our civilization would destroy and make mockery whatever spirit of ISFET that was used to make the black skinned humanity the embodiment of evil. This our civilization would uphold and celebrate the Truth of human freedom. This our civilization would subordinate the forces of ISFET and make the forces of MAAT the dominant consciousness in the universe of life. This our civilization would make the worship of the One Creator of the universe the ultimate reality of human life.

The Ekwueme civilization of Kemet would strive to renounce evil and restore good as the Truth of human morality. This our civilization is against every form of agreement with Nsi. This our civilization would fight against ignorance, falsehood and deception as the basis of justifying its existence. This our civilization would strive to overcome evil by doing good in the Holy Name of AMUN in whom we trust. This our civilization would be a blessing in eternity to the righteous humanity. This our civilization is the human paradigm of the Ekwueme. This our civilization is against every form of Ekwensism of any kind. This our civilization would advance human thought and behavior. This our civilization would expand the knowledge of what it means to be fully human. This our civilization would honor both the male and female principles of life. Now, this our civilization is Here in the Almighty Spirit of EKUMEKU. OTUA-KA-ODI!

CHAPTER TWELVE

THE MOVEMENT OF NZOPUTA UWA IS UNIVERSAL

There is nothing in creation that expresses the truthfulness of life far greater than the human spirit. In other words, the human spirit is the root of all values, good and evil, spirit and matter. If we do not have value for the human spirit, whatever value we may give to other things is baseless.
-----The Chosen One

The human spirit has to die to his or her Ekwensu beliefs in order to be born again as an Ekwueme. We must cast off the Ekwensi condition of living a life so that we may come into the awareness of the Ekwueme Universal Life.
-----The Chosen One

Human freedom consists not in living in agreement with Nsi, not in abnormal dreams and fantasies, but in the actuality of being disagreeable with Nsi through the devotion of purpose to the Divine Plan of the One Creator of the universe. Since the advent of the Mission of Nzoputa Uwa, human freedom has become an undeniable reality that is self-realized by every devoted follower of the Divine Plan of AMUN in whom we trust. The Ekwueme People of Truth are free and equal in their devotion of purpose to the supreme principle of EKUMEKU. The widening gulf separating the Ekwueme from the Ekwensi is the human freedom of being in disagreement with Nsi. The Ekwensi living in agreement with Nsi is ignorant of EKUMEKU; and as a result, the Ekwensi is the embodiment of evil.
....THE HOLY ANKHUWA

The Movement of Nzoputa Uwa who is it for? What is the spark that can ignite the vast body of the world of Ekwensu to the ultimate reality of **Nzuko,** *blackened* enough to melt the old world of skin color contraption that the new Ekwueme Order of the world may be established into form?

The Movement of **Nzoputa Uwa** is the Deliverance from the world of death for everybody that lives in agreement with Nsi. Since every human spirit is born in the world of Ekwensu in agreement with Nsi, the Movement of Nzoputa Uwa is the everlasting call to all humanity to repent from Nsi.

The first step is **Nkuzimatism**, whereby the human spirit is Nkuzimatized to develop the morality of repentance from Nsi. Repentance begins with the awareness of evil through the knowledge of self. Once the human spirit becomes aware of Nsi, the individual realizes the consciousness of Nsi as the root of all evil.

The second step therefore is to empower the human spirit by elevating its consciousness to the self-realization of the eternal Truth of the divine birth of EKUMEKU, liberating the individual consciousness of the Chi as the human spirit declares publicly the **Nkwekolita** of the Ekwueme Universal Life in fellowship with the living Haremakhet that it may be *Harembetized* in the Almighty Spirit of EKUMEKU.

The third step is the Life of the converted or transformed human being, the Ekwueme, who lives MAAT by renouncing ISFET through the devotion of purpose to the supreme principle of EKUMEKU. Without any doubt, the Movement of Nzoputa Uwa is universal and has come for the redemption of the human spirit from the dead end nature of the world of Ekwensu.

In other words, the Ekwueme is at war with the immoral condition of *Ekwensism*. We are at war with the condition of living in agreement with Nsi. The struggle to overcome evil by doing good is the divine ordinance of the One Creator of the universe. **Therefore, the fight against Ekwensism demands a fight against superstitions, against old habits and prejudices, and against previous conceptions and traditions. It is the**

struggle against the poisoning of the heart by the religions of ISFET in ignorance, falsehood and deception. It is the struggle against the moral plague of the skin color contraption of the religions of ISFET. Without any doubt, the Movement of Nzoputa Uwa is the struggle against the abuse of human morality of the followers of the religions of ISFET.

REPENT FROM NSI

The Creator is One. The One is AMUN and the Divine Plan is EKUMEKU . There is no other Creator of the universe but AMUN in whom we trust.

Repent from Nsi and be converted to the eternal Truth of the divine birth of EKUMEKU. With repentance, you can no longer afford to keep collaborating with the systems that have been created by the Ekwensu people to undermine your human potentials. **Without any doubt, the skin color contraption of the religions of ISFET is a death trap, a monstrous evil.**

Let it be known that the high melanin pigmentation is a blessing and not a curse. The followers of the religions of ISFET have tried in vain to transform what is apparently a blessing from the One Creator of the universe to seem like a curse. They are in error because blackness is the archetype of humanity.

THE UNIVERSAL AIMS OF EKWUEMEISM

The universal aims of *Ekwuemism* constitute an integral part of the configuration that animates the **Movement of Nzoputa Uwa**. The decisive factor in human life is the eternal Truth of the divine birth of EKUMEKU on the Second year of **Nzoputa Uwa**. **The Holy Cause of Nzoputa Uwa** is the motivation, means and opportunity to fight for human freedom in the struggle to overcome evil by doing good in order to displace ISFET and restore MAAT as the dominant consciousness in the universe of life.

Since the world of Ekwensu is perishable, it is the world of

EKUMEKU, which is the World of Life, that represents the true aim of human existence. Therefore, whosoever is not an Ekwueme is an Ekwensi who is ignorant of EKUMEKU. The Ekwensi lives in agreement with Nsi in ignorance, falsehood and deception. Without repentance from Nsi, the Ekwensi is not a human being morally speaking. Without the attainment of the devotion of purpose, every Ekwensi is mortal and perishable. Without following in the footsteps of the Chosen One for the mission of Nzoputa Uwa, the condition of every Ekwensi is destined to be acted upon by the Ekwueme. Without being a devoted follower of the Divine Plan of the One Creator of the universe, every Ekwensi is the diametrical opposite of the Ekwueme. Without the public declaration of **Nkwekolita** and **Harembetism,** every Ekwensi is the embodiment of evil. Without renouncing ISFET by living MAAT, an Ekwensi cannot be converted or transformed to become the devoted follower of the Divine Plan of AMUN in whom we trust. **In other words, the Ekwensi is the Unbeliever who lives in a spiritual void, in a wasteland, and is yet to conceive of or realize the eternal Truth of the divine birth of EKUMEKU which exists in the wholeness of eternity.**

The Ekwensi preaches what can never be practiced and practices what has nothing to do with human morality. Without any doubt, the universal Aim of Ekwuemeism is to worship only the One Creator of the universe in opposition to the Ekwensism of the Ekwensi who worships the created images of the human mind.

Let us use the three dominant religions of ISFET as an example to illustrate how human morality has been abused and is being abused by the Ekwensu people.

THE THREE DOMINANT RELIGIONS OF ISFET

The whole world of Ekwensu is ignorant of EKUMEKU. As a result, the three dominant religions of ISFET have disqualified themselves from the future of humanity because their mythologies have been justified with blood. Their so-called word of God is nothing but a self-fulfilling mythology that exists in opposition to the Truth of the One Creator of the universe. No doubt, their different socially oriented mythologies are all based on the nomadic principle of constant warfare, constant raiding, constant corruption, constant looting, pillaging and destruction, constant anarchy, constant reaping where they never sowed, constant violence by blood and terror, etc. This ruthless hunting culture of the religions of ISFET is the basis of the tension and anxiety that exist in the world of Ekwensu with its preoccupation of destroying the ecology of the planet and the annihilation of the defenseless peoples without any regard to human morality. **The divine birth of EKUMEKU has come to displace the field of animal action and to bring humanity into the field of human action according to the Divine Plan of AMUN in whom we trust.** Although the animalistic tendency of the hunter and the herder may have contributed to the domestication of animals and yet its cultural conditions have no doubt encouraged the abuse of human morality. Wherefore, we must die of our animal nature in order to become truly the human being: Death to the Ekwensi nature and the birth of the Ekwueme universal life is the Truth of the divine birth of EKUMEKU.

The three dominant religions of ISFET have proven morally incapable of transcending beyond the field of animal action. **As a result, the religions of ISFET are stuck in their metaphors of darkness and lightness, interpreting them erroneously and associating them with their skin color contraption. They are stuck in their make-believe world of associating darkness with high melanin pigmentation and lightness with low melanin pigmentation.** The religions of ISFET are stuck in the false image that they have projected against the Black skinned humanity without knowing that their exclusive image of blackness as the embodiment of evil has suggested something sinister about them. But they do not know what they are doing because they are stuck in the metaphor of darkness as being evil and lightness as being good.

The followers of the religions of ISFET do not have the true knowledge of good and evil because they are stuck in their metaphors of darkness and lightness, interpreting them erroneously as factual truths. The followers of the religions of ISFET are very ignorant of EKUMEKU for they use their dark/light dichotomy literally in itself as the sole referent of their bloody actions. They do not use dark/light metaphors as something transcendent; instead, the followers of the religions of ISFET use their darkness and lightness metaphors literally and erroneously, misusing them in their abuse of human morality. They pretend not to know that low melanin pigmentation is akin to darkness, while high melanin pigmentation is akin to lightness. They misinterpret and misuse the metaphoric nature of life, obscuring their message in order to gain cheap advantage against the other.

The followers of the religions of ISFET need to throw away their metaphors of darkness and lightness for they have misused them in their abuse of human morality. They must also throw away the false notion of the physical resurrection of a dead body that ascended into the sky for it is untruthful and a life impossibility. In ignorance, falsehood and deception, they are using outward images outwardly, without knowing that in metaphor outward images are used inwardly while inward images are used outwardly. They are fixated with the material condition and that is why they were unable to understand that darkness and lightness are two aspects of the same thing.

There can be no connotation of a struggle between darkness and lightness. The denotation that there is a struggle between darkness and lightness is the skin color contraption of the religions of ISFET. The Ekwensu people have fallen into the abyss, trapping the minds of those who are ignorant of EKUMEKU. How can the inner and the outer meet, when the inner has been trapped in the bottom pit of the abyss? How can we realize the Chi-Ukwu-Di in us when the individual Chi is in bondage and slavery without even knowing it?

Regardless of their skin color pigmentation, the followers of the religions of ISFET are in the abyss for they made a grave

moral error of associating darkness and lightness with skin color pigmentation. The religions of ISFET have disqualified themselves from the future of humanity because of their abuse of human morality. They no longer have the moral authority nor the ethics to speak to the heart of humanity because they are stuck in their immoral metaphors of darkness and lightness. Their doctrine of intolerance is based solely on the skin color contraption that they had devised to brand the Black skinned humanity to be the embodiment of evil.

Without any doubt, skin color must never and can never be the basis of human morality. A non-black person can never be superior to a black person just because the former has low melanin pigmentation and the latter has high melanin pigmentation. **It is absurd for anybody to claim superiority merely on skin pigmentation.** Whosoever claims superiority over another person solely based on skin pigmentation is not worthy to be called a human being. Such a spectacle is an animal figure which has not developed as a full human being and must be isolated from the human community.

To the extent of the Unbeliever's claim that the dark skin has no relationship with light, it is to that extent that the non-black skin has no relationship with the light-giving sun. If the dark skin is the embodiment of evil, where does the goodness of the non-black skin come from? We must never allow ourselves to fall into the same trap that the followers of the religions of ISFET have entrapped themselves. If they claim superiority from the other based on skin pigmentation and from the lightness of the sun, question them to explain how the light-giving sun is more akin to the non-black skin than to the black skin? Without any doubt, the light-giving sun is favorable to the Black skin than to the non-black skin. Let them explain very thoroughly what makes low melanin pigmentation superior to high melanin pigmentation without any link to the light-giving sun, for the light-giving sun must never be used to support the artificial notion of skin whiteness. Let them explain how whiteness is superior to blackness without any link to the light-giving sun.

We are the People of Truth, who recognize both darkness and lightness as two aspects of the same thing. Let there be Truth for without the Truth the lightness of the day and the darkness of the night would have no real meaning because we would have continued to live in agreement with Nsi. It is the Truth which has enabled us to realize that the metaphor of lightness is an image that can suggest an inward state of actualization. It is to the same extent can the metaphor of darkness be understood as the inward state of potentiality, realization and transformation. We must never associate the image of darkness or lightness as a metaphor to become the image of a particular skin color. **We reject the false notion that associates the Black skin with darkness. Therefore, we reject the false notion which promoted the illusion of darkness representing evil and lightness representing good.**

The religions of ISFET are obsessed with "light" not because they are devoted to the Truth of the One Creator of the universe; but instead, the followers of the religions of ISFET are obsessed with the "light" of the skin color contraption which they had devised in error. The "light" of the skin color contraption is white magic which has no truth within it. The followers of the religions of ISFET are not obsessed with the light of the life nourishing sun; rather, they are obsessed with the destructive light of fire that burns and destroys the spiritual appetite for the Truth, the flame of torment. **The followers of the religions of ISFET are obsessed with the "light" or "fire" that goes with death, Okumuo.** For their "light" is the harbinger of death, the fire of pain and destruction.

However, what the human spirit needs is the Living Truth, the life of Truth or the living of Truth which comes with the World of Life and yet cannot exist without darkness and lightness; and not the "light" that is the harbinger of death, the fire of pain and destruction, which can only exist in tension with darkness. When the followers of the religions of ISFET believe that life is a conflict or struggle between the forces of darkness and the forces of lightness, their forces of darkness become the dark skinned humanity by association and that is morally wrong. What is darkness but a place or situation that has no reflection of the light of the sun. What has that got to do with a dark skinned body? The dark skinned body is the exemplar of a body that typifies the reflection of the light-giving sun. The Ekwensu people have misused the basic principle of darkness and have misapplied the basic principle of lightness without knowing that both represent the process of conversion of potentiality into actuality. No doubt, it is from the rhythmic motion of darkness and lightness in the **Eternal Wheel of Nzoputa Uwa** that the potentiality inherent in the seed of life becomes an actuality.

To the extent that good or evil is not inherent with darkness, it is to the same extent that good or evil is not inherent with lightness. But darkness and lightness must never be identified with any particular skin color for they can only be used as metaphors and not as the focus of consciousness. **On the contrary, the religions of ISFET had placed darkness and lightness as the focus of consciousness in their dichotomy or polarization of the objective phenomenal appearance and have erred by associating darkness with the high melanin pigmentation.** This has led to their creation of many fabulous myths in order to justify their skin color contraption, which made the Black skinned humanity the embodiment of evil.

Wherefore, there is a widening gulf between the Ekwensu people and the World of Life, between those who are stuck in false images of life and those who are the manifest expression of the Living Truth that is the Higher Self.

Let it be known that as long as the followers of the religions of ISFET believe that life is a struggle between the forces of darkness and the forces of lightness, they would continue to lack the moral certainty to practice what they preach. That is why, the followers of the religions of ISFET preach one thing and practice another thing because they lack the true knowledge of good and evil. It is from the bottom of this abyss that the voice of salvation was heard when the inward life meets with the outward life at the center of being.

Without any doubt, the eternal struggle that would always exist between the forces of MAAT and the forces of ISFET represents the true principle of good and evil and not a specific historical situation or a particular skin color pigmentation. The eternal struggle between the forces of MAAT and the forces of ISFET is the operation of the principles of good and evil that is not identified with any specific people or skin pigmentation. It is an abstract principle that would always exist both within and without, and it is fundamental in explaining the clash of good and evil and the moral certainty to overcome evil by doing good. It is morally wrong to identify a specific people or a particular skin color as the absolute exemplification or the embodiment of evil. The abstract principles of good and evil are universal in their operational application to human life. These abstract principles of good and evil exist within the life of every human spirit and can only be applied correctly through the devotion of purpose in EKUMEKU, when one has been liberated from the dead end nature of the world of Ekwensu.

The religions of ISFET are in error in their identification of darkness as evil for their "darkness" has been misapplied to mean the dark skinned people. We do not see an exclusive evil in our knowledge of the reality of darkness. There is nothing evil with darkness for every human life comes into being from the darkness of the womb. The thought of darkness as absolutely evil is the basis of the myth of the dark skin as evil. Whenever the followers of the religions of ISFET claim to be confronting the evil that is darkness, it is the high melanin pigmentation, the dark skinned people, that is meant by association. But nobody can confront darkness in the true sense of the word, just as nobody can confront lightness. Their confrontation with darkness has historically been a confrontation with the dark skinned people.

The unique potentiality to experience life as the Living Truth is the essential meaning of the darkness of life. No doubt, darkness and lightness are fields of experience in time which are neither good nor evil and their images should evoke attitudes that make us to appreciate the ultimate reality of the Truth of the One Creator of the universe. Let it be known that the abyss is a wasteland where out of fear the human spirit lives in agreement with Nsi, in the vicious circle of eternal death.

The world historical emergence of the Ekwueme represents the realization of the eternal Truth of the divine birth of EKUMEKU that is the fulfillment of the highest spiritual potential of what it means to be fully human. For, it is the death of the Ekwensi condition of living a life that leads to the birth of the Ekwueme Universal Life. The recognition of the human identity of the other without regards to skin color differences and the entrenchment of the Truth of the One Creator of the universe in disagreement with Nsi would confirm the struggle between the World of Life and the world of death. The separateness of being the Ekwensi when converted from its ignorance, falsehood and deception, from the living in agreement with Nsi, realizes the oneness of being the Ekwueme, the Universal Being.

In order to go beyond the subject and the object categories of thought, the human spirit must be born again. The images of darkness and lightness are the reflections of the spiritual potentialities and actualities of human life and are two aspects of the same thing. There is no struggle between darkness and lightness as the religions of ISFET have been known to have propagated; and it is a grave moral error to put them in a dichotomy by splitting one from the other. Darkness and lightness are pairs of opposites and separately they have no meaningful referent even when used with substantive images. There is no antagonistic contradiction between darkness and lightness. The antagonistic contradictions that exist within the skin color contraption of the religions of ISFET have been a self-fulfilling prophecy that is embedded in their mythologies of the concept of one God. There is unity between darkness and lightness, the unity of opposites, and that is from where we take our stand against the skin color contraption of the religions of ISFET.

Let it be known that darkness and lightness are neither place, thing, nor person. So, why do the Ekwensu people associate darkness with a particular place, thing or person? This is because of ignorance, falsehood and deception. The Ekwensu people live in agreement with Nsi in the dead end nature of the world of Ekwensu.

The Ekwueme People of Truth are morally and mentally aware and ready to denounce the spiritual terrorization and the abuse of human morality of the followers of the religions of ISFET. The Ekwueme People of Truth are fighting against the Ekwensism of the Ekwensu people, fighting for life against death, fighting for human freedom against human bondage and slavery. The evil of Ekwensism is neither a place, thing nor person; instead, it is the condition of living in agreement with Nsi, the condition of being agreeable to Nsi, and that is what the Ekwueme must fight steadfastly against according to the conviction of the Truth of the divine birth of EKUMEKU.

The sincerity or righteousness of this conviction is the moral certainty of the Ekwueme that the Chosen One was chosen by the One Creator of the universe for the mission of **Nzoputa Uwa**. Unwavering, uncompromising, unflinching and single-mindedly devoted, year in year out, in the wholeness of eternity, the World of Life would emerge to dominate the world of death as the Ekwueme bears witness to the Living Truth of the One Creator of the universe.

The followers of the religions of ISFET have created dichotomies between ideas of identical nature by neglecting the fact that it is the interrelationship between opposites that makes them applicable to human life. They have split the reality of darkness from the reality of lightness by giving them absolute values. For example, they impose absolute value on lightness which is a lower gradation of the universal energy level which cannot exist without darkness, i.e., the complementary opposite energy level in the universe. By so doing, the followers of the religions of ISFET fail to understand that the existence of lightness presupposes the existence of darkness because both complementary and opposite energy levels are identical in nature. In other words, the followers of the religions of ISFET conceive morality as make-believe, as a gimmick that is capable of concealing their vested interest. The morality which they preach cannot be confirmed by their actions as a result. It then becomes a moral gimmick rooted in the rhetoric of deceit used as a front to disarm and pacify those who are ignorant of EKUMEKU.

We must no longer listen to them talk of morality since their actions have already shown them to be immoral. They must repent from Nsi and accept EKUMEKU as their eternal Savior and Redeemer from the dead end nature of the world of Ekwensu. The followers of the religions of ISFET practice Ekwensism; while they preach something that might seem akin to human morality to those who are ignorant of EKUMEKU.

THE CONCEPT OF ONE GOD IS NOT UNIVERSAL

Since the skin color contraption of the religions of ISFET evolved historically from a polarized framework of sectional presuppositions, its implicit ideology became explicit with time as white supremacy and black subordination. The identification of purity, beauty, virtue or excellence with whiteness and impurity, ugliness, vice and dirt with blackness created the false notion that white is absolutely good and black is absolutely evil. This extremism of whiteness, white magic, rooted in the skin color contraption of the dominant religions of ISFET, tied together and brought into focus a negation of what was misconstrued to be embodied in the actuality of the dominant historical relationship that it had eclipsed. But it is from the skin color contraption of the religions of ISFET that we can derive the meaning of the historical context upon which the implicit idea became an explicit ideology.

In the metaphor of the struggle between the forces of darkness and the forces of lightness, the thought of darkness as absolutely evil was entrenched. What was then necessary was how to tie darkness with the dark skinned people by association. Although by correct application in metaphor, dark skin would represent the embodiment of light, the association of darkness with the dark skin was done by splitting darkness from lightness. By using outward images outwardly, the followers of the religions of

ISFET, began to misrepresent the high melanin pigmentation by associating the Black skin color with darkness. To the contrary, it is the low melanin pigmentation that is the embodiment of darkness in the human body. Since darkness is the absence of the light from the sun, the melanin deficiency factor, the skin pigmentation that correlates with the absence of the light from the sun is the low melanin pigmentation.

Bearing that in mind, the adoption of the idea of whiteness could not have supplanted what preceded it without the constant association of itself with the light-giving sun. Even though it is bizarre, it worked for almost two millennia of black degradation because of ignorance, falsehood and deception. As the thought that darkness is absolutely evil became the focus of consciousness of the religions of ISFET, lightness became absolutely good. The followers of the religions of ISFET then began to associate lightness with whiteness. Since whiteness is the opposite of blackness, it became very easy by association to tie darkness to blackness. As a result, darkness and blackness became synonymous in the mind of the followers of the religions of ISFET. Without any serious challenge by anyone, this skin color contraption evolved and became frozen in time and has been used as a weapon of destruction in the abuse of human morality.

The abuse of the humanity of the Black skinned people began to be justified with fabulous myths that have been codified in the mythologies that are embedded in the concept of one God. Whatever that the followers of the religions of ISFET could conceptualize as evil began to be associated with blackness for they have in error tied darkness with blackness. From this contraption, white and light became synonymous. Then, the false notion that lightness supersedes darkness became the theoretical assumption upon which the supremacy of whiteness was built against blackness. But whiteness and lightness are not synonymous. At the same time, blackness and darkness are not synonymous. But to the followers of the religions of ISFET, darkness is absolutely evil ; and as a result whatever that is black is the embodiment of absolute evil for to them darkness and blackness are synonymous.

In the Ekwensi mind, the orchestrated struggle between darkness and lightness is in actuality a preconceived struggle between blackness and whiteness. In other words, the bogus claim that white is superior to black can be traced to the skin color contraption of the religions of ISFET, to the root where the idea was implicit before it became an explicit ideology. What is obvious is that the followers of the religions of ISFET do not have the true knowledge of good and evil because their concept of good and evil is based on the skin color contraption. However, skin color or its contraption must never be the basis of human morality.

Therefore, the concept of one God has been based on the skin color contraption and could not have been universal because it excluded the Black skinned humanity and condemned them to perish in eternal doom due to their skin pigmentation. Let it be known that the concept of one God has been very far from being universal because of the skin color contraption which made the Black skinned people the sole embodiment of absolute evil. **In other words, to accept the concept of one God is to accept that the Black skinned humanity is less than human just because of their skin pigmentation. It is to accept the false ideology that has made blackness to become exclusively what is impure, ugly, dirty, evil, etc.** The concept of one God is a hoax from the beginning of its development and it has always been a sectional and polarized ideology, with an anti-black frame of reference, that purports to speak to the heart of humanity, misleading those who are ignorant of EKUMEKU with the peculiar value it attached to whiteness which precluded black exclusion and degradation.

Without any shadow of doubt, the concept of one God has been superseded by the Truth of the One Creator of the universe. It is the divine birth of EKUMEKU on the Second year of Nzoputa Uwa that has made us to realize that the concept of one God is a hoax. The concept of one God is immoral for it excluded the Black skinned humanity from its peculiar notion of what it means to be fully human by condemning them to everlasting doom. The consequences of the concept of one God are self-evident in the historical relationship that existed over the past two millennia of black degradation in the time of Oge Nzuzu. Wherefore, the concept of one God has been superseded because it is not universal in its morality and awareness of what it means to be fully human.

Without any doubt, the Truth of the One Creator of the universe is universal in its awareness of what it means to be fully human. Let us bear witness to the Truth of the divine birth of EKUMEKU on the Second year of Nzoputa Uwa. The Creator is One. The One is AMUN and the Divine Plan is EKUMEKU. There is no other Creator of the universe but AMUN in whom we trust.

THE IDEOLOGY OF WHITENESS

The content or manner of thinking which is based on the belief that there is an effortless virtue in the low melanin pigmentation, which is absent in the high melanin pigmentation, that has made those who possess such a skin color to be free from moral impurity is the ideology of whiteness. Let it be known that the Ekwueme is completely in disagreement with this ideology not just from the point of view of its basic assumptions but also its presupposition of what is blackness. Why? This is because everybody is born in the world of Ekwensu in agreement with Nsi. But let us deal with how it came to be built on the anti-black frame of reference.

As we can now ascertain, the origin of the skin color contraption of the religions of ISFET is rooted in their erroneous metaphoric belief that there is an eternal struggle between the forces of darkness and the forces of lightness. Simply stated, it has now been unequivocally revealed about how what is an implicit idea gradually became an explicit ideology.

It is the historical fact of how a metaphor has been erroneously applied to become an explicit ideology. Without any doubt, the ideology of whiteness began as a reaction to the historical reality of blackness. Before the ideology of whiteness became white supremacy, it was a reactionary ideology which has the sole preoccupation of making blackness to be synonymous with darkness. Because the ideology of whiteness has no greater access to light than blackness, the ideology of whiteness became obsessed with light in its attempt to exclude blackness from the light giving sun. This led to the distortion and degeneration of the true meaning of blackness. Since blackness in skin color can never be understood without linking it to the light giving sun, the strength of the ideology of whiteness is hitherto derived from its ability to exclude the dark skin from the light giving sun by associating blackness with darkness.

If people could accept in ignorance, falsehood and deception that the low melanin pigmentation is synonymous with lightness and that the high melanin pigmentation is synonymous with darkness, then the ideology of whiteness has succeeded in supplanting and degrading blackness---in order to become white supremacy. Anyone who has not understood this underlying assumption is yet to understand white supremacy as an ideology.

No doubt, white is the opposite of black. Both black and white have positive and negative qualities. But if the positive quality in blackness can be appropriated to give added value to whiteness, then blackness would become inferior---at least theoretically from the point of view of the ideology of whiteness. The penchant drama to attribute and ascribe all the negative qualities in both black and white to a contrived created image of blackness is the basis of white supremacy. **For if a contrived image of blackness can be imposed with the negative qualities of whiteness and the negative qualities of blackness and is made to become the embodiment of absolute evil, then such a distorted image is bound to be inferior for it cannot have any positive quality. It would not have any will of its own, for it would be an instrument created to serve the will of its master. If you can understand that, then you can understand why white supremacy is based on the platform of black inferiority.**

That is to say, that white supremacy is based on the penchant drama to make black inferior, consciously and unconsciously. Indeed, it is a penchant drama because in color reality black is a dominant color than white. So, in order to avoid becoming subordinated to black, the white supremacists with the peculiar value that they have attached to whiteness have created a make-believe world which has been programmed to determine black exclusion by its exaggerated power to define and regulate the condition of the black humanity as being the most exploited and despised humanity. The assumption that black in color and in condition must be degraded, despised and rejected is therefore the underlying principle of the ideology of whiteness. It is a system of thought and behavior that would have been impossible to be established without the skin color contraption of the religions of ISFET. For, it is the skin color contraption of the religions of ISFET that is the undeniable structural matrix that made the implicit idea to become inevitably the explicit ideology of whiteness.

In other words, the ideology of whiteness did not emerge from a vacuum; instead, it is rooted in the skin color contraption of the three dominant religions of ISFET, in their vain attempt to make blackness a badge of dishonor, ridicule and domination. Without any doubt, the skin color contraption of the religions of ISFET is a crime against humanity. It is a crime against humanity to devalue the humanity of the Black skinned people without any moral justification whatsoever.

Let it be known that the alleged effortless virtue that is derived from the skin color contraption of the religions of ISFET is immoral and it is not free from moral impurity. No doubt, the skin color contraption of the religions of ISFET is not only immoral, it is indeed built on the total negation of the humanity of the Black skinned people. Nevertheless, by striving to degrade the humanity of the Black skinned people, the followers of the religions of ISFET have distorted the moral values that bind all humanity together.

THE MOVEMENT OF NZOPUTA UWA

The Movement of Nzoputa Uwa has come into universal expression, according to the Divine Plan of the One Creator of the universe, in order to restore the essential equilibrium of the human life that was disrupted through the skin color contraption of the religions of ISFET during the time of Oge Nzuzu. The Movement of Nzoputa Uwa, whose main content is the universal aim of Ekwuemeism, has inaugurated the age of human freedom from all forms of Ekwensism of any kind.

As a result, the Movement of Nzoputa Uwa would displace ISFET and restore MAAT as the dominant consciousness in the universe of life. Without any shadow of doubt, the Movement of Nzoputa Uwa is universal. Wherefore, the unity of existence can only be realized when the human spirit surrenders unconditionally to the Divine Will of AMUN in whom we trust. Championing the universal aim of *Ekwuemism*, the Movement of Nzoputa Uwa would not only change the way the human beings think about black and white but also would unite humanity based on the conviction of the Truth, by restoring the moral fabric that holds humanity together. In other words, the monomania of the skin color contraption would be uprooted from its roots as the Movement of Nzoputa Uwa restores the moral fabric that holds humanity together.

Let it be known that the skin color contraption of the religions of ISFET and the Movement of Nzoputa Uwa are irreconcilable. Consequently, the former must give way to the latter. No doubt, the skin color contraption of the religions of ISFET must die a natural death through the Movement of Nzoputa Uwa. The Movement of Nzoputa Uwa would bring order against disorder, and restore the oneness of being against the separateness of being. It would destroy the previous conceptions that had sought to divide humanity into the categories of effortless virtue and irredeemable vice.

From the beginning of creation, the struggle between good and evil has been the foundation of human life. If choice was not part of the divine ordinance, we would have existed either in absolute good or absolute evil. But the religions of ISFET have tried in vain to propagate the false notions of an effortless virtue and an irredeemable vice with their skin color contraption. However, without the choice to renounce ISFET by living MAAT, human morality could never have existed. Therefore, the human spirit who is the manifest expression of EKUMEKU can only represent the reality of the equilibrium between the forces of MAAT and the forces of ISFET.

Thus, the restoration of the equilibrium which had been disrupted and broken can only be realized through the Movement of Nzoputa Uwa---by subordinating the forces of ISFET and restoring MAAT as the dominant consciousness in the universe of life. In other words, the Movement of Nzoputa Uwa advances the truth that there is no skin color that possesses the monopoly for virtue or vice, beauty or ugliness, intelligence or stupidity, righteousness or unrighteousness, etc. Wherefore, the skin color contraption of the religions of ISFET is immoral and a monstrous evil. Indeed, the religions of ISFET are more concerned with their attempt to perpetuate the skin color contraption than with good conduct and human morality. Without any doubt, to fight for the Holy Cause of Nzoputa Uwa in the Almighty Spirit of EKUMEKU is morally more superior than the Ekwensism of the Ekwensi, more intelligent than living in agreement with Nsi.

THE MOVEMENT OF NZOPUTA UWA IS UNIVERSAL

The eternal struggle that exists between MAAT and ISFET, the rise and fall of one conditional process against another conditional process, is the fundamental basis upon which good triumphs against evil in human life. **But the clash between the forces of MAAT and the forces of ISFET is quite clear and decisive to those who are the devoted followers of the Divine Plan of AMUN in whom we trust**. Let it be known that the faculty of ISFET is within and without every human spirit. It cannot be eliminated but can be subordinated through the devotion of purpose in EKUMEKU. Life is the battlefield of the clash between MAAT and ISFET.

The human life is an eternal struggle between the forces of MAAT and the forces of ISFET, between the oneness of being and the separateness of being, between the interdependent order of the universe and the independent condition of living a life, between the Higher self and the Lower self, between the good life and the evil condition, an eternal victory of the Ekwueme against the Ekwensi.

Let it be known that human life is not a struggle between the forces of darkness and the forces of lightness as has erroneously been propagated by the dominant religions of ISFET. There are neither the forces of darkness nor the forces of lightness in human life. It is without any shadow of doubt that on a daily basis darkness transforms itself into lightness and lightness transforms itself into darkness without any struggle. **So there is no struggle at all between darkness and lightness. The struggle of the religions of ISFET to transform the dark skin to become the embodiment of evil has been the skin color contraption that is devoid of human morality.** In other words, the human life is a struggle between those who exist in disagreement with Nsi and those who live in agreement with Nsi, between the World of Life and the world of death, an eternal victory for those who have realized the human freedom from every form of agreement with Nsi against those who are dead in Nsi. No doubt, the Movement of Nzoputa Uwa is universal.

CONCLUSION

The supreme principle of EKUMEKU is the ultimate reality because it exists in the wholeness of eternity at the point of equilibrium between MAAT and ISFET. It is through the devotion of purpose to the supreme principle of EKUMEKU can ISFET be displaced and MAAT restored as the dominant consciousness in the universe of life. Indeed, it is through the devotion of purpose to the supreme principle of EKUMEKU can the human spirit renounce ISFET by living MAAT. Without any doubt, it is only through the devotion of purpose in EKUMEKU can the faculty of ISFET exist in a state of subordination with the faculty of MAAT as the dominant consciousness.

In other words, the moral capacity to extend the consciousness of life beyond the present cannot exist without the devotion of purpose to the supreme principle of EKUMEKU. It is the devotion of purpose to the supreme principle of EKUMEKU that can reconcile the clash between the forces of MAAT and the forces of ISFET. Wherefore, it is only through the devotion of purpose to the supreme principle of EKUMEKU can the human spirit worship the One Creator of the universe instead of the created images of the human mind.

Repent from Nsi and accept EKUMEKU as your eternal Savior and Redeemer from the dead end nature of the world of Ekwensu. OTUA-KA-ODI!

www.ingramcontent.com/pod-product-compliance
Lightning Source LLC
Chambersburg PA
CBHW071311110426
42743CB00042B/1255